W9-CYT-450

Forms of Uncertainty

Essays in Historical Criticism

Forms of Uncertainty

Essays in Historical Criticism

David Levin

University Press of Virginia
Charlottesville and London

THE UNIVERSITY PRESS OF VIRGINIA
Copyright © 1992 by the Rector and Visitors
of the University of Virginia

First published 1992

Library of Congress Cataloging-in-Publication Data
Levin, David, 1924–
   Forms of uncertainty : essays in historical criticism / David
Levin.
      p.   cm.
   Includes index.
   ISBN 0-8139-1379-9
   1. American literature—History and criticism—Theory, etc.
2. Historical criticism (Literature)—United States.   3. Literature
and history—United States.   4. United States—Historiography.
I. Title.
PS121.L48   1992
810.9—dc20   91-32563
                                                       CIP

Printed in the United States of America

For Monroe and Betty Levin

Ah, brother! only I and thou
Are left of all that circle now

Contents

PART THREE
Fiction and History

Forms of Uncertainty

Essays in Historical Criticism

We Are All Critics, We Are All Historians

Reflections on Method in the Study of Literature and History

> *We are all Republicans, we are all Federalists.*
> —Thomas Jefferson

In 1959, several months after agreeing to publish my book on nineteenth-century American historians, the Stanford University Press confronted me with a perplexing decision: whether *History as Romantic Art* would appear in the series called Stanford Studies in Language and Literature or in the series called Stanford Studies in History and Political Science. Had I foreseen that my reluctant choice of Language and Literature (because I was teaching in an English department) would forever give my book a philological call number in the Harvard College Library, so that nobody browsing through the stacks in historiography or American literature would ever come across it, I might have chosen History and Political Science. But the major premise of my book declared that it was both literary criticism and intellectual history, and a major theme insists throughout the book that the histories written by George Bancroft, William H. Prescott, John L. Motley, and Francis Parkman are works of literature. I did not want to choose at all.

Thirty years after that reluctant decision, I still consider such choices to be as meaningless as Hobson's choice, even though I now have a much better sense of the utility and the inevitability of departmental budgets. Of course I perceive differences between what people trained in a history department and people trained in an English department usually do. Yet even if I had not been trained in both departments, I would have to insist that, long before the advent of the New Historicism, the fundamental differences between them were often ex-

aggerated. Besides a few hybrids like me who are interested in historical literature or American Studies, a large section of the greenhouse in
almost every English department faculty consists of historians, scholars
who write and teach the history of English and American literature,
ideas, philology, critical theory and practice. Throughout the decades
that supposedly were dominated by the New Criticism, with its scorn
for history and its reputedly exclusive concentration on individual
texts, many literary scholars worked historically. Few of their diplomas
contain the word *history* (as all of mine do), but these scholars not only
profess expert knowledge in the history of literature. Many of them
actually write biography, social history, intellectual history. Among my
colleagues at Stanford, for example, Ian Watt wrote *The Rise of the Novel*
and a biography of Joseph Conrad, Wilfred Stone a biography of E. M.
Forster. William Irvine wrote a study of the fight to make Charles
Darwin's ideas acceptable in nineteenth-century England, William
Chace a book on *The Political Identities of Ezra Pound and T. S. Eliot.* My
colleagues at Virginia have included biographers of Jonathan Swift,
Van Wyck Brooks, Henry Fielding, W. E. B. Du Bois, and D. H.
Lawrence, and authors of books about relationships between art and
literature as well as *A History of English Literature, A Genealogy of Mod-
ernism,* and *The Idea of the Renaissance.*

Without underestimating distinctions, then, we should acknowledge that some literary scholars have always had much more in common with some historians than either group shares with other scholars
in its own supposed discipline. Some quantitative historians and some
linguists or deconstructionists in the English department will find
little to approve in the methods of their respective colleagues who
write intellectual or literary history. Let us concede cheerfully that the
combination of history and literature has value chiefly for those who
recognize that the border between the two disciplines is indistinct.

Rather than prescribe a single method for the study of literature
and history, I should like, in this introductory statement and in the
chapters that follow, to illustrate the value of studying the one with an
awareness of the other, and some of the dangers of studying either one
without some understanding of the other. Historians ought to seek and
then try to express, even though they cannot perfectly attain, a just
understanding of the past. I use the word *just* not in the sense of de-

claring verdicts but in commitment to fairness mixed with human sympathy, trying to perceive (as in reading literature) how the experience of other people differed from our own and how it resembles our own. Limited though our perception and our language certainly are, and aware of how easily our sight and our words may deceive us, historians and literary scholars have little choice (even as we abandon claims to objectivity) but to strive to see the subject with the clearest awareness of its context and of our own perspectives. We acknowledge that no version or interpretation can be absolutely complete or correct, but we take some comfort from knowing that some at least can be absolutely wrong (a declaration, for example, that *Moby-Dick* is a novel about the World Series of 1850). Awareness of how much we cannot know, and of how imperfect our knowledge often is, does not deny us the privilege of discovering and preserving what we *can* know. And in reading a literary work or any historical document, historians and literary scholars will seek first to understand its language.

As R. G. Collingwood observed long ago in his essays on historiography, we bring to bear on our subject all that our personal experience as well as our scholarship has taught us about human life.[1] Whether we are asking questions as critical interpreters of literature or as inquirers into historical change, we ought to know as much as we can about the context of the documents we study. Even the explicit meaning of words may depend on our knowledge or ignorance of that context.

Cotton Mather, for example, called his first wife his "good thing" in a number of the entries in his private journal, and he used that phrase several times during the last months of her young life, as he prayed for her recovery. The modern novelist Katherine Anne Porter, in a brilliant but to my mind unjust chapter of her unfinished biography of Mather, used the phrase "good thing" to help prove that Mather regarded his wife as what we would now call a sex object, a mere thing to be used. But a concordance to the Bible leads to a different meaning of "good thing": One of the Proverbs (18:22) declares that "whoso findeth a wife findeth a good thing," and the eighty-fourth Psalm (84:11) promises that "no good thing will be withheld from them that walk uprightly." In a prayer a few days before his wedding, moreover, Mather had paraphrased that very promise without explicitly citing

Psalm 84. Katherine Anne Porter misread the meaning of *thing* because she was too quick to apply a conventional attitude of her own time to the early eighteenth century, and because she neglected the kind of scholarly tool that might have helped her recover the biblical context in which Mather lived. Except for its emphasis on words, the error differs hardly at all from Porter's miscalculation when she wrote that Increase Mather had ridden his horse all the way from Boston to Plymouth and back on a Saturday afternoon to consult his brother-in-law John Cotton about a crisis in young Cotton Mather's first year at Harvard College. Since the young John Cotton who was tormenting Increase Mather's eleven-year-old son was *not* the son of his namesake in Plymouth, it seems unlikely that Increase Mather would have ridden a horse eighty miles just to consult another of the tormentor's uncles, even if he could have stayed overnight. To anyone who thinks of the horses and of unpaved roads in 1674, the ride in one afternoon is inconceivable.[2]

The point of these little examples is not that Porter was peculiarly inclined to err, but that any of us might easily misread words and facts, and that we therefore need all the help we can find. The chief advantage of studying literature and history, as in studying economics or any other social science along with history, is that literature widens the range of experience we can bring to our study of history.

And of course the benefits are sometimes reciprocal. Students of American political history who know that in the nineteenth century canals, toll roads, and railroads connecting the coastal states to the interior were called internal improvements will appreciate Henry Thoreau's jocular declaration in *Walden* that all such "improvements" are "external and superficial."[3] The most striking benefit of incidental historical knowledge in my own experience came to me as I was preparing to teach an undergraduate class about Nathaniel Hawthorne's great story "Young Goodman Brown." I had read the story several times in English courses, but only after a seminar in early American history had led me into research on the Salem witchcraft trials did I understand some of Hawthorne's most important words. Along with most other modern commentators, I had noticed that in writing from Brown's point of view Hawthorne often uses such words as "figure," "image," or "shape" when Brown perceives a new traveler on the path from Salem

Village into the heart of the dark forest, where the Devil tries to entice Brown to participate in a witches' sabbat.[4] I had always assumed that these terms were merely appropriate to Hawthorne's emphasis on the dimness of the light in the woods, and to Brown's discernment of a new person who comes vaguely into view before Brown or his wily companion announces the newcomer's identity. When I learned that in the Salem trials of 1692 a major issue had been the reliability of spectral evidence, and that after spectral evidence had been declared inadmissible in the court no more witches had been executed, I saw that, whether or not Hawthorne's story describes a dream, it is much more explicitly spectral than any modern commentator had understood. By this time I knew that the most illiterate of witnesses for the prosecution in 1692 had repeatedly distinguished between a defendant's bodily person and a defendant's "image," "figure," "shape," "specter," or "apparition." The many defenders and the few articulate critics of the court had concurred in this distinction, but the court and many of its supporters had insisted during three lethal months that the Devil, by whose power specters and shapes were made visible to human victims, could not impersonate a man or woman who had not signed his evil covenant. Or if he could manage that deceit, they said, Providence would expose the deception.

It became evident to me then that Brown commits in Hawthorne's story the very mistakes that many people in Boston and Salem had made in 1692. He does not see real people going to worship at the Devil's altar in the forest. He sees the shapes of people, some of which disappear, and the whole spectral assembly vanishes when Brown, at the climax of the story, calls on "the slender form" of his wife to "look up to heaven and resist the wicked one!"[5] Brown never learns whether any of the people actually had given the Devil permission to represent them spectrally in his effort to seduce young Goodman Brown. For the rest of his gloomy life Brown lives in doubt whether the most virtuous people in his community, including his wife, are as wicked as he discovered himself to be when for a time he abandoned himself in the forest to be led by his basest instincts to the Devil's place of blasphemous worship.

My task as a historical critic of literature was not completed in that analysis until I had shown that Hawthorne himself had known very well the significance of spectral evidence both as a concept and as an issue in the actual Salem trials. And I had to show how the language of shapes and figures functions in the story itself—what difference my historical information makes in both the narration (the point of view, the psychological exposition or development) and the theme. For historians trying to understand the incorporeal nature of a seventeenth-century witness's conception of a spectral appearance, moreover, I know of no better text to recommend than Hawthorne's imaginative re-creation in "Alice Doane's Appeal." There the narrator declares that the apparitions in a cemetery were "too shadowy for language to portray; for here would be the moonbeams on the ice, glittering through a warrior's breastplate, and there the letters of a tombstone, on the form that stood before it; and wherever a breeze went by, it swept the old men's hoary heads, the women's fearful beauty, and all the unreal throng into one indistinguishable crowd together." [6]

Besides enlarging my knowledge of the historical context, the study of literature gave at least two large benefits to my methods of historical inquiry, and for both of these I am permanently indebted to Perry Miller. The first was respect for the past, a willingness to take seriously ideas and forms of expression that we may think our own age has outgrown. Good literary training encourages us to read attentively, to be alert for shades of meaning, changes in tone. Here again, as in considering the passages that Katherine Anne Porter misread, we need to avoid the condescending or resentful judgments that our prevailing attitudes might encourage. Armed with our suspicion of Benjamin Franklin's canniness and his notorious advice about how to manipulate others, we may be too quick to batter the effigy of that historical character unless we listen to the cadences with which, in his *Autobiography,* he introduces his narrative of his course in the art of virtue. If we do hear the language, we will see that Franklin's ironic self-criticism is unmistakable: "It was about this time [he says] that I conceived the bold and arduous project of arriving at moral Perfection." [7] Even if it stood alone, that sentence could hardly be read aloud without ironically humorous emphasis on "bold," "arduous," and "project," for those words of worldly striving move in comically rhythmic parallel to the rhetorically (and spiritually) climactic "arriving at moral perfection." Bold and arduous project indeed! Even in what Jonathan Swift called

"this projecting age,"[8] arriving at moral perfection ought to have required language much more grand, and Franklin underlines the comic
incongruity by the casual attitude implicit in his introductory words:
"It was about this time."

Now the answer to the riddle of Benjamin Franklin is far from
simple. We cannot dismiss his course in the art of virtue or any other
subject that he presents ironically. But we will not come close to solving the riddle unless we try to understand his uses of irony and the
subtleties of his language. He and Thomas Jefferson and John Adams
and Cotton Mather and Jonathan Edwards and Abraham Lincoln—
these and many others exerted much of their influence on historical
events through their literary craft. The historian who is knowledgeable
about that craft will know his subject better than the colleague who
has not studied literature.

The second, and to my life even more important, literary truth
that Perry Miller's example helped me to apply profitably to historical
study is a corollary of the first. In evaluating the histories written by
William Bradford and Cotton Mather, I put this axiom in the form of
a question about the seventeenth century: "What *good* did it do the
Puritan historian to be a Puritan?"[9] But it was in Miller's course on
romanticism in American literature that the central principle first
came through to me. Miller taught students not to regard conventional
characters, not even stereotypes, as figures of fun, but to try to see
what value they had for both the author and the reader. Miller was not
above eliciting an easy laugh with allusions to Mark Twain's lugubrious
poet Emmeline Grangerford, fictitious author of "Ode to Stephen
Dowling Bots, Deceased," when Miller spoke about the actual Lydia
Sigourney, author of a poem on the baptism of an infant at its mother's
funeral. Long before Jane Tompkins began defending the value of *Uncle
Tom's Cabin* and other sentimental works by nineteenth-century
women, nonetheless, Miller's lectures on romanticism insisted that we
consider the cultural work of Stowe and Susan Warner. At a time when
several of his colleagues, in the composite study *Literary History of the
United States* (1948), dismissed some romantic American works as too
imitative of European models, and dismissed some characters as "Byronic ghosts,"[10] Miller taught that one's task had only begun when one
had speared and identified the Byronic ghost or isolated the dark hero-

ine. He insisted on asking why James Fenimore Cooper or Hawthorne or Herman Melville had used that conventional figure, what the convention might have meant when it was a way of giving life to characters rather than of making them into rigid silhouettes. To discover that Hawthorne's Hester Prynne and Beatrice Rappaccini were dark heroines, then, was to see an opportunity for variety rather than to expose mere imitation. And in the characterization of both women, I came to see, Hawthorne had made his awareness of the convention a major source of strength. The "rich, voluptuous, Oriental" quality in Hester Prynne gains credibility from her conventional appearance, and so does the great scene in the forest when, after seven years of isolation and self-restraint, she removes her cap and lets her loosened black hair fall glistening around her shoulders in the sunlight.[11] In the story "Rappaccini's Daughter," the beautiful Beatrice is believably frightening as well as attractive to her shallow lover not only because her breath appears to be deadly to insects but also because she appears to be a typical dark heroine. That appearance, which the lover misreads, is belied by her spiritual nature, a quality that Hawthorne and his readers knew was usually reserved in fiction for fair-haired young women.

In the study of historiography this principle led me to look for the value as well as the limitations in conventional representation, and to perceive that value both on a relative scale—How useful were the conventional characters and techniques in expressing the judgments of a historian's own time?—and a less variable scale—How well do the conventional characters and techniques express historical judgment that I still consider valid? It was the recognition of this double set of standards that especially complicated the problem of methods. I saw that in *The Conquest of Mexico,* for example, W. H. Prescott had emphasized the conquistador Cortés's aggressively energetic decisiveness and that in pictures of vigorous activity Prescott had set that quality against equally repetitive pictures of Montezuma's indecisive passivity. I had to admire the insight that these conventional choices enabled Prescott to express—first as an embodiment of his own culture's judgment: The self-reliant, brave, Christian adventurer, newly committed to useful action in the world, overcomes the superstitiously fatalistic pagan, whose "semi-civilized" culture (as Prescott called it) could not survive its encounter with European civilization.[12] As my choice of twentieth-century terms in that last phrase suggests, I also had to admire Prescott's recognition of a continuity between the values of modern commercial enterprise and some qualities in Spanish "knight-errantry," the "spirit of romantic enterprise." [13] Without approving of Cortés's action or all of Prescott's rhetoric, I still admire as valid, too, some of the connections that Prescott's nineteenth-century attitudes helped him to see between Aztec religion and Cortés's astonishing victory. (If the Aztecs had not tried to preserve Cortés for the human sacrifice, they might easily have killed him. If their priests had not prophesied a victory in eight days, Cortés's native allies might not have returned to him after the eight days had passed.) Nor did my qualified admiration oblige me to overlook the considerable cost of Prescott's methods. I ignore the costs here because it is much easier to see the distortions in outdated standards than in our own.

As a critic of history and as an intellectual historian, then, I was especially interested in how historians turn their predicament into their opportunity, and I felt a special attraction to ways of conceiving and portraying character. Rather than expose a historian's sins, I hoped to show, even in some twentieth-century histories, how a historian's literary techniques enhance the value of the historical interpretation. This I tried to do by studying some histories with which my experience had more or less incidentally acquainted me, in brief commentaries on Erik Erikson's *Young Man Luther,* Perry Miller's *The New England Mind,* Oscar Handlin's *The Uprooted,* and Richard Hofstadter's *The Age of Reform.* [14] In my judgment the method worked best for a modern history that I did not write about until 1974, Garrett Mattingly's *The Armada* (1959), and for John Demos's prizewinning *Entertaining Satan* (1983).

Since both of those critical essays are reprinted here (the Mattingly in chap. 2, "Forms of Uncertainty"), I need only point out now that Mattingly's work attracted me both because of our mutual interest in some legendary historical characters and because of its strong ethical emphasis. A remark in my essay "Trying to Make a Monster Human" (chap. 8) bears anticipatory paraphrase in this introductory statement: I agree heartily with Mattingly that although our revisions of historical justice cannot do much for a dead character, they can do much for us. The very enterprise of seeking a fairer reading of the past implies a willingness to reconsider our premises, to think self-critically.

Nearly all these chapters—even the few in which questions of historical fact stand at the center—consider issues of literary form or technique along with issues of historical judgment and interpretation. I have grouped them roughly according to genre in order to underline my conviction that formal and substantive questions often illuminate one another. Although arranged without regard to the chronological order of their composition and previous publication, the chapters from different decades may remind readers that writing, *écriture,* discourse outside the limits of fiction, was receiving critical attention in the United States for some time before the tidal vogue of French theory washed up on the American strand. The reputations of Perry Miller, Henry Nash Smith, and M. H. Abrams in the 1950s and 1960s flourished right beside the "hegemony" of the New Critics. Although few of us who were trained in American literature in the 1940s and 1950s were untouched by the New Criticism, our reading of William Bradford, Jonathan Edwards, Thomas Paine, James Madison, Thomas Jefferson, Margaret Fuller, John C. Calhoun, and Thorstein Veblen opened our classrooms and our critical inquiries to discourses about history, theology, constitutional law. In respect for historical differences as well as continuities, I have noted the date and place of publication, or the date of composition, for each chapter, and for the same reason I have allowed some inevitable repetition to stand.

Notes

1. R. G. Collingwood, *The Idea of History* (New York: Oxford Univ. Press), pp. 215–16.

2. See David Levin, "The Hazing of Cotton Mather: The Creation of a Biographical Personality," *New England Quarterly* 36 (1963): 147–71.

3. Henry D. Thoreau, *Walden; or, Life in the Woods* (Boston and New York, 1894), p. 145.

4. David Levin, "Shadows of Doubt: Specter Evidence in Hawthorne's 'Young Goodman Brown,'" *American Literature* 35 (1962): 344–52.

5. Nathaniel Hawthorne, "Young Goodman Brown," in *Mosses from an Old Manse,* ed. William A. Charvat et al. (Columbus: Ohio State Univ. Press, 1974), p. 88.

6. Nathaniel Hawthorne, "Alice Doane's Appeal," in *The Snow Image and*

Uncollected Tales, ed. William A. Charvat et al. (Columbus: Ohio State Univ. Press, 1974), p. 277.

7. Benjamin Franklin, "The Autobiography," in *Franklin, Writings,* ed. J. A. Leo Lemay (New York: Library of America, 1987), p. 1383.

8. Jonathan Swift, "A Project for the Advancement of Religion and the Reformation of Manners," in *Swift's Writing on Religion and the Church,* ed. Temple Scott, 2 vols. (London, 1898), 1:28.

9. See below, chapters 1 and 2.

10. Robert E. Spiller et al., *Literary History of the United States,* 2 vols. (New York: Macmillan, 1948), 1:262.

11. Nathaniel Hawthorne, *The Scarlet Letter,* ed. William A. Charvat et al. (Columbus: Ohio State Univ. Press, 1962), pp. 83, 202.

12. See, for example, William H. Prescott, *History of the Conquest of Mexico,* 3 vols. (Philadelphia, 1860), 1:107.

13. Ibid., 3:353–54.

14. See David Levin, *In Defense of Historical Literature: Essays on American History, Autobiography, Drama, and Fiction* (New York: Hill and Wang, 1967), pp. 17–31.

Part One

Histories and History

1.

William Bradford

The Value of Puritan Historiography

Famine once we had, wanting corn and bread,
But other things God gave us in the stead,
As fish and ground nuts, to supply our strait,
That we might learn on providence to wait;
And know by bread man lives not in his need,
But by each word that doth from God proceed.
But a while after plenty did come in,
From His hand only who doth pardon sin.
And all did flourish like the pleasant green,
Which in the joyful spring is to be seen.
. . . . .
Another cause of our declining here,
Is a mixt multitude, as doth appear.
Many for servants hither were brought,
Others came for gain, or worse ends they sought;
And of these, many grow loose and profane,
Though some are brought to know God and His name.
But thus it is, and hath been so of old,
As by the Scriptures we are plainly told.
> Bradford, "Some Observations of God's Merciful
> Dealing with Us in the Wilderness" (1654)

Reprinted by permission from Everett Emerson, ed., *Major Writers of Early American Literature* (Madison: Univ. of Wisconsin Press, 1972), Copyright © 1972 the Regents of the University of Wisconsin System.

I

In the body of tradition that stands between modern readers and the best literary works of seventeenth-century New England, William Bradford holds an honorable place both as a political leader and as a writer. Three hundred and fifty years after the founding of Plymouth, we respect him as the faithful governor of Plymouth during the colony's first decades and as the writer whose unfinished history *Of Plymouth Plantation* helped to give the tradition literary form. It is in Bradford's history that we read of "pilgrims" who obey their calling to leave the known European world for a wilderness, seeking comfort in the biblical reminder that heaven is their dearest country. It is Bradford's history that appeals to law as the true foundation of liberty and to "the simplicity of the gospel, without the mixture of men's inventions," as the right model for worship. It is Bradford's history that unites religious, political, and aesthetic value by celebrating "the primitive order, liberty, and beauty" of the first Christian churches.[1]

Bradford's literary reputation rests entirely on the history that he began to write ten years after the founding of Plymouth. His awkward verses and his long, skillfully written dialogues defending Congregational church government against Roman Catholic, Episcopal, and Presbyterian theory and practice have not gained admission to our literary anthologies. It is his admirable prose style, his role as governor, and his representative quality as one of the mildest and most magnanimous of Puritan spokesmen that have won him his honored place in our literary history. Thousands of students who never see the entire volume *Of Plymouth Plantation* know Bradford as the writer, formerly a participant in the historical action, who "cannot but stay and make a pause" to reflect, in the most famous of all his passages, on "this poor people's . . . condition" during their first wintry days on Cape Cod; there "all things stand upon them with a weatherbeaten face," and "which way soever they turned their eyes (save upward to the heavens) they could have little solace or content in respect of outward objects" (61–62). The Bradford modern readers know best is the participant who writes that he respected some newcomers' conscientious refusal to work on Christmas Day—until he found them playing games. (He then told them that it was against his conscience for them to play while others worked.) The Bradford we all know best is the Old Founder who laments the dispersal of original church members and the decline of their original commitment to maintaining one loving, covenanted community.

Yet the distinction between Bradford the eminent colonial leader and Bradford the writer can too easily be blurred in a way that underestimates the achievement of Bradford the historian. The few commentators on Bradford's "conscious art" tend naturally to concentrate on his literary style rather than on his historical imagination.[2] Historians of history and literature, moreover, are inclined to emphasize changes, development, and differences in the ways of writing history, especially when they address a contemporary audience about seventeenth-century historians who had no great influence on the development of the art, the science, the profession. In explaining strange ways to modern students, it is only reasonable to concentrate on differences between the Puritans and ourselves, to show what was "puritan" about them. The very nature of the subject seems to impose a condescending perspective on the study of old histories. It is so important to notice predestination, Providence, and authorial piety that one has little chance to look for much complexity in the individual Puritan's work. And if one does write at some length about Bradford or Cotton Mather, one is tempted to concentrate on the historical facts and the author's remarkable character.

Students of literature need also to pay some attention to the substantive value of the histories they study. The question that has too rarely been asked about Bradford and others is not how Puritanism limited their histories but what good it might have done a historian to be a Puritan. What does Bradford the historian understand, interpret, portray in a way that no other historian has surpassed? Bradford was a Puritan not only when he committed narrow-minded errors but also when he acted meritoriously and wrote perceptively. His Puritan preconceptions gave him some special kinds of historical insight. The literary value of his book depends as much on the quality of his historical intelligence as on the virtues of his style. As an interpreter of Puritan piety, for example, he seems to me a better historian than George Langdon, Peter Gay, or John Demos, all of whom have written more effectively than Bradford about other qualities in Puritan life. Anyone who doubts Bradford's value as a historian needs only to set *Of Plymouth Plantation* beside George Langdon's recent history of the colony. Langdon's excellent book repeatedly uses Bradford's information, and he often follows Bradford's interpretations, but he never treats Bradford as a fellow historian.

The mistake of much commentary—an error more damaging to literary evaluation than to historical narrative—is to treat Bradford only as an example of piety but not to stress the achievement of Bradford the historian in portraying Puritan piety. Bradford's purpose in the first book of his history seems to be to represent the Pilgrims' sufferings in a way that will show how frequently circumstances allowed them nothing else to rely on except their piety. In a very early scene, for example, he dramatizes their predicament under an English authority that refused to let them stay as they were but also refused to let them emigrate. To show the full range of Bradford's use of piety here, I shall have to quote at unusual length.

When the first boatload of emigrant men boarded a Dutch ship near Hull for the voyage to Holland, the sudden appearance of hostile English authorities forced the Dutch captain to "hoise sails, and away." Bradford shows us the plight of both the separated groups of Pilgrims from the point of view of the men being carried to sea

> in great distress for their wives and children which they saw thus to be taken, and . . . left destitute of their helps; and themselves also, not having a cloth to shift them with, more than they had on their backs, and some scarce a penny about them, all they had being aboard the bark . . . and anything they had they would have given to have been ashore again; but all in vain, there was no remedy, they must thus sadly part. And afterward endured a fearful storm at sea, being fourteen days or more before they arrived at their port; in seven whereof they neither saw sun, moon nor stars, and were driven near the coast of Norway; the mariners themselves often despairing of life, and once with shrieks and cries gave over all, as if the ship had been foundered in the sea and they sinking without recovery. But when man's hope and help wholly failed, the Lord's power and mercy appeared in their recovery; for the ship rose again and gave the mariners courage again to manage her. And if modesty would suffer me, I might declare with what fervent prayers they cried unto the Lord in this great distress (especially some of them) even without any great distraction. When the water ran into their mouths

and ears and the mariners cried out, "We sink, we sink!" they cried (if not with miraculous, yet with a great height or degree of divine faith), "Yet Lord Thou canst save! Yet Lord Thou canst save!" with such other expressions as I will forbear. Upon which the ship did not only recover, but shortly after the violence of the storm began to abate, and the Lord filled their afflicted minds with such comforts as everyone cannot understand, and in the end brought them to their desired haven, where the people came flocking, admiring their deliverance; the storm having been so long and sore, in which much hurt had been done, as the master's friends related unto him in their congratulations.

But to return to the others where we left. The rest of the men that were in greatest danger made shift to escape away before the troop could surprise them, those only staying that best might be assistant unto the women. But pitiful it was to see the heavy case of these poor women in this distress; what weeping and crying on every side, some for their husbands that were carried away in the ship . . . ; others not knowing what should become of them and their little ones; others again melted in tears, seeing their poor little ones hanging about them, crying for fear and quaking with cold. Being thus apprehended, they were hurried from one place to another and from one justice to another, till in the end they [the authorities] knew not what to do with them; for to imprison so many women and innocent children for no other cause (many of them) but that they must go with their husbands, seemed to be unreasonable and all would cry out of them. And to send them home again was as difficult; for they alleged, as the truth was, they had no homes to go to, for they had either sold or otherwise disposed of their houses and livings. To be short, after they had been thus turmoiled a good while and conveyed from one constable to another, they [the authorities] were glad to be rid of them in the end upon any terms, for all were wearied and tired with them. Though in the meantime they (poor souls) endured misery enough; and thus in the end necessity forced a way for them. [13–14]

To avoid becoming tedious, Bradford says, he will omit "many other notable passages and troubles which they endured and underwent in these their wanderings," but he understands that he "may not omit the fruit that came hereby," and he saves it for the conclusion of his chapter:

by these so public troubles in so many eminent places their cause became famous and occasioned many to look into the same, and their godly carriage and Christian behaviour was such as left a deep impression in the minds of many. And though some few shrunk at these first conflicts and sharp beginnings (as it was no marvel) yet many more came on with fresh courage and greatly animated others. And in the end, notwithstanding all these storms of opposition, they all gat over at length, some at one time and some at another, and some in one place and some in another, and met together again according to their desires, with no small rejoicing. [14–15]

This eloquent passage has been justly praised for its embodiment of the Pilgrim spirit in images of departure, peril, and arrival that foreshadow both the voyage across the Atlantic and the Christian's journey to heaven. The intervention of Providence draws as much modern notice, if less praise. What I wish to stress in addition is Bradford's attention to worldly as well as Providential cause. Bradford's refusal to see any conflict between Providential and natural causes has admirable as well as regrettable consequences. It requires him to look into the natural and human means through which Providential will usually works. In a North Sea storm the Lord may quiet the waves in answer to faithful prayers, but in narrating human events the Puritan historian must attend to the earthly causes by which "necessity forced a way" for the Lord's covenanted people. Bradford shows us the Pilgrims' misery, but also the logic of their emancipation (what else could be done with them?), the psychology of their victory (their cause became famous, and many more came on with fresh courage). Both examples of deliverance merit the "admiration" of the people, and it is Bradford's Puritan piety that obliges him to examine worldly causes and forbids him to "omit the fruit that came hereby."

Throughout the history, moreover, Bradford's piety functions not chiefly to attribute all causes to Providence but rather to motivate a full report and a strict inquiry into historical complexity. Commentators too often notice his partisanship and his early allusions to Providence, and then cite the doubts he later expressed as he lamented the decline of piety in the second decade after the founding of Plymouth. It is hard for us to believe that historians who portrayed God as their people's faithful shepherd would reveal much doubt in their study of his interventions in history, and we find it easy to emphasize such striking passages as the lament in which Bradford, troubled by the exposure of shocking enormities in 1642, guesses that the Devil may mount especially powerful assaults among God's covenanted people. In truth, the Puritan was expected to be always alert for ambiguity in the historical revelation of God's will. From the opening pages of the history, Bradford depicts the saints in considerable perplexity.

Before considering several examples, I must insist that Bradford's portrayal of Puritan uncertainty is a historical interpretation of great importance, an interpretation that follows from his own inquiry into the significance of events. This valuable interpretation thus follows from his piety, his special way of seeing, his interest in discovering the Providential design in history. It will not suffice to portray him occasionally as a writer whose puzzled comments exemplify uncertainty about a particular phenomenon. We must recognize that he himself portrays the Pilgrim community in its perplexity. He recognizes the faithful search for God's will as the major quest of the Pilgrim's life.

At the very beginning of his history Bradford shows us his conviction that after Satan had failed to destroy the faithful with burnings and open warfare "in the days of Queen Mary and before, he then began another kind of war and went more closely to work . . . to ruinate and destroy the kingdom of Christ by more secret and subtle means, by kindling the flames of contention and sowing the seeds of discord and bitter enmity amongst the professors and, seeming reformed, themselves" (4). In his account difficulties pursue the Marian exiles to the Continent; and the effort of Puritans to hold firm against seductive pleas for retention of "divers harmless ceremonies" is described as a lengthy battle continuing several years until the poor people are enabled by "the continuance and increase of these troubles, and other means which the Lord raised up in those days, to see further into things by the light of the Word of God" (8). It is only those believers who "saw the evil" in Anglican ceremonies who, according to Bradford, at first shake off "this yoke of antichristian bondage"; they join "as the Lord's free people" in a church covenanted to walk not merely "in all His ways made known" but also in all his ways later "to be made known unto them" (9). Bradford reports that division occurred almost at once, and that one of the two congregations fell afterwards "into some errors" in the Netherlands and "there (for the most part) buried themselves and their names" (9).

Even though in doctrinal agreement, the covenanted remnant to which Bradford devotes the rest of his history spends great quantities of time and intelligence studying worldly evidence to find God's will. Bradford the historian shows us that the Lord's free people regarded their new covenant as a genuine liberation, and he is happy to narrate the debates through which (they trusted) God's ways were later to be made known to them. It is respect for the difficulty of knowing that leads him to record the arguments for and against emigrating from Holland to America. Just as he sees it is no marvel that "some few shrunk" at the first conflicts in England, so his piety leads him to describe fully the objections to the great emigration and the fears of good men as the negotiations proceed after the crucial decision has been made. He knows that "in all businesses the acting part is most difficult, especially where the work of many agents must concur" (39). It is no disgrace that good Pilgrims doubt the validity of the calling to emigrate or that the courage of faithful men like Robert Cushman fails for a while on the English side of the Atlantic. The Puritan's liberation frees him to struggle in the world for the glory of God. Some saints are braver than others. The doubts, fears, perplexities, and follies of good men can only add to the glory of the God that has brought the community through the dangers they feared.

This attitude allows Bradford to shape his narrative so that the most persuasive of worldly arguments against proceeding with the colonial adventure lead to a convincing restatement of his Providential theme. He can thus show conscientious men arriving at the conclusion that their best and only hope lies in reliance on Providence. His arrangement has a convincing tenor even for skeptical readers, because his representation of the contrary arguments is both generous and reasonable, and because it is informed with sound political knowledge. When King James tells the Pilgrims' agents that the crown cannot officially grant them liberty to worship in their own way in America, but lets them know that he will "connive at them and not molest them" so long as they behave peaceably, many of the Pilgrims fear (Bradford says) that they should not risk their estates and their lives on such vague assurances. With extremely skillful use of indirect quotation, Bradford dramatizes the most forcible arguments on both sides in a way that leads us through intricate political understanding to dependence upon Providence:

> Yea it was thought they might better have presumed hereupon without making any suit at all than, having made it, to be thus rejected. But some of the chiefest thought otherwise and that they might well proceed hereupon, and that the King's Majesty was willing enough to suffer them without molestation, though for other reasons he would not confirm it by any public act. And furthermore, if there was no security in this promise intimated, there would be no great certainty in a further confirmation of the same; for if afterwards there should be a purpose or desire to wrong them, though they had a seal as broad as the house floor it would not serve the turn; for there would be means enow found to recall or reverse it. Seeing therefore the course was probable, they must rest herein on God's providence as they had done in other things. [30–31]

II

The great value of the Puritan historian, then, is that he can show us piety functioning uncertainly but faithfully in the world, along with other motives. In his portrayal of John Robinson and William Brewster, Bradford achieves one of the best versions we have of the Congregational pastor's and elder's relation to their flock, and he deliberately introduces his characterization of Robinson for its representative social value. Sweetened by twenty years of nostalgic recollection, Bradford's portrait begins with Robinson's "able ministry and prudent government" and with the

> mutual love and reciprocal respect that this worthy man had to his flock. . . . His love was great towards them, and his care was always bent for their best good, both for soul and body. For besides his singular abilities in divine things (wherein he excelled) he was also very able to give directions in civil affairs and to foresee dangers and inconveniences, by which means he was very helpful to their outward estates and so was every way as a common father unto them. And none did more offend him than those that were close and cleaving to themselves and retired from the common good; as also such as would be stiff and

rigid in matters of outward order and inveigh against the evils of others, and yet be remiss in themselves, and not so careful to express a virtuous conversation. [18]

The pastor teaches, so that his people grow "in knowledge and other gifts and graces," and he governs, so that disagreements and offenses are "ever so met with and nipped in the head betimes, or otherwise so well composed as still [to preserve] love, peace, and communion." Bradford thus helps us to enter a world in which there is no necessary conflict between economic and pious motivation. Perhaps one reason we find it difficult to enter such a world without the help of such a historian is that our own view of religious motivation is narrower than his.

Bradford, of course, wanted his narrative to record a valid model of Congregational church government (and to justify his generation) for an uncertain posterity, as well as to achieve an accurate, coherent history and to celebrate the glory of God. He frankly believed, and we ought gratefully to concede, that these different purposes are often served by the same methods. John Robinson's place as the admirable Congregational pastor would not be so effectively achieved in these pages if it depended solely or even primarily on the moving paragraph that I have just discussed. Even in 1630, about fifteen years before he actually wrote the bulk of his narrative, Bradford finishes that paragraph by foreshadowing Robinson's death: dearly as the people loved Robinson while he was alive, they "esteemed him . . . much more after his death, when they came to feel the want of his help and saw (by woeful experience) what a treasure they had lost." Robinson will figure throughout the rest of his life as a major character in the narrative, and much of the narrative that Bradford will later write as annual chapters dramatizes the congregation's painful failure "to find such another leader and feeder in all respects."

What brings to life the Robinson of Bradford's laudatory rhetoric is the abundant circumstantial evidence of his continuing influence in the rest of the history. Bradford shows Robinson debating with an Arminian professor in Leyden, preaching "a good part of the day very profitably" on the eve of the Pilgrims' departure from Leyden, falling down on his knees and tearfully commending his people to God as their ship prepares to sail (47–48). But the chief material of Bradford's historical success in this central characterization is the rich, incontrovertible supply of Robinson's letters. Bradford's judicious, extensive quotation reveals John Robinson as a forceful negotiator on economic and other issues and as an adviser on community government even after the congregation has emigrated to America. Robinson's moral power stands out most admirably in a letter to Bradford more than three years after the founding of Plymouth, when the pastor rebukes the colonists for having killed several Indians; Robinson understands at least some feelings of colonists and Indians alike, and the breadth of his understanding makes his rebuke and his prudential warning all the more persuasive:

> Oh, how happy a thing had it been, if you had converted some before you had killed any! Besides, where blood is once begun to be shed, it is seldom staunched of a long time after. You will say they deserved it. I grant it; but upon what provocations and invitements by those heathenish Christians [that is, not members of Plymouth Plantation or the congregation]? Besides, you being no magistrates over them were to consider not what they deserved but what you were by necessity constrained to inflict. [374–75]

Several of the long letters that Bradford copies into his text impress the reader as footnotes to the narrative, and S. E. Morison, in the best recent edition of the book, relegates many of the letters, including the one that I have just quoted, to an appendix. It seems to me very important, however, to consider all the letters as part of Bradford's narrative. Although a few of them do serve chiefly as documentation, many others deepen the characterization, build the larger structure, and provide unique narrative details. Only through a letter of Robinson's does Bradford let us see Captain Miles Standish's usual humility and meekness as civil traits that probably issue "merely from an humane spirit" rather than from Christian grace. Robinson's fear that under provocation Standish may lack Christian "tenderness of the life of man"—and his warning that "it is . . . a thing more glorious, in men's eyes, than pleasing in God's or convenient for Christians, to be a terror to poor barbarous people"—these help to characterize both Robinson and Standish (375). Only through one of Robert Cushman's many fine letters does Bradford first show us that the treacherous preacher John Lyford was sent to the colony at the insistence of several English stockholders, and that the two Pilgrim agents in England reluctantly consented to this arrangement with the express understanding that Lyford "knows he is no officer amongst you" (374). And it is one of Robinson's early letters that shows us the ideal of the church covenant: "We are knit together as a body in a most strict and sacred bond and covenant of the Lord, of the violation whereof we make great conscience, and by virtue whereof we do hold ourselves straitly tied to all care of each other's good and of the whole, by every one and so mutually" (33).

As the narrative develops, these apparently small matters grow in significance. The letters of Robinson and Cushman show us the complexities of negotiations for the original voyage to Plymouth. They also establish the pattern of governmental affairs for the first decades of life in America. Instructions received in good faith must be loosely interpreted or flatly disobeyed by agents under the immediate pressure of unforeseen decisions—sometimes apparently dishonest and evidently self-interested—made by the Englishmen who control the money on which the whole enterprise depends. Bradford, who as a participant had actually been with the colonists, uses the letters in his history to show us a remarkably complete picture of all four groups: the colonists, the agents, the investors (Adventurers), and (after the founding of Plymouth) the prospective colonists who never did manage to leave the Netherlands. His choice and placement of the letters not only give us essential information but convey the genuine plight and the vivid feelings of men caught in their historical situation. Each of the main figures in this correspondence speaks in his own characteristic language, and Bradford's shrewd arrangement of the inconstant Adventurer Thomas Weston's letters among those of Robert Cushman, John Robinson, and Bradford himself demonstrates brilliantly that character and circumstance make up the essential substance of early colonial history. Weston's blustering accusations that the colonists have let him down appear in the record only after we have seen, through the death of half the colonists in the first winter, how utterly unjust those accusations are, and how desperately the colonists need the help that he has promised but has failed to deliver.

Throughout the first fifteen years of colonization, it is not only the content but the actual historical importance of slow communication that gives the letters their greatest value in Bradford's history. The letter of Weston to which I have just alluded was dated (as Bradford carefully notes) July 6, 1621, and addressed to Governor John Carver. By that time Carver had been dead for more than two months, and his successor, William Bradford, did not receive the letter until November 10. Letters arrive belatedly, and their contents show that correspondents on both sides of the Atlantic have contradictory expectations of one another. Letters prove to be important not only for what they say but because they were often the essential stuff of the new colonists' experience. Eagerly awaited from England, they name new conditions imposed by the Adventurers or announce the French capture of a shipment of American furs from Plymouth. Intercepted by Governor Bradford on their way from Plymouth to England, the Reverend Mr. John Lyford's letters reveal his plans to destroy the Adventurers' confidence in the infant colony's religious and political government, and when he insists that he has been completely loyal to the colonists his own letters are suddenly produced in a grand confrontation to expose him. Letters about his scandalous conduct in Ireland arrive too late to serve as warning. It is letters, too, that bring chilling news of 50-percent interest rates in the early years, and even chillier news a decade later—when colonists awaiting supplies receive instead word that their ship has been sent on a disastrous fishing expedition, and when the Adventurers belatedly confess that for years they have kept no clear records of thousands of pounds of furs and other goods received in payment from the colony.

As evidence from the letters has already suggested, Bradford, in delineating the Pilgrims' struggle against adversity, gives close attention to the diversity of human character. He also displays abundant evidence that the Pilgrims found it difficult to know human character. The Puritan saints who act in this history believe that men are divided into the elect and the damned, but they know that they themselves are often unable to perceive the distinction. They know, too, that an elected Christian can behave incomprehensibly. They do not really understand the character of Robert Cushman, their own agent and friend, or that of Isaac Allerton and James Sherley, until it has been revealed through action, and even then their knowledge is inconclusive. Roger Williams remains a mystery to Bradford long after error has led Williams out of Plymouth and into trouble elsewhere; yet Bradford can thank God for Williams's teachings and can "hope he belongs to the Lord" (257).

It is to Bradford's credit as a narrator that his consistent efforts to justify the Pilgrims and to dramatize their sufferings fill his pages with the bewildering actions of a succession of confidence men. Reading character is an essential quality in any successful colonizer and in Puritan religious life. Bradford's Puritan insistence on justifying his evaluation for the reader assures us of plentiful evidence from the letters of these men themselves, and his sympathy with the community that he portrays as their victim gives memorable power to the difficulties of all colonization. We can see in his account numerous practitioners of Simon Suggs's famous dictum: It is good to be shifty in a new country.

In portraying these confidence men, Bradford as narrator once again not only exemplifies but perceptively requires us to observe important qualities in seventeenth-century Puritanism: the passion for fairness and the liking for scenes of confrontation. The passion for justice (mixed though it often is with self-justification and even self-righteousness) flows powerfully through the letters about misunderstandings, and the combination of open rebuke with recapitulation of evidence sometimes makes the letters themselves serve as confrontations. A number of scenes in the history, moreover, represent Puritan leaders, armed with evidence or at least with the conviction that they must speak out for the truth, directly confronting their antagonists. In Leyden, John Robinson confutes an Arminian professor in public debate of theological issues. In New England, Pilgrims march to demand that Indian leaders verify or deny rumors of a plan to murder Squanto and attack the English settlements; and several of the rogues who figure so entertainingly in the narrative eventually appear in New England to face the indignation of their victims. The most celebrated of these scenes is the attack on Thomas Morton's "pagan" colony at Merrymount, but the most important is the "trial" of John Lyford, the preacher who betrayed the colonists in 1624.

Lyford's story gains force through his pretentious hopes of replacing John Robinson, whom Bradford has already characterized as the ideal Congregational pastor. Bradford shows us how the actual scene of the trial was prepared, through the interception of Lyford's letters to England and the concealment of their discovery until they could be revealed as a public denunciation of his claims to be the Pilgrims' loving friend and pastor. (These letters, by the way, also disclose that Lyford had been intercepting Bradford's letters.) The incident would be impressive enough if Bradford had merely dramatized the revelation, Lyford's confusion, and Lyford's confession and repentance. Bradford's account deserves especial praise because it shows how lenient Puritan justice could often be and because it emphasizes the political consequences. Even at this point, the Plymouth authorities and the congregation are willing to accept Lyford's repentance—until he writes yet another secret letter against them. Then Lyford's wife reveals that he has betrayed her, too, and belated reports from London declare that his original departure from Ireland had been precipitated by the discovery that he had seduced a young parishioner who had sought his counsel before her wedding. Bradford, of course, does not underplay this denouement, but the justification for his attention to the Lyford story has other, historically more significant grounds: his next chapter argues that the banishment of John Lyford provoked a majority of the original Company of Adventurers to break off their relationship to the colony.

As a judge of the diverse characters who enliven his history, Bradford, though often magnanimous and often puzzled, is by no means timid. He roundly condemns the behavior of Weston, Allerton, Lyford, Morton, Sir Christopher Gardiner, and others. But his high standards do not stifle his interest in reading character, and the variety itself supports two of his chief historical observations: (1) that other colonies perished while the religious colony at Plymouth survived, and (2) that the growing proportion of nonreligious settlers in the Plymouth colony reduced the original congregation's influence and its commitment to unity.

III

The perplexity that Pilgrim leaders feel throughout Bradford's history as they struggle to understand character and circumstance seems to me more important than the persuasive theories of lament and decline with which several scholars have tried to explain Bradford's composition of the book. Bradford began writing the history in 1630, the year that the Massachusetts Bay colony was founded by a large group of influential English Puritans. Some scholars believe that the likelihood of Plymouth's being overshadowed by the populous new colony may have moved him to write the first quarter of his narrative in 1630, almost twenty-five years after the first specific event in which he had participated, and that the decline of the original congregation's exemplary unity may have prompted him to resume writing again and to compose the last three-fourths of the narrative in the years between 1645 and 1650. (By 1646 he had reached only the year 1621.)

My own view is that although Bradford does lament evidence of decline in the 1640s, and although these passages are among the most famous that he wrote, the pattern of his historical organization is perennially dialectical, cyclical, alternating, as in the early passage that I have quoted in the departure from England for the Netherlands. Success is followed by failure, safety by danger, disaster by fortunate escape and recovery. Financial tormentors among the colonial agents and Adventurers seem to succeed one another; Weston is followed by Allerton and Sherley in bitter correspondence with the colonists about the debt that seems to grow larger with each payment.

Difficulties exist from the beginning, then, and successes increase along with losses throughout the decades of the history. Insofar as there is a clear direction in the entire narrative, that too is ambiguous. It is a dual story of flourishing growth "from their first beginnings" (46) and of decline from original purity (33n). That, in Bradford's view, is the pattern of all Christian narrative. The same historian might consistently see both threads in the pattern, but he might at different times concentrate on one or the other. Only with the Millennium would the larger pattern be clear to human eyes. Bradford tells us in 1646 that when he began writing the history he did not see how near was the downfall of English bishops, and we can see for ourselves in the section composed in 1630 (and in the verses, written in 1654, which I have used as an epigraph) that he felt as much encouraged as threatened by the friendly settlements in Massachusetts Bay.

It is in this context and with an eye toward the occasional pessimism of old age that we should consider Bradford's comments on the execution of young Thomas Granger (along with several animals) in 1642 for sodomy. Although apparently only the third capital sentence in twenty-two years, this gruesome episode leads Bradford to consider possible explanations for the recent growth of outrageous crimes in Plymouth. Rather than cite these passages as sufficient evidence of a controlling historical disappointment, we must notice the chronology of composition. Bradford did not write the last three-fourths of the history until after the events of 1642 and the death of his friend William Brewster. Granger's execution had occurred several years before Bradford wrote optimistically of the perplexity into which the colonists had been thrown by news of John Robinson's death in 1626:

> it could not but strike them with great perplexity, and to look humanly on the state of things as they presented themselves at this time. It is a marvel it did not wholly discourage them and sink them. But they gathered up their spirits, and the Lord so helped them, . . . as now when they were at [their] lowest they began to rise again, and being stripped in a manner of all human helps and hopes, He brought things about otherwise, in His divine providence as they were not only upheld and sustained, but their proceedings both honored and imitated by others. As by the sequel will more appear, if the Lord spare me life and time to declare the same. [181]

Bradford and other Puritan historians recognized that belief in Providence raised as many difficulties for them as it solved. Indeed, there is one moment in which two sets of Congregationalists in *Of Plymouth Plantation* see Providence on opposite sides. In 1635–36 a group from Plymouth and a rival group from Massachusetts Bay enter conflicting declarations that Providence has entitled them to the same land on the Connecticut River. "Look," says one Congregational group to the other, "that you abuse not God's providence in such allegations" (282–83). The Plymouth group agrees to negotiate only on condition that Thomas Hooker's invaders first grant Plymouth's right to the land, and then the sale is accepted. Where, then, a reader might ask, does the Providential choice finally rest? Plymouth's Providential title is acknowledged, but those who acknowledge it gain the Providential consolation of actual possession.

Knowing that Providence sometimes favored the saints by granting them prosperity did not blind Puritan historians to the wondrous ambiguity of even that blessing. Perhaps the best illustration of how Puritan beliefs encouraged rather than discouraged the study of historical evidence is Bradford's account of the prosperity that came from wampumpeag in 1628. His description of prosperity leads to a puzzle. The trade in wampum makes the Narragansetts and Pequots rich along with the English, and Bradford suggests that it may soon cease to be profitable.

> In the meantime [however], it makes the Indians of these parts rich and powerful and also proud thereby, and fills them with pieces, powder and shot, which no laws can restrain, by reason of the baseness of sundry unworthy persons, both English, Dutch and French, which may turn to the ruin of many. Hitherto the Indians of these parts had no pieces nor other arms but their bows and arrows, nor of many years after; neither durst they scarce handle a gun, so much were they afraid of them. And the very sight of one (though out of kilter) was a terror unto them. But those Indians to the east parts, which had commerce with the French, got pieces of them, and they in the end made a common trade of it. And in time our English fishermen, led with the like covetousness, followed their example for their own gain. [204]

It is these reflections that introduce the most famous rogue in the history, Thomas Morton of Merrymount, whom Bradford excoriates for selling arms to the Indians.

Prosperity, moreover, has a major role in causing conflict among the Pilgrims themselves. Although Bradford is naturally troubled by the events, he seems to have a clear understanding of their causes, economic and social, and he presents them unmistakably as natural consequences of human actions in a world that is just as complex for Pilgrims as for others:

> Also the people of the Plantation began to grow in their outward estates, by reason of the flowing of many people into the country, especially into the Bay of the Massachusetts. By which means corn and cattle rose to a great price, by which many were much enriched and commodities grew plentiful. And yet in other regards this benefit turned to their hurt, and this accession of strength to their weakness. For now as their stocks increased and the increase vendible, there was no longer any holding them together, but now they must of necessity

go to their great lots. They could not otherwise keep their cattle, and having oxen grown they must have land for plowing and tillage. And no man now thought he could live except he had cattle and a great deal of ground to keep them, all striving to increase their stocks. By which means they were scattered all over the Bay quickly and the town in which they lived compactly till now was left very thin and in a short time almost desolate.

And if this had been all, it had been less, though too much; but the church must also be divided, and those that had lived so long together in Christian and comfortable fellowship must now part and suffer many divisions. First, those that lived on their lots on the other side of the Bay, called Duxbury, they could not long bring their wives and children to the public worship and church meetings here, but with such burthen as, growing to some competent number, they sued to be dismissed and become a body of themselves. And so they were dismissed about this time, though very unwillingly. But to touch this sad matter, and handle things together that fell out afterward; to prevent any further scattering from this place and weakening of the same, it was thought best to give out some good farms to special persons that would promise to live at Plymouth, and likely to be helpful to the church or commonwealth, and so tie the lands to Plymouth as farms for the same; and there they might keep their cattle and tillage by some servants and retain their dwellings here. And so some special lands were granted at a place general called Green's Harbor, where no allotments had been in the former division, a place very well meadowed and fit to keep and rear cattle good store. But alas, this remedy proved worse than the disease; for within a few years those that had thus got footing there rent themselves away, partly by force and partly wearing the rest with importunity and pleas of necessity, so as they must either suffer them to go or live in continual opposition and contention. And other still, as they conceived themselves straitened or to want accommodation, broke away under one pretence or other, thinking their own conceived necessity and the example of others a warrant sufficient for them. And this I fear will be the ruin of New England, at least of the churches of God there, and will provoke the Lord's displeasure against them. [252–54]

Clearly, then, the Puritan historian was able to recognize a pattern that has become common in our secular history. Mobility and prosperity harm the community. New remedies bring on new diseases. Throughout the history, Bradford also records a dialectic in which the chosen people (acting out Christian typology) struggle to find God's will as they move between the perils of disease and remedy, adversity and prosperity, enemy and friend. In the long passages I have cited here the people are often trapped in a logical predicament that finds superb expression in the coordinate antitheses of Bradford's rhythmic syntax. That admirably flexible instrument is capable of showing us the Puritan's ideal community, the covenanted church "knit together as a body" (33), the Pilgrims whose "dearest country" was in heaven (47), and the pious but inevitably troubled reality in the actual country of the New World, where complex historical forces transform church and commonwealth.

Bradford's style also serves him admirably in many pages of circumstantial description. Though often abstract, and though occasionally confused by ambiguous pronoun references, his prose has a tough particularity that regularly grounds his typology in explicit biblical references and specific facts of New England life. His typological reading of the smallpox epidemics that devastate Indian nations but pass over the English would be much more vulnerable to criticism if he had not balanced it with a sympathetically detailed picture of the suffering Indians, and with some effort to explain the terrible consequences:

> they fear [smallpox] more than the plague. For usually they that have this disease have them in abundance, and for want of bedding and linen and other helps they fall into a lamentable condition as they lie on their hard mats, the pox breaking and mattering and running one into another, their skin cleaving by reason thereof to the mats they lie on. When they turn them, a whole side will flay off at once as it were, and they will be all of a gore blood, more fearful to behold. And then being very sore, what with cold and other distempers, they die like rotten sheep. The condition of this people [in Windsor, Connecticut,] was so lamentable and they fell down so generally of this disease as they were in the end not able to help one another, no not to make a fire nor to fetch a little water to drink, nor any to bury the dead. But would strive as long as they could, and when they could procure no other means to make fire, they would burn the wooden trays and dishes they ate their meat in, and their very bows and arrows. And some would crawl out on all fours to get a little water, and sometimes die by the way and not be able to get in again. [270–71]

An amazing hurricane; a dying sailor cursed by his own shipmate for expiring too slowly; a fatal shoot-out over fur-trading rights in the Penobscot River; a rogue whom the Indians (with Bradford's consent) capture when he loses control of his canoe as he tries to shoot at them—these and other phenomena come through to the modern reader with equal vigor and detail.

It would be foolish to claim that Bradford's history is faultless. The book is marred at times by an appalling indifference to the Indians and by the kind of narrow perspective and partisanship that one might expect of the "puritanical." But it is an admirably faithful work as well as an eloquently "mythical" statement about plain pilgrims on a journey through the world, and its continuing value depends as much on Bradford's historical intelligence and skill as on his celebrated modesty and style. It gives the best picture that I know of Puritan piety in action in the New World, and it owes much of its success to the obligations imposed on every believer by that piety: to search faithfully for an understanding of God's revealed will in the ambiguous evidence of the historical world.

Notes

1. William Bradford, *Of Plymouth Plantation*, ed. Samuel Eliot Morison (New York: Alfred A. Knopf, 1953), pp. 6, 3.

2. Since these words were written, Alan B. Howard has moved to avoid that distortion. See his "Art and History in Bradford's *Of Plymouth Plantation*," *William and Mary Quarterly*, 3d ser., 28 (1971): 237–66.

2.

Forms of Uncertainty

Representation of Doubt in American Histories

One of the more valuable ways to trace changes and continuities in American historiography is to study how historians have treated the fact of uncertainty, by which I mean both their own doubt or unavoidable ignorance and that of their subjects. Every historian shares with his subjects at least an occasional doubt about the direction in which history moves—or at least about the significance of particular events in his own lifetime—and of course every historian perceives some limit to his ability to discover what happened in the past. Even in the seventeenth century, when a historian could call his book *The Wonder-Working Providence of Sion's Savior in New England,* or *Magnalia Christi Americana,* or *The Triumphs of the Reformed Religion in America,* the anxious serpent of doubt lay coiled in the study. Providence controlled destiny, but no one could really know which of man's accidents revealed which of God's purposes. As Hawthorne demonstrated brilliantly two centuries later in *The Scarlet Letter,* a seventeenth-century comet might be read as the sign of a hypocrite's secret Adultery or as the coincidental sign that Angelic Governor Winthrop was dying. And the witchcraft crisis or King Philip's War might be read either as a divine retribution for past sins or as a test of faith, for which the correct response was utter confidence that Providence would deliver a faithful nation. Perry Miller catches these extreme variations of response in his account of King Philip's War: the ineffectiveness of many Days of Humiliation and Fasting, Miller writes, led the authorities to try a Day of Thanks-

Reprinted by permission from *New Literary History* 8 (1976): 59–74, this essay was first delivered at a conference on American historical thought, at Cornell University, in 1974.

giving, which was immediately rewarded by news of King Philip's death. We do not diminish Miller's achievement when we notice that Increase and Cotton Mather made the same point in their own contemporaneous histories.[1] The two best Puritan historians, William Bradford and Cotton Mather, wrote in considerable perplexity because the Providentially nurtured communities whose survival their histories celebrate seemed to be declining even as the histories were being composed. Indeed, one reason for our own revival of interest in Puritanism may well be a sympathetic recognition of that very perplexity.

For some years now I have been arguing that we can learn much by considering Puritan and other outdated historians not primarily as Puritans or Romantics or Whigs but as historians. What good did it do historians to be Puritans? What can we learn from them that no other historians tell us more effectively? More than three hundred years after his death William Bradford has not been superseded or excelled as an interpreter of Puritan piety in the Plymouth colony. His is still the best account that I know of the Congregational minister's function in the covenanted community, of Puritan piety in action, and of a tiny new colony's experiences in the first years of almost total dependence on supplies from overseas. Bradford understood what historians after Hawthorne scarcely discovered again till our own anxious age—not only that, in Emerson's wistful phrase, the Puritan saw God face to face and enjoyed an original relation to the universe, but also that the Puritan's essential life was a daily battle to strengthen and preserve his faith, and that Puritans found it extremely difficult to know human character, one's own true motives and those of one's closest friends and neighbors.[2]

Bradford's understanding of those subjects has a powerful effect upon the very form of his history. His organization of the narrative gives us not only the sufferings of the saints but their perplexity; as they struggle between assurance and doubt, prosperity and adversity, peace and war, health and disease, the unmistakable pattern of alternation reflects Bradford's conviction that in the uncertain world they often had nothing to rely on except God's providence. Even those of us who don't believe in Providence are thus enabled by Bradford the skilled historian to see what kind of evidence and circumstances confirmed the Pilgrims' faithful reliance upon it. Bradford's heavy use of documentation, moreover, his regular incorporation of long letters into the text and his elaborate rehearsal of conflicting arguments, issue from the same uncertainty about how to judge historical events. Other motives do contribute to these devices—Bradford himself expresses a characteristically Puritan desire to justify his choices and those of his people, and for the glory of God he wishes to compile a full record. But equally strong is the need to have the record available for reinterpretation, or to show why the Pilgrims took a seemingly incomprehensible position, or to represent individual character directly rather than through the less reliable judgment of a perplexed historical interpreter.

Here we need to consider only one brief example of the ways in which Bradford's prose style is suited to his patterns. He portrayed the Pilgrims as a small band oppressed by the English authorities and later nearly overwhelmed by the impossible demands of their financial backers in Old England and the great dangers in the New England wilderness. In that delineation his recourse to a pattern of biblical antitheses is beautifully appropriate. Consider two sentences describing their plight in 1609, just after his exposition of the military and urban dangers that the prospect of life in the Netherlands threatened for these brave, simple English farmers: "Yet this was not all, for though they could not stay, yet were they not suffered to go; but the ports and havens were shut against them, so as they were fain to seek secret means of conveyance, and to bribe and fee the mariners, and give extraordinary rates for their passages. And yet were they often times betrayed, many of them; and both they and their goods intercepted and surprised." The same sort of device is admirably effective in Bradford's analysis of the spiritual cost of prosperity, when he must report that thriving trade enriched the Indians as well as the Pilgrims, and enabled the former to buy guns and ammunition, and again later when the growth of the community into larger and more prosperous farms breaks up the original ideal of a single covenanted church. Perry Miller noted that the logic of Peter Ramus, with its emphasis on disjunctive syllogisms and the mere naming of dialectical qualities which argued their opposites, was a logic for dogmatists.[3] The style encouraged by such thinking was often a rhetoric for the perplexed.

I contend, then, that while Puritan attitudes prejudiced historians they also disposed them to strive for a faithful record of the past and to recognize its ambiguities. It is perfectly acceptable to study Puritan historians for their emphasis on a wonder-working Providence, their pervasive search for biblical typology, and their prejudicial distortions. It is also necessary to study their efforts to write true history. Austin Warren illuminates *Magnalia Christi Americana* when he calls it "Grandfather Mather's Wonder Book"; Sacvan Bercovitch lights up the same book when he treats it as an epic, an early work of the expansive American literary imagination. Perry Miller clarifies its intended function when he calls it a grand jeremiad.[4] Despite all its faults and its other aims, however, the work cannot be adequately understood unless it is also regarded as a history, a genuine effort to achieve what Mather called an impartial record.[5]

Mather seems at first a historian more difficult to take seriously than Bradford, whose personal detachment and unusually generous temperament have always been apparent to even the most skeptical readers. Every page of Mather's huge folio volume seems to call attention to the historian's own personality. Mather writes as a defensive provincial, addressing the great world of English readers, whom he "entertains," especially in his elaborate General Introduction and in the opening paragraphs of his innumerable biographies, with learned parallels and allusions. "Readers of History," he declares (quoting Polybius), "get more good by the Objects of their Emulations, than of their Indignation." And he frankly writes to celebrate virtue. "How," he asks, "can the lives of the commendable be written without commending them?" ([xxvi]). He warns us that he will suppress the names and some of the deeds of evil men, and many of the controversies between worthy men. And he writes the lives of the New England saints, his revered father's and grandfathers' generations, who by the dozen may seem to modern readers no more distinguishable from one another than all those portraits of Madonnas in Italian museums seemed to Mark Twain's innocents abroad.

Yet Mather was essentially a faithful historian. Both in questions of fact and in interpretation he is still a valuable observer, despite his obvious limitations. On the Pilgrims' departure from England to Holland, for example, or John Winthrop's now celebrated speech explaining the differences between civil and natural liberty, or the Salem witchcraft trials of 1692, in which Mather himself was a participant—

on these and many other subjects we can now watch Mather following his sources. When I do so, I find him a consistently intelligent editor and reporter, whose paraphrases and summaries are remarkably free of distortion. Although we must be careful with documents that he himself wrote, because he sometimes remembers (or wishfully supplies) a different intention from the one our judgment would prefer, I believe it is fair to say that we would lose very little if his report of the documents we can now check were the only surviving version of them. I believe he was genuinely concerned for accuracy when he invited every reader to point out errors of fact in his mammoth work, and that when he declared himself an impartial historian he did not mean to deny his passionate allegiance, but rather to declare a standard of justice.

Mather was also a more sophisticated thinker about historical objectivity than his reputation would lead us to expect. He understood and rejected, for example, the argument that in order to claim impartiality a historian had to restrict himself to "bare *Matters of Fact,* without all Reflection." On that issue he cited Tacitus, who had declared the historian's privilege of narrating past actions with praise or blame, and Mather was also familiar with other classical, Christian, and seventeenth-century debates on objectivity and partisanship. Although he did not completely anticipate modern debates about relativism, he certainly understood that it would be ridiculous for a Christian, who had sworn a covenant of faithful service after renouncing his own sins, to pretend that he saw no difference between virtue and vice. It is in this context that we must read the rhetorical question that I have already quoted: How can the lives of the commendable be written without commending them? It was not partial, he believed, to praise what objectively deserved to be praised.

As an interpreter of New England church history, moreover—from church government and membership to the character of governors John Winthrop, Sir Henry Vane, William Bradford, and Sir William Phips—Mather stands up surprisingly well even today. If we make minor allowances for the lapse of time, I believe that most of us will set his characterization of John Winthrop beside those of Samuel Eliot Morison, Perry Miller, and Edmund Morgan—Mather was, after all, the first historian to see the importance of reprinting Winthrop's speech on civil and natural liberty—and that we will find his interpre-

tation of seventeenth-century changes in church memberships rather
close to the thesis of Edmund Morgan's fine study.[6]

If my main purpose here were to rehabilitate Cotton Mather, I
would make similar claims for his interpretation of the Salem witchcraft trials and the colonists' grievances before the Glorious Revolution
of 1689, but I must return to the question of representing uncertainty,
to which all this discussion of Mather has been merely preliminary.
Credulous though he sometimes was, Mather of course understood that
neither Christian historians nor eyewitnesses were always reliable authorities. He warns us, for example, that John Winthrop's journal is
not an adequate source for the character of Sir Henry Vane (2:18).
Mather tried to collect the most reliable information he could find, by
circulating requests throughout the colony, and he complained emphatically that some descendants of figures in his history had neglected
to answer his requests, so that he simply left some biographies blank,
with nothing but the name and epitaph to mark the man's presence in
history.

But what has hagiography to do with uncertainty or doubt? The
first point to notice is that Mather's lives of the New England saints
are set in a frame which allows him to celebrate the complexity of
God's historical plan even as he sometimes uneasily concedes that the
glorious experiment may fail and that the Golden City prophesied in
Scripture may not after all be found in America. His first book, called
"Antiquities," describes the founding of New England. Historical
knowledge, Mather implies here, is progressive. Christian writers had
superseded the pagan chroniclers who had located in Joppa the bones
of the sea monster from which Perseus had rescued Andromeda. Christians knew about the true story of Jonah and the whale, and the bones
of Joppa were probably those of Jonah's whale.[7] In the same way, Christian writers ignorant of America's existence are corrected by a frankly
provincial, explicitly American historian who boasts that he now writes
from a region whose very existence could not have been proclaimed
during the time of Pope Zachary without the risk of excommunication.
Mather rejoices that he is not only beyond the range of the pope's
excommunication but also beyond any need to be protected by such an
authority (1:2).

The idea of progressive historical knowledge is built into the history itself, and Mather knows that he too is subject to it. He argues that the concealment of America's existence over the centuries was a more remarkable Providence than the actual discovery. But he reserves especial admiration for the timing of the Providential revelation to Columbus. The three key events that transformed the world near the beginning of the sixteenth century, he writes, were the "Resurrection of Literature," the discovery of America, and the Reformation (1:2). The Pilgrims and Puritans who act in Mather's history are not merely defenders of a completed Reformation; they actively pursue the ideal of continuing reformation. Near the end of his brief chapter on Plymouth, Mather quotes a very important sermon by John Robinson, pastor of the Plymouth congregation in Leyden, exhorting his flock, as they embarked for England and America, to be ready to receive further truth that would surely break forth out of God's Holy Word. In that sermon Robinson criticizes the Lutherans and Calvinists for their refusal to go beyond what Luther or Calvin saw. He reminds the departing Pilgrims that the Covenant which binds them together binds them also to "be ready to receive whatever Truth shall be made known unto you from the Written Word of God" (1:14). The rest of Mather's vast history reports what New England Congregationalists had learned in the last eight decades of the century.

Mather's fundamental uncertainty influences the form of this first book and many of the later ones in the *Magnalia*, reinforcing the pattern of alternation that we have already noticed in Bradford. Faith in the progressive destiny of God's people does predominate; even the jeremiad assumes that God's favor will be restored if his people truly reown their covenant with him. The wonders of the Christian religion in America include demographic triumphs: while the population of the world doubled in the last 360 years, Mather notes, in little more than fifty years 4,000 New England immigrants somehow managed to multiply into more than 100,000 (1:23). They converted a "desert wilderness" into "a garden" (1:17, 18, 23); and these desert colonies that had boasted an extraordinary number of Cambridge and Oxford graduates among their clergy in the first generation can now (only sixty years later) count 104 Harvard graduates preaching in their churches (1:27–28). The historian of these wonders can also point to physical abundance, which he typifies most grandly in the whale fishery's recent capture of a fifty-five-foot cow with a twenty-foot calf: "for unto such vast *Calves,* the *Sea Monsters draw forth their Breasts.* But so does the good God here give his People to suck the Abundance of the Seas!" (1:13).

Against this celebration of abundance Mather sets the contrary theme of declension both spiritual and (at times) physical. He concedes that for more than twenty years now since the days of King Philip's War "the *Blasting Strokes* of Heaven" have fallen "upon the Secular Affairs" of New England (1:27). And from the early years of the Plymouth colony he establishes an old Latin proverb as the counterpoint that has been taken up, in the three centuries since he wrote, as the main theme of many studies of colonial New England: "The chief *Hazard* and *Symptom of Degeneracy*" in the churches, he says, "is in the Verification of that Old Observation *Religio peperit Divitas, et Filia Devoravit Matrem;* Religion brought forth *Prosperity,* and the *Daughter* destroy'd the *Mother.*" One would expect gratitude to the God "who *gives them Power to get Wealth,*" but "the Enchantments of this World make them to forget their *Errand into the Wilderness*" (1:14). So we alternate. Sometimes we concentrate on the blasting strokes: a great fire destroys many homes, 1,000 people die of smallpox in a town of 4,000. Sometimes we stress the Providential blessings: the town afflicted by smallpox has now grown to number 7,000, with more than 1,000 houses (1:31). If no new towns have been founded since the devastating Indian wars of the 1670s, the old towns have doubled in population nonetheless (1:29).

Mather strives to find some rational coherence in the evidence. At first he insists that the sole motive for colonizing Massachusetts was religious zeal, and by way of contrast he candidly reports the protest of a group of colonists in Maine who would not allow a visiting preacher to rebuke them for betraying the religious purpose of their colony: "Sir," one of them protests, "You are mistaken, you think you are Preaching to the People at the Bay; our main End was to catch Fish." For such worldly motives, Mather argues, the northern people suffered one disaster after another, while the early Puritans of Massachusetts have often "thriven to admiration" (1:15). And in Massachusetts itself calamities have not been evenly distributed. Providence does not merely intervene to reward those towns that are blessed with "a good Ministry"; in this matter, as in many others, the divine purpose is attached to mundane reasoning. Mather contends—as Larzer Ziff has recently done[8]—that the cold climate and barren land might not have allowed New England towns to flourish better than more fertile colonies if they had not enjoyed the extraordinary discipline of their churches and congregations. But then Mather also concedes that one subsidiary motive for the founding of Massachusetts included both disgust with European corruption and a conviction that "the whole Earth is the *Lord's Garden,* . . . to be Tilled and Improved by" the sons of Adam: why then, his English Puritans ask, "should we stand starving here for places of Habitation, and in the meantime suffer whole countries so profitable for the use of man, to lye waste without any Improvement?" (1:18). Here, as in Max Weber's version of Puritanism, a worldly motive was acceptable and implicitly more effective if subordinated to a religious one.

The alternating pattern gives our doctrinaire historian freedom to incorporate all kinds of evidence without abandoning his essential faith. When he highlights the "blasting strokes" and the threat of disaster, he is like the preacher who calls for repentance. Indeed, he expresses not the slightest discomfort about incorporating into the text of his history several entire sermons of his own. In these he is the immediately present pastor, exhorting his flock to improve. At other times, in the more disinterested stance of the historian, he can calmly report that like Jesus in the wilderness the people of New England have been "*continually* tempted by the Devil" in their wilderness—with "a new Assault of Extraordinary Temptation" almost every five years (7:4). And when he sings his theme of the Christian wonders in America, he is holding up past models for emulation and celebrating the glory of the God who will yet deliver New England. Doubts of the future appear in the framing introductory book and more insistently in the last book on the Wars of the Lord. The lives of the saints, which fill Mather's second, third, and fourth books, are balanced later on by chilling circumstantial narratives of executions, confessing yet unrepentant murderers, Indian wars, witchcrafts, and an astonishingly well depicted succession of confidence men who invade Boston at the very end of the century and utterly deceive some congregations. The complexity of the secular world, and many of the controversies that Mather frankly underplays in his biographies, appear in these later books along with a large number of original documents which emphasize Mather's conviction—iterated and refined in our own century by scholars from Perry Miller and Samuel Eliot Morison to Edmund S. Morgan and Michael Kammen[9]—that New England church government was a mixed government, that embattled and perplexed seventeenth-century synods repeatedly sought and followed a middle way, as Mather insists in his account of what we have come to know as the Half-way Covenant (5: chaps. 10 and 17).

Even in Mather's lives of the saints uncertainty plays a major role. Every reader must share to some degree Peter Gay's resistance to the sameness in those lives, to the pattern not only of similar conversions but of happy endings, exemplary Christian deaths.[10] But here, as in the study of Italian portraits of Madonnas, familiarity enables one to see important distinctions. It is precisely Mather's intention to show that so many of the lives of first-generation ministers were outwardly and inwardly similar. When one reads the entire history consecutively, the resemblances among these lives may become monotonous, but they are also impressive and even moving, and it is Mather's great theme of variation within essential uniformity that makes both his emotional and his historical case. To the allegorical Puritan mind and to the casual modern reader, all these men are saints. To the historian glorifying God in his narrative and instructing posterity by their example, these men are unique versions of an essential type. The challenge is to make their uniqueness evident and memorable within the allegorical forms.

Before we consider the differences, I believe it is important to look more closely at the value of the repetition. As we see one after another in the first generation of ministers and governors experience the crisis of conversion, of resistance to Anglican ceremonies, and of persecution by Archbishop Laud, we receive a convincing impression of a central historical reality: Many accomplished men had to experience this religious and social crisis individually. For the secular reader of history, the impression of that fact is more memorable than the Providential deliverances that Mather sometimes underlines. And of course one of the main similarities among some of the most eminent lives is the recurrence of perplexing, often terrifying doubt. Richard Mather, John Cotton, Thomas Hooker, Thomas Shepard, Nathanael

Rogers, Jonathan Mitchell—Mather gives strong evidence to show that every one of those men was seriously troubled by major challenges to his faith and to his assurance of his own salvation years after he had already been preaching the Gospel. Thomas Hooker remarks as he takes his last look at England from his departing ship that in his lifetime true religion may never again be defended with the same genuine ardor as in the days of the English oppression. And in the same brief speech he prophesies the declension of piety that has been noted by American historians ever since the seventeenth century: Some of the churches will decline when they have liberty in America, Hooker declares in Mather's narrative as he leaves England; "Adversity had slain its Thousands, but Prosperity would slay its Ten Thousands!" (3:63). Ezekiel Rogers, an extraordinarily successful preacher in England, fears nonetheless that he is unregenerate, and his "Lively Spirit" has the misfortune to inhabit what Mather calls "a crazy body." Mather depicts him in a memorable image during his old age in Rowley, Massachusetts, as a tree of knowledge stooping to let the children "pick off the Apples ready to drop into their mouths" (3:103). William Thompson, suffering what Mather calls the prevalent New England disease of "splenetic maladies," is sometimes tempted like many others to suicide. While preaching at Braintree, he falls into "a black Melancholy" which disables him for many years, and only as Thompson approaches death does the Devil flee and "God himself draw near" (3:118–19). John Warham is so afflicted by a "deadly . . . Melancholy" that he refuses to accept communion himself while serving it to his congregation. "Some," Mather scrupulously reports, say that Warham was still "in a Cloud" when he died, "tho' some have asserted, that the Cloud was dispelled, before he expired" (3:121). Nathanael Rogers laments his brief subscription in 1627 to articles of Anglican conformity in England. It had seemed only prudent, Rogers wrote at the time, "but it was my weakness as I now conceive it; which I beseech God to pardon unto me." Four years later Rogers added a note which Mather prints: "This I smarted for, 1631. If I had read this, it may be, I had not done what I did." "Readers," Mather comments, "in this one Passage Thou hast a large History, of the Thoughts and Fears, and Cares, with which the *Puritans* of those Times were exercised" (3:106).

In no other historical work that I know can we find so pervasive and so well integrated a representation of doubt and uncertainty in the individual Puritan's life. Mather's strength as a historian grows out of the range and the number of his examples, and the persistence of his theme—the piety, the faith, the struggle, the perplexity, and the resignation in so many. However we may discount his partisanship, the unquestionable reality of their losses, their suffering, and their anxiety comes through as a major achievement of his narrative method, which, of course, owes something to John Foxe's Book of Martyrs.[11] To know that dozens of successful, learned ministers left England is to be impressed by their danger and their commitment; to read dozens of their lives as in various circumstances they decide to leave is quite another, more powerful experience. The variety and the specific detail of Mather's individualizing anecdotes make their historicity generally unquestionable. Of all the characters who die exemplary deaths in the *Magnalia,* only Richard Mather struggles to get off his deathbed and into his study on the day before his death, for fear of wasting time; and only Thomas Parker, the celibate, sweet-voiced singer, retains his excellent voice until "very Old Age" because, Mather reasons, "his Teeth held sound and good until then; his Custom being to wash his Mouth, and rub his Teeth every Morning." Having always feared a palsied tongue and the loss of his voice, poor Parker comes at last to an infirmity that prevents him from speaking words but allows him to speak letters, and one of Mather's unforgettably unique anecdotes recounts Parker's laborious narration of a geriatric dream by the only method available to him—spelling it out.

The lives of the governors, though perhaps the best of Mather's historical achievements, need not take so much space here, but it is important to notice that in the *Magnalia* even the most assured of those men also labor at times in perplexity. Perhaps the best example is Sir William Phips, whose absolute conviction that destiny will make him rich leads him to persevere in his search for a wrecked Spanish treasure ship, and who, when he finds it, cries out, "Thanks be to God; we're made!" (2:41). Even that favorite of Providence comes to fear, since he is not yet a church member, that by granting him extraordinary prosperity Providence may have decided to "put him off with a portion" here on earth, without saving his soul hereafter (2:47). He does repent of his sins and join the church, and as governor of Massachusetts he trusts Providence and again finds extraordinary success in the capture of the French fort at Louisbourg. Emboldened then to attack Quebec with a much greater force later on, he suffers a humiliating disaster. Neither he nor his biographer can understand what signs might have told them that the siege of Quebec would fail, although neither one questions the conviction that an English conquest of Quebec would serve to advance true Christian liberty.

It is right here, of course, that we see the key distinction between Puritan uncertainty and that which prevails among many of ourselves. Puritans, too, had trouble understanding their own motives and the motives of historical and contemporaneous characters. Mather could even describe himself in one uncharacteristic moment as a "Seeker" in his effort to understand the conflicting reports of the character of Sir Henry Vane (2:18). They also had great difficulty in reading the intentions of Providence, the direction of history: one of Mather's most poignantly valuable passages describes the ironic misery of saints who had emigrated to America for the religious benefit of their descendants but who eventually found that some of their own grandchildren could not even be baptized, because neither parent in the intermediate generation had joined the church. Sometimes Puritan historians could show that Providence rebuked the strictest interpreters of Scripture: the most vehement leaders who insisted that the Devil cannot appear in a person's shape without that person's consent are confuted in Mather's history by sworn testimony that victims have been afflicted by specters in the shapes of those very leaders themselves! And ultimately the entire community can make gross errors in the name of the Lord—as when they fight the Devil's assault in the form of witches, only to discover too late that his real strategy has been to mix lies with truths and thus throw them into utter confusion by fomenting universal suspicion, wild accusations, and at least some false convictions as he seduces the courts into accepting his testimony. In all these difficulties, however, Cotton Mather and other Puritan historians never doubted for long that history was moving toward a good ending decreed by the wisest of beings. Nor in all the reporting of villains, backsliders, and confidence men did Mather doubt that heroes and saints had really existed. The *Magnalia* is full of qualifications. "*Suffering* as well as *Doing* belongs to the Compleat Character of a Christian," Mather says, and the "Excellent Lives" of his saints are limited by the faults of human nature. Yet among Christians at least there *are* exemplary lives, and it is one of Mather's chief aims to establish them as models for his readers. Even in that Copernican universe Puritan historians knew the temptations of ultimate doubt, from atheism to despair, but they felt sure that such doubts tormented them only for their instruction, or as the Lord's way of testing them—or perhaps of damning them—for the glory of God.

In the twentieth century, of course, all the kinds of uncertainty and doubt that I have discussed function in innumerable ways to affect the writing of history. The very proliferation of historical writing in the last hundred years is probably both cause and consequence of intensified uncertainty and doubt. A great quantity of solid, confident history is of course published with little attention to self-doubt or to theoretical uncertainty, and we ought to remember that just as Cotton Mather in the beginning of the eighteenth century had some insight into the historian's subjectivity, so Washington Irving in the beginning of the nineteenth century asked ultimate questions about the historian's bias and reliability. [12] What seems to me plainly distinctive nonetheless in the eighty years since Henry Adams wrote his history of the Jefferson and Madison administrations is the pervasiveness of theoretical and personal questioning among historians, and the acceleration of challenges to interpretations. My revered mentor and friend Oscar Handlin fears that that acceleration has been wrecking the profession. [13] Others have noticed a remarkable gap between the theoretical modesty and self-awareness of twentieth-century American historians and the persistence of "scientific" assumptions about method in their actual historical work. [14] What I wish to consider now are a few literary, or formal, consequences of the new self-awareness in the work of some historians who have been almost universally acclaimed as masters. I shall offer a few general comments upon a mode of almost comic self-deprecation that has characterized some of our best writers from Henry Adams to Robert R. Palmer, and I shall look in a little more detail at a major work by Garrett Mattingly.

The mode to which I refer—I hesitate to call it a tradition—is that of the critical inquirer who often represents himself to us as the curious, skeptical, self-critical investigator of received assumptions, interpretations. The phrasing of new questions, and especially new kinds of questions, can be undertaken in many different ways, but in the works of writers as different as Henry Adams, Carl L. Becker, and David M. Potter—and especially in the essays of the latter two—it has been done with striking effectiveness through an ironic, humorous, self-effacing understatement. The manner, of course, is not new in the twentieth century. It is Socratic; it is Franklinian; it comes out of the Missouri, Nevada, and California of Mark Twain as well as the Midwest of Carl Becker and the rural New England of Brother Jonathan and Robert Frost. Nor do we need to call upon modern psychoanalysis in order to appreciate the usefulness of an understated, questioning manner for forcible, even aggressively adventurous assertions of personal conviction. There is a long tradition in American literature of self-critically provincial appeals to humor which are also declarations of strong personal conviction, self-assertion against the presumptuousness of established prejudices. Benjamin Franklin, Joel Barlow, Washington Irving, and Mark Twain all understood at least part of this quality in their own work. One of the best exemplars of the attitude among modern historians is Carl Becker, especially in his essays and letters on historiography and in his lectures on the *Heavenly City of the Eighteenth-Century Philosophers.*

My first example, however, comes from a letter by one of Becker's most distinguished students, Robert R. Palmer. Not originally written for publication, the letter was printed at the end of Palmer's essay in *Generalization in the Writing of History.*[15] Other contributors, and members of the committee charged by the Social Science Research Council to prepare that report, had raised some objections to Palmer's essay. The nature of the debate will become clear in my quotation from his letter, after I have pointed out that he had quoted some maxims of La Rochefoucauld which he believed to be as valid and useful (though as incapable of positive proof) "as any we are likely to get in social science." These were the maxims: "A bourgeois manner may sometimes be lost in the army, but never at court." "Self-interest blinds some and gives light to others." "There are bad men who would be less dangerous if wholly lacking in goodness."

In his letter of January 29, 1959, Palmer conceded that the commentators on his essay had described important problems, which he felt he could at least partially understand:

> I simply do not know how to go about answering them. [David] Potter, for example, . . . finds my statement ambiguous or silent on the relation between ideas and social conditions. He finds that "ideas are regarded as secondary." Perhaps they are. I do not know. I have not settled this relationship in my own mind. I expect to die without having settled it. . . . I know, of course, about "borrowing concepts from other disciplines" for use in history; I have at times made reasonable efforts to do so, but to tell the truth I have never felt very successful. With a few exceptions such as "social mobility" or "functional rank," there are few such concepts that I have felt conscious of employing. I do not doubt the need of concepts; but, as I remarked in the letter of June 16, the concepts of social science, with certain exceptions, have not, to my knowledge, entered much more into my work than those stated in the maxims of La Rochefoucauld. As for . . . "limited generalizations that can be proved or disproved," I am also in the dark. I do not know whether propositions about human affairs can be "proved" or not. I am not so presumptuous, or naive, as to suppose that my book, consistent, logical, and persuasive as I hope it is, actually "proves" either its main thesis or any of its subordinate points.

The disarming attitude of skeptical faith and self-effacing self-reliance in this kind of writing is perfectly adapted to an understated, ironic, comic quality in the prose itself, the short declarations of ignorance and doubt, the frequent choice of plain, colloquial diction. We can see the qualities in Carl Becker's letter to Henry Johnson. Becker insists that "the mass of the nation cares nothing for history until they have a particular purpose to carry through which can be justified by reference to the past, to their traditions, (American 'principles,' etc.) and then they proceed to make these traditions, this past, to suit their purpose. In other words the 'history' that actually has an effect on the course of events is almost always an idealized history." [16]

The last sentence of Becker's brings me to the themes and form of my last example, Garrett Mattingly's *The Armada*.[17] Mattingly indicates from his opening paragraph that he intends his book to be more than a fresh narrative of the disaster that according to legend changed

Western European and American history. In his preface he locates the genesis of his book in his reflections on the danger that Adolf Hitler might invade the British Isles in 1940, near the beginning of a war over conflicting systems of ideas. Mattingly begins by suggesting that a historian who has lived through World War II is better equipped than the generation of A. T. Mahan to understand the people embroiled in an ideological, total war (v). And he concludes with a slightly different version of the last sentence that I have quoted from Carl Becker. The destruction of the Armada, he says, did little in itself to change history, but the use that was made of that disaster—the belief that it had been influential and the legends based thereon—had very important historical consequences (401–2).

Between the preface and the epilogue, then, Mattingly's *The Armada* is thoroughly modern in the sense that I have been trying to delineate. The author frankly tells us of his self-awareness, that he stands within a particular time and place and that tolerant knowledge of its own limitations, traditions, prejudices, and ignorance is the wisest lesson that his civilization brings to the study of the past. As J. H. Hexter has demonstrated in an admirable essay, Mattingly was passionately dedicated to the quest for justice in historical writing, and that commitment gave him a special advantage in understanding historical figures whom Hexter calls losers.[18] Mattingly's conviction that the living have an obligation to correct unfair judgments upon the dead is as emphatic as Cotton Mather's commitment to another version of magnanimous historical judgment. *The Armada* is filled with insistent, learned, positive corrections of historical error. But from the moment that a prefatory note on sixteenth-century ships and guns shows us the great confusion over defining the precise range and weight of culverins and their ammunition (xviii), Mattingly's learned instruction comes to us through evidence and technique which subtly remind us of how little men know, how much they err, how often they must act on imperfect or false information.

One formal way of building that insistent theme into the very organization of the book is to employ the modern device of limiting the point of view. Beginning with Mary's execution at Fotheringhay in 1587, an execution which was hurried through because none of those responsible "knew which of the others might not weaken if they waited another day" (1), Mattingly brings the news of her death to each important place—London, Greenwich, Paris, Brussels, Rome, the Escorial—as the respective figures whose actions will be affected by the message learn about it. As we learn more about the significance and background of the events, then, we see the ignorance of the chief historical figures. And the knowledge that we gain of their characters often reinforces the theme that I have stressed.

Mattingly is even able to exploit some of the conventional, historical characterizations that he is correcting. Elizabeth I has traditionally been characterized as the eternally unpredictable Woman, and so Mattingly describes her here (while underplaying the male condescension that one can find in the portraits by Sir Walter Scott and John Lothrop Motley).[19] We ought not to insist, Mattingly says, that Elizabeth's expression of grief was "all acting. About a character so complex as Elizabeth's it is safer never to be too sure of anything" (22). And again, a little later: "Her consistency was in being always inconsistent. . . . Elizabeth did more than merely profit by time; she baffled it; she seemed sometimes to annul it altogether" (23). Her deliberate unpredictability baffles other statesmen, too, men who have to act on conjecture about her future conduct. Philip II, though hardly diabolical in Mattingly's book, functions here with the same elaborate attention to detail, the same indefatigable, secretive, and astonishingly petty scribbling that John Lothrop Motley had portrayed unforgettably. Alexander Farnese, duke of Parma, is as subtle and dangerous in Mattingly's history as in Motley's. Sir Francis Drake and the Dutch commander Justin appear, too, with their traditional daring, bluster, and skill. But the key to the action is in the vast complexity of the enterprise and the ignorance in which people must act, and the central figure is the Armada's commander, the duke of Medina Sidonia.

Mattingly's portrayal of Medina Sidonia obliterates one of the most comforting figures in our national mythology, the bungling Spanish nobleman whose incompetence ruins a proud navy. Instead of that conventional character, Mattingly depicts an intelligent, conscientious man who manages extraordinarily well in impossible circumstances. But at the crisis of the narrative we learn that both Philip II and the duke of Parma have concealed from Medina Sidonia the impossibility of fulfilling one of his essential requests. The entire plan for invading

England has depended from the beginning on a convergence of the Armada with the duke of Parma's army waiting in Dunkirk and Nieuport. Medina Sidonia has written several unanswered letters to Parma as the Armada has made its way north, and now, anchored near Calais, he writes once again, this time to request "forty or fifty flyboats" from Parma's supposed fleet; with these, he says, "I can defend myself here until you are ready to come out" (318). Only then does he learn, and Mattingly's readers learn with him, that Parma has no such maneuverable boats to send him, but only a group of "canal boats, without masts or sails or guns," which might be able to transport the army across the English Channel on a perfectly calm day, if unchallenged by hostile forces. The only flyboats, Mattingly says, are "where Parma knew they would be, standing off and on between Dunkirk and Ostend, the tough little ships of Justin of Nassau, treating the treacherous banks and shoals of Flanders with the contemptuous familiarity of children on their own playground" (319). Here at last are those lively little craft that each of us has known since childhood as the "true" conquerors of the Spanish Armada. Mattingly shows us that both Parma and Medina Sidonia, far from relying on the sluggish galleons of our tradition, knew perfectly well that they, too, needed such boats. Parma, we learn, has been telling Philip II all along that the invasion is impossible— that he can never get out of Dunkirk without small swift ships of shallow draught, but neither he nor King Philip has ever informed Medina Sidonia (320). As Mattingly tries to solve the riddle of Parma's behavior, then, he has to concede that even if Parma had had 100 flyboats he would have had to bring them out one by one under the superior guns of the Dutch (322). Mattingly leaves us with a feeling of delight in his cool employment of the best modern scholarship to invalidate erroneous interpretations and legends. Yet he applies the greatest weight of that scholarship to reveal the limited knowledge not only of historical figures but of modern historians. His duke of Parma goes through a charade in preparing for the invasion, even to the extreme of packing his men into the canal boats—after the winds that drive the Armada off have already begun to blow (321–22). Clearly, Mattingly implies, Parma never really intended to bring his army out, and beyond that inference there is no explanation of his strange conduct. Parma is as unknowable as Elizabeth.

I certainly don't mean to leave the impression that Mattingly bases his history on what we would call a nonevent. With superior guns and ammunition, the English do win a naval battle (though not a total victory) against the Armada, and although Medina Sidonia has arrived in time for the action to have been unaffected by the weather (if only the expected flyboats had been properly available!), the Armada *is* eventually damaged by its legendary flight north and west around Scotland and Ireland before stormy winds. Thousands of lives, including Medina Sidonia's, are lost or ruined before the survivors arrive back in Spain. Good leaders on both sides are blamed, not only in Spain but in England. Typhus kills almost as many in Harwich and Margate and Dover as dysentery and other ailments have killed in the Spanish fleet. Neglected English sailors, discharged without adequate funds or nutrition, die in the streets of Dover and Rochester. Hawkins and Howard feel almost as mistreated as Medina Sidonia, who compounds the misjudgments by blaming himself too much. With his cool intelligence and his mastery of the evidence, Mattingly is able to respect even as he drastically revises the legend, and he uses a rebuke which he finds in an undated anecdote about Philip II to sound his own secular theme in the religious language of the times. Mattingly has already tried to explain the startling fact that Spanish historians adapted the erroneous English legend of a Grand Armada providentially ruined by a monstrous storm; it might be easier, he reasons, to accept defeat by Providence than by the enemy. And now King Philip rebukes a gardener in the Escorial for saying that God will surely reward his labor with healthy fruit trees. God's will, Philip declares, cannot be predicted. "Even kings," he says in Mattingly's translation, "must submit to being used by God's will without knowing what it is. They must never seek to use it" (392).

In Mattingly's *Armada,* as in many other twentieth-century histories, we can see clear evidence of how far historiography has developed since the days of Cotton Mather. Perhaps the most striking contrasts appear in Mattingly's far greater concern for technical and thematic unity, in his respect for the value of the legendary errors that he corrects, and in his far more pervasive skepticism concerning the direction of history. But in his devotion to historical justice, his emphasis on human limitations, confusion, perplexity, he is recognizable as a citizen of a comparable scholarly world. I agree with him and with Cotton Mather that the historians of certain generations may understand some periods and issues better than their predecessors could understand them. One reason for our special effort to understand Puritans is our own uncertainty, particularly about our capacity to know our own motives, the direction of history, and the relation thereunto of our national covenant, our national mission, or our self-inflated national destiny. If the study of Puritan histories does little to help us solve those mysteries, it may at least remind us that other historians have had to live with them and have derived some good, even some wisdom, from the experience.

Notes

1. Perry Miller, *The New England Mind: From Colony to Province* (Cambridge: Harvard Univ. Press, 1953), p. 21; Increase Mather, *A Brief History of the War with the Indians in New-England* (London, 1676); Cotton Mather, *Magnalia Christi Americana* (London, 1702), 7:53.

2. See chapter 1 above.

3. Perry Miller and Thomas H. Johnson, *The Puritans* (New York: American Book Company, 1938), p. 30.

4. Austin Warren, "Grandfather Mather and His Wonder Book," *Sewanee Review* 72 (1964): 96–116; Sacvan Bercovitch, "New England Epic: Cotton Mather's *Magnalia Christi Americana*," *ELH* 33 (1966): 337–50; Miller, *From Colony to Province,* p. 33.

5. Mather, *Magnalia,* [xxvii]. The pages of Mather's General Introduction are not numbered in the first edition (London, 1702).

6. Compare ibid., 2:8–15; Samuel Eliot Morison, *Builders of the Bay Colony* (Boston and New York: Houghton Mifflin, 1930), pp. 51–104; and Edmund Morgan, *The Puritan Dilemma: The Story of John Winthrop* (Boston: Little, Brown, 1958) and *Visible Saints: The History of a Puritan Idea* (Ithaca: Cornell Univ. Press, 1963). Compare also Mather and Francis Parkman on Sir William Phips, Count Frontenac, and the siege of Quebec: Mather, *Magnalia* 2:47–49, and Parkman, *Count Frontenac and New France under Louis XIV* (Boston, 1892), pp. 235–85.

7. Cotton Mather to James Jurin, June 5, 1723, Royal Society, London. Mather attributes the hypothesis to "Mr. William Jameson, a late Professor in the University of Glasgow." Although this letter was written more than

twenty years after the *Magnalia* had been published, similar historical and "scientific" skepticism appears throughout Mather's adult life. I am grateful to the Royal Society for permission to examine and quote from Mather's letters.

8. Larzer Ziff, *Puritanism in America: New Culture in a New World* (New York: Viking Press, 1973), p. 113.

9. See Michael Kammen, *People of Paradox: An Inquiry concerning the Origins of American Civilization* (New York: Alfred A. Knopf, 1972), pp. 171–72.

10. Peter Gay, *A Loss of Mastery: Puritan Historians in Colonial America* (Berkeley and Los Angeles: Univ. of California Press, 1966), pp. 64–65.

11. John Foxe, *Acts and Monuments of These Latter and Perilous Dayes* (1563).

12. Washington Irving, *A History of New York, from the Beginning of the World to the End of the Dutch Dynasty,* by Diedrich Knickerbocker (New York, 1812), bk. 1, chap. 5.

13. Oscar Handlin, "History: A Discipline in Crisis," *American Scholar* 40 (1971): 447–65.

14. See, for example, *Generalization in the Writing of History,* ed. Louis Gottschalk (Chicago and London: Univ. of Chicago Press, 1963).

15. Ibid., pp. 75–76.

16. *What Is the Good of History?: Selected Letters of Carl L. Becker, 1990– 1945,* ed. Michael Kammen (Ithaca and London: Cornell Univ. Press, 1973), p. 86. Compare Becker's letter to the *Cornell Daily Sun,* in answer to "Five Bewildered Freshmen" who had complained that after two months of intellectual life they still didn't know "what it was all about." Becker replied that "the professors are in the same boat. They don't know either what it's all about. . . . Most of them, if they are wise, don't expect ever to find out, not really" (ibid., p. 110).

17. Garrett Mattingly, *The Armada* (New York: Houghton Mifflin, 1959).

18. J. H. Hexter, "Garrett Mattingly, Historian," *From the Renaissance to the Counter-Reformation: Essays in Honor of Garrett Mattingly,* ed. Charles Howard Carter (New York: Random House, 1965), pp. 22–23.

19. Sir Walter Scott, *Kenilworth* (London, 1821); John Lothrop Motley, *History of the United Netherlands from the Death of William the Silent to the Twelve Years' Truce 1609,* 4 vols. (New York, 1888), vol. 2.

3.

The Form and Sources of Cultural History

An Essay on Entertaining Satan

In *Entertaining Satan,* an excellent history, John Demos boldly ventures both substantive and formal innovation. He demonstrates that in many New England towns and villages witchcraft functioned for decades before the notorious Salem "delusion" of 1692, functioned not only as a sudden menace but also as a part of the community's way of understanding reality and acknowledging mystery. He reports that ninety-three witchcraft cases in Massachusetts and Connecticut, and another two dozen civil cases of slander that included accusations of witchcraft, were actually brought to the point of formal complaint outside the period of the Salem trials, and he demonstrates that "a clear majority" of the trials ended in some kind of acquittal.[1] Surprisingly, a fair number of those accused of witchcraft won judgments against their accusers for slander. And several of those who were acquitted received only a grudging verdict, in which the court either admonished the defendant to walk carefully in the future or actually declared (as at Ipswich in 1659) that the evidence "rendered [him] suspicious" (39). One of the most cantankerous defendants, a man who brought to court dozens of separate suits besides his thirty appearances as defendant in civil suits and his thirteen indictments on criminal charges, seems to have been accepted back into the household of his accusers immediately after being acquitted of witchcraft (42–43). Even a convicted witch from Newbury, Massachusetts, who had been condemned in Boston and jailed there in 1680 to await her execution, was reprieved several times by the Court of Assistants and was allowed, in 1681, to return to her home, on condition that she not leave the immediate neighborhood—

Reprinted by permission from *Early American Literature* 18 (1983): 95–101.

except to attend church services (137)! Another woman, convicted in the autumn of 1669, was simply told to move away from Wethersfield after the magistrates had declared that they could not concur in a sentence of death (363). Yet Massachusetts and Connecticut did hang twenty-one people as witches, besides the twenty who died in Salem in 1692. Others under suspicion were forced to flee, and some were harassed and repeatedly accused for decades.

Witchcraft, then, was at once more pervasive, more leniently treated, and more severely punished in seventeenth-century New England than any scholar before Demos has noticed. To address the complexity of the historical phenomenon, Demos has brought to bear on the surviving evidence an impressive range of interdisciplinary learning. To keep us aware of his insistence on asking various kinds of questions, he has divided his book into four parts, each emphasizing a particular method or discipline. He begins with biography, narrative, the lives of the witches. Part Two, concentrating on victims and accusers, stresses psychology. Part Three, sociology, "relates witchcraft to the shapes and structures of group life in early New England," and demonstrates that "witchcraft cases formed an integral part of social experience" there (14). And the last section concentrates on history, relationships between the witchcraft cases and changing historical circumstances, which may help to explain why there were more cases in some times and places than in others.

Since Michael Kammen is surely correct in predicting (on the dust jacket) that *Entertaining Satan* will "become a classic in the literature of social and cultural history," the costs of Demos's method warrant special attention. His investigation of the record is so admirably thorough, his search for explanations so persistent, his many disclaimers so straightforward, and his speculations so unfailingly interesting, that some of the difficulties in his method might otherwise be neglected. Let us begin with questions of form.

Demos wisely regards the mixture of narrative and analysis as essential to historical understanding. The historian who wants to understand witchcraft must eventually stand at some distance from individual lives in his search for patterns, but in his own investigation and in his exposition for the reader some of the most valuable evidence is inextricably entangled in the sequential experience of an individual life. Demos repeatedly shows, in the most purely narrative parts of his study, not only that the people seemed alert for fraudulent and erroneous accusations, but also that a fair proportion of those accused of witchcraft made unmistakably suggestive claims of special powers or used threatening language. His narratives of Elizabeth Knapp, John Godfrey, Rachel Clinton, Mary Parsons, Caleb Powell, Elizabeth Garlick, and Elizabeth Morse show us through the combination of intelligent sympathy and psychological understanding the intricate relationships between accusers and defendants. The defendant was sometimes the aggressor, threatening the accuser's livestock or children. The "possessed" or afflicted person, on the other hand, might all too readily be blamed for her own supposed familiarity with the Devil.

This kind of truth has been available in Nathaniel Hawthorne's works and in individual accounts of the Salem and Boston cases ever since Barrett Wendell wrote *Were the Salem Witches Guiltless?* (Boston, 1892). In our own century George Lyman Kittredge and half a dozen others reinforced our awareness of it. What makes Demos's narratives so impressive is the depth of psychological understanding and the abundance of circumstantial detail about a wide variety of people and places. I welcome his inference and his scrupulously identified conjecture, but I repeatedly find that when the record is spotty it is rather the tact of his narrative sense, his implicit appeal to my historical imagination, than his citation of statistical tables or psychoanalytic authority that takes me safely across the gaps in the historical evidence.

A narrator relies on an implicit understanding with the reader: that all literary sequence is selective, incomplete, filling in or crossing gaps in the record not by inventing fictions but by connecting the known particulars in ways that do not violate our common sense of what people are like or what they were like then. A narrator knows more than he can tell, and sometimes a narrative implicitly explains much more than it can either prove or explicitly say. Sometimes, therefore, narrative is a better form than analytical exposition for embodying complex, tentative, or multiple explanation.

Both the analytical exposition and the narratives in *Entertaining Satan* are enriched by Demos's learned commitment to the behavioral sciences. But Demos the narrator is less narrowly insistent on demanding explanations than Demos the psychohistorian, the sociological historian, the anthropological historian. Again the problem is both substantive and formal. I cannot remember that any historian has taken more care than Demos to identify his speculative reasoning. Again and again Demos warns us that "the evidence is not conclusive on this point" before he claims that the evidence "does allow certain inferences." But the thrust of his entire venture, on large questions and small ones, can be seen in the word that he has italicized immediately before the warning that I have just quoted: "*Why* was William Morse so quick to accuse Caleb Powell?" (134). The insistent form of the question implies that there is an answer out there, in theory and in the particular psyche.

If conclusive answers cannot be found in the evidence, Demos's interpretation of the behavioral sciences seems at least to assume that answers must be explicitly ventured, and it is in representing such inferences that his rhetorical practices raise serious questions. Even when he introduces a conjecture as a "best guess" (76), the statistical form of his argument gives the percentages that he uses a greater authority than his scrupulous disclaimer. Here he asks, for example, whether the people accused of witchcraft had already been "associated with other (and prior) criminal proceedings," and he finds that forty-one of them definitely had been and the remaining seventy-three had not. But "many" of the seventy-three, he acutely notices, "can scarcely be traced at all beyond their alleged involvement with witchcraft." We have "some evidence of *ongoing* experience" for only sixty-five (76). The forty-one, then, represent at the least 36 percent of all the 114 persons accused of witchcraft, or at most 63 percent of the sixty-five about whom some other biographical evidence exists. Demos's "best guess" is to imagine a "midpoint": "In short, approximately one-half of the people accused of practicing witchcraft were also charged with the commission of other crimes" (76).

Now one could well question the numbers in this calculation, for the opposite extreme from the 36 percent would be much larger than 63 percent if one considered the possibility that all forty-nine of those about whom we have no other biographical information had already been accused of other crimes. (In that unlikely eventuality, ninety of the 114, or 79 percent, would have been previously accused, and the midpoint might be nearer to 60 percent than to 50 percent.) Since

Demos, however, is obviously proceeding in good faith, showing us the essential numbers and at least suggesting his method of interpreting them, my uneasiness about this example does not focus on his statistical method. What troubles me is the difficulty of maintaining an awareness of the tentativeness, the complexity of such calculations after one has laid out the individual tables, combined similarly indeterminate groups of them, and translated them into the kind of prose that builds arguments.

Can language be found that, as the argument builds, will retain our sense of the provisional without becoming too cumbersome? Historians who use *Entertaining Satan* may well be excused if, on this small question of prior criminal record, they overlook Demos's original phrase "associated with other . . . criminal proceedings" and use as fact not only his "approximately one-half of the people accused" but also his much more decisive translation in the summary sentence: "the commission of other crimes" (76). Even if the accompanying table (headed "Crimes of the witches") did not show that half of those crimes turn out to be "assaultive speech" and "lying" (77)—offenses that Demos himself associates closely with the witch's traditional *Maleficium*— I would fear that in this instance as in others the use of numbers and tables and the translation of tentative or speculative language into usable summary give debatable interpretations an authority much stronger than the introductory disclaimers would justify.

On some issues the power of the evidence in an individual narrative tends to undermine the significance of statistical inferences, either by unquestionable particulars that fall outside the statistical patterns or by simply leading us to a mystery. Demos has presented very strong numerical evidence that a large portion of the people accused of witchcraft were childless or menopausal women. His superb accounts, then, of charges against two men, John Godfrey and Caleb Powell, are so convincing, and these masculine defendants so free of qualities prominent in the menopausal explanation, that one may wonder how much the menopausal hypothesis really explains. No individual case, of course, can refute a statistical argument. Yet when the husband of Elizabeth Morse responds promptly to charges against her by saying that Caleb Powell is the actual witch, one notices that Morse did not strike out at another middle-aged woman. I see nothing in the quality of accusations against Powell to differentiate his case from those of women (132–37). And in the splendid narrative of Mary Parsons of Northampton, who was first accused in her late twenties, relatively early in her twenty-five years of bearing fourteen children and her forty-five years of rearing the nine who survived, Demos emphasizes the persistent rumors and accusations over half a century rather than an emphatic challenge to his theory that childlessness and the menopause characterize the targets of rumor and accusation. Here it is the chief accusers, envious of Mary Parsons's fertility and good health, who have been barren or have recently stopped bearing children (249–74).

Demos's narratives of individual characters are better able than his analytical passages to embody one of the strongest generalizations in his fine chapter on "The Social Matrix of Witchcraft": The "personal element," he says there, "stands out in all the materials. The relationships of witches and accuser/victims were not defined by, or limited to, any single strand of experience." They were "complex, many-sided, and altogether dense" (284). When "increasingly rumor declares," in the superb narrative of Elizabeth Garlick, that she is "in league with the Devil" (240), I feel a stronger understanding of intricate relationships in the vague word "rumor" than in the sociological analysis of motives.

The greatest cost of Demos's interdisciplinary method is his relative neglect of theological and literary evidence. Not until three hundred pages have passed do we find here any strong emphasis on religious belief. The social function of witchcraft includes a balancing of hatred against charity or goodness (304–5), Demos says, and of course witchcraft may have been thought to allow the clergy, especially in the latter half of the seventeenth century, a hope of preserving their social power. But even here, as in Boyer and Nissenbaum's *Salem Possessed,*[2] social history usually seems to exclude religious belief, God's command (Exodus 22:18) to execute witches, the fear of tolerating witchcraft, as a major cause of behavior. Demos does come around to such matters in his fourth section, but only very briefly, and his use of seventeenth-century literary documents is much more selective than his exhaustive study of the local accusations. Not even in his tardy reference to "the cosmic struggle between" God and Satan does he mention the imminence of the millennium—nor even when he mentions Cotton Mather's belief that the Devil will be most actively hating where he is most passionately hated (310). Demos quotes this passage from Mather's shrill defense of the Salem judges, *The Wonders of the Invisible World,* but seems unaware of its prior appearance in the English preacher Richard Baxter's preface to the London edition (1691) of Mather's *Memorable Providences;* unaware, too, of the immediate historical relevance of a text that Mather used for a sermon in 1692: "Woe to the inhabitants of the earth, for the Devil is come down in great Wrath, knowing his time to be but short."[3]

It would be unjust to demand of so resourceful and learned a scholar as Demos that he read as thoroughly in seventeenth-century historiography as he has done in the genealogical and criminal records. Yet in their reaction against the heavy reliance of Perry Miller and others on the literary evidence left by intellectuals, the social historians who have accomplished prodigies in the last twenty years have too often mistrusted or neglected the literary evidence. One cannot believe that Demos, the author of *A Little Commonwealth,* neglected to read Bradford's history *Of Plymouth Plantation,* but by the time he came to write *Entertaining Satan* he had forgotten Bradford's eloquent meditation on the extraordinary longevity of the Pilgrims, and he seems to have overlooked similar passages in the biographies in Mather's *Magnalia Christi Americana.* He declares that he has "not encountered a single reference in contemporary writings to the extraordinary longevity of early New Englanders" (520n.8). And he cites a statement by Cotton Mather in 1726 that "scarce three in one hundred live to three score and ten" (520). If he had recognized that Mather and other ministers, especially in the seventeenth century, habitually worked both sides of the Providential street, citing Providential mercies and retribution as the occasion demanded, he might have looked for a different kind of evidence in Mather's earlier writings as well as Bradford's.

This kind of omission is most costly in one of Demos's boldest speculative ventures, his effort to "plot the curve" of local or regional crises against witchcraft accusations. The "pattern" that he finds, though "rough and incomplete along its edges" (386), regularly displays "a reverse correlation" between episodes of social conflict and witchcraft proceedings, the two phenomena waxing and waning "in alternating sequence" (369). He argues that witchcraft follows other social conflict, that "witchcraft and conflict exclude one another at any given point in time" (370). Both the Goodwin-Glover case in Boston, during the climactic weeks of the Andros administration's conflict with the people of Boston, and the notorious Salem outbreak evidently contradict the pattern. Demos ignores the Goodwin-Glover case in this part of his book, and it is here that his understandable decision to exclude the Salem outbreak from his central focus seems to me most costly. He seems aware of the probable argument that the Salem madness erupted in the midst of conflict rather than afterward, but he argues that "the imperial crisis was partially eased [because] Massachusetts had just received a new charter" (384). That charter itself was the subject of intensive social conflict, however, even before Increase Mather agreed to accept it, and we cannot be sure that the people in Salem knew about the charter's formal existence before the first accusations and the first confession on February 29, 1692. Arrests and indictments proliferated in the months before the new governor arrived, and the first prisoners were sent from Salem to the Boston jail as early as March 7.

Entertaining Satan does gain valuable flexibility by excluding Salem from the local research. Demos's study would have been overwhelmed by the extensive research already done on the Salem episode and by the magnitude of the Salem numbers: nearly as many executions there in one summer as in the whole of New England in the seventeenth century; in less than one year, more accusations in Salem than in all New England in that century. Yet the cursory effort to fit the Salem evidence into the historical pattern in Demos's last chapters underlines the difficulty of omitting Salem from any general study of New England witchcraft. Atypical as Demos and Perry Miller—from their radically different perspectives—wisely believe that the Salem delusion was, it cannot be omitted from a study of witchcraft and the culture of early New England, and it cannot be effectively included without threateningly close attention to its abundant evidence. Once again the historian's rhetorical problem seems virtually insoluble.

I cannot conclude these caviling reflections without reaffirming my admiration for this excellent book. I am happy to applaud the achievement, grateful for the insights and the information, delighted by much of the social analysis. I would be happily surprised if Demos or any other historian had been able to solve all the difficulties lurking, as if by diabolical plan, in this subject. The answer, if any paragon should find one, is not to abandon social history for narrative, but to strive for an even better combination than Demos has fashioned here.

Notes

1. John Demos, *Entertaining Satan: Witchcraft and the Culture of New England* (New York: Oxford Univ. Press, 1982), p. 11.

2. Paul Boyer and Stephen Nissenbaum, *Salem Possessed: The Social Origins of Witchcraft* (Cambridge: Harvard Univ. Press, 1974).

3. Cotton Mather published the sermon in *The Wonders of the Invisible World* (Boston, 1692), after he had preached it on Aug. 4. The biblical text is Revelation 12:12.

4.

Did the Mathers Disagree about the Salem Witchcraft Trials?

The question that I have posed may seem at first to be antiquarian in the narrowest sense. One of my colleagues suggested that I make the title more provocative by asking, Did the Mathers disagree about the Salem trials, and who cares? What could be more parochial than asking whether two embattled ministers, serving in the same congregation, disagreed toward the end of one of the most shameful episodes in early New England history? I could argue that this topic deserves to be reexamined because the Salem trials have already held a disproportionately large place in American historical consciousness for nearly three centuries. Somehow we choose the historical topics that will become notorious. Everyone knows that twenty people were executed in Salem in 1692, whereas I had a doctorate in the history of American civilization before I learned that in the city of New York, nearly half a century after the Salem trials, many black people were actually burned at the stake for an alleged conspiracy to revolt.[1] The question that I shall pursue instead concerns fairness to historical characters, and it asks us, in examining these recondite materials, to reconsider how it is that historical villains, and especially historical heroes, are made. The documentary evidence is small enough to be examined carefully in a brief space, and debatable enough to remind us that the answer to questions about such evidence often depends on our own desires. Learned historians and biographers, sophisticated in our self-awareness, we can still occasionally resemble Huckleberry Finn, the simple boy who decided to forgo "borrowing" two of the fruits that he

Reprinted from the *Proceedings of the American Antiquarian Society* 95 (1985): 19–37, by permission of the Society.

had been taking from people's trees. He decided to borrow no more crabapples or persimmons, so that he could believe that his borrowing of other fruits really did differ from stealing. "I was glad the way it come out, too," he says, "because crabapples ain't ever good, and the p'simmons wouldn't be ripe for two or three months yet."[2]

I cannot say that the scholars with whom I disagree are rationalizing quite so baldly as Huck Finn, but perhaps they have allowed their healthy skepticism about one kind of documentary evidence to betray them into credulous neglect or dismissal of other evidence that is equally explicit in the record. They put far too much emphasis on a postscript to Increase Mather's book on the Salem trials, and by shining their flashlights on one paragraph in that postscript itself, they leave other sections—and many of their trusting readers—in the darkness. Perry Miller and Kenneth Silverman, for example, have portrayed Increase Mather as a reasonable critic who belatedly demolished the reliability of the witchcraft court's procedures and verdicts in the autumn of 1692. The same scholars have argued that Cotton Mather, by persisting in defending the court, broke dramatically with his father and the other leading ministers of the colony;[3] that Cotton Mather thus tied to his own name the tin can that has rattled through history for nearly three centuries because he failed to stand with his father and their colleagues against the misguided judges, but chose instead to write a book in defense of the court.[4]

Let me warn readers, too, against my own desire. Ever since I first studied these materials forty years ago, I have believed that Increase and Cotton Mather worked cooperatively in this crisis, as they did on nearly every other major and minor issue during their forty years as colleagues in the Second Church in Boston. Both father and son had written books in the 1680s to encourage the recording of "illustrious" or "remarkable providences," and several nineteenth- and twentieth-century historians blamed those books as major causes of the Salem delusion. Modern scholarship has generally acknowledged that the lore, fear, and accusations of witchcraft were well known in Massachusetts through surer and earlier sources than the books of any ministers. Virtually nobody in Massachusetts denied, before it was much too late, that witches exist and that the state is obliged to execute them. I believe it is also fair to say that, although judgments of individual ministers range from severe criticism to praise, a modern consensus acknowledges the Boston clergy's efforts—equivocal and ineffective though they surely were—to protect the rights of the defendants and to warn judges against procedures that might convict defendants who were not guilty.[5] Cotton Mather wrote a long letter of this kind to one of the judges on May 31, 1692, three days before the first trial, and when Governor Phips asked the ministers for advice soon after that trial, Cotton Mather copied and paraphrased his letter in the document that he drafted and the other ministers, including his father, signed on June 15, 1692.[6]

This document is known to scholars as the Ministers' Return—that is, their answer to Governor Phips's request for advice. Five of its eight numbered paragraphs argue forcibly for great care. They urge "a very critical and exquisite caution, lest by too much credulity for things received only upon the Devil's authority, there be a door opened for a long train of miserable consequences, and Satan get an advantage over us, for we should not be ignorant of his devices." They insist that nobody should even be arrested, let alone convicted, on the mere testimony that a specter (or ghostly form) appeared to an afflicted person in the form of a real human being, for the ministers said it was both "undoubted" and "notorious" that a demon could appear to human beings in the shape of innocent and virtuous people. (Such evidence was called spectral evidence or specter evidence.) The ministers even went so far as to recommend that the people and the court try to insult the Devil by refusing to believe any evidence "whose whole force and strength is from [the devils] alone"—evidence such as startling changes that seemed to be caused in "the sufferers, by a look or touch of the accused." Both Increase and Cotton Mather endorsed these warnings, and both also endorsed the final article of advice, which began with a big "nevertheless" and called for "the speedy and vigorous prosecution of such as have rendered themselves obnoxious, according to the direction given in the laws of God, and the wholesome statutes of the *English* nation, for the detection of witchcrafts."

My reason for reminding readers that both Mathers signed this equivocal document is to underline Cotton's participation in the plea for caution and Increase's endorsement of vigorous prosecution. From the beginning of the crisis, they both expected, or at least hoped, to protect the innocent and prosecute the guilty. But as we all know, the door was indeed opened for a train of miserable consequences. By autumn, twenty men and women had been executed, others had been convicted, and many more were in jail awaiting trial. The accusations seemed to be spreading uncontrollably, and at the same time a growing feeling of doubt and resentment was questioning the fairness and the procedures of the special court, which had tried the cases without following the ministers' advice against spectral evidence. By the beginning of September, both Increase and Cotton Mather were writing books about the trials.

Increase Mather called his book *Cases of Conscience concerning Evil Spirits Personating Men,* and he read it to a group of ministers early in October. This eloquent statement demolishes the validity of spectral evidence. Increase Mather not only establishes the truth that all the ministers had called notorious at the beginning of the summer. He declares that it would be better for ten guilty witches to go free than for one innocent person to be condemned.[7] He insists that "the father of lies is never to be believed," because that master of deceit will utter twenty truths in order to make us believe one of his lies (40). And Increase Mather also demands that the court stop accepting testimony from the alleged victims of the witches, for these afflicted witnesses are admittedly possessed by the Devil, and therefore under his control in their testimony as well as in their dreadful fits.

Cotton Mather's book, *The Wonders of the Invisible World,* was completed no more than eight days after his father's *Cases of Conscience,* and the son's book was actually published first.[8] Here, too, one finds unmistakable acknowledgment that the Devil's purpose in the entire affair may have aimed at getting the Lord's people to maul one another "hotly and madly . . . in the dark" (43), and that spectral evidence may well have led the court into grave error. But Cotton Mather's *Wonders* has a purpose that more than one modern historian has called odious. This book sets out to "countermine the whole PLOT of the Devil, against New-England, in every branch of it, as far as one of my *darkness* can comprehend such a *Work of Darkness*" ([vi]). Here Cotton Mather argues that, whatever their perplexities and errors, the judges acted in good faith and did convict a number of real witches—a position that Increase Mather's book stated just as clearly, though much more briefly.

The theme of *The Wonders of the Invisible World* resounds in the five trials that Cotton Mather summarizes, with detailed quotation and paraphrase from the depositions and from transcripts of oral testimony before the magistrates and the special court. He tries to show that in every one of these five convictions spectral evidence was less important than reliable kinds of incriminating evidence, ranging from the defendant's perjury or self-contradiction to explicit curses, puppets with pins stuck in them found in the defendant's house, and feats of the defendant that could not have been performed without supernatural aid. Cotton Mather also asked for the help of William Stoughton, the deputy governor and chief justice of the special court, who returned the courtesy by writing a prefatory letter of commendation and signing (with Judge Samuel Sewall) an endorsement of the narratives.[9]

Here we have the essential division on which our little historical problem is based. Increase Mather, the father, presents a thorough argument, both scriptural and rational, for excluding all evidence that is in any way influenced by the Devil. Increase's son Cotton publishes a shrill, sometimes incoherent mixture of arguments, sermons, and narrative to show how the people became perplexed, why one should still believe in the Devil's power to set witches loose on human victims, and how a well-meaning, though fallible court could have justly convicted and condemned guilty defendants. Increase Mather demands an immediate, drastic change in procedure; Cotton Mather tries to persuade the people not to condemn the court.

The question for us to consider is whether these two books were complementary parts of a cooperative venture, or whether they represent an ill-concealed split between the Mathers. Besides the tones and themes of the two books themselves, the chief seventeenth-century evidence of a clear disagreement is of a negative kind: both Mathers explicitly deny that they disagree, and both explicitly say that others have attributed the disagreement to them. So far as I know, no documents survive that actually attribute disagreement to father and son. We cannot examine the rumors or any contemporaneous arguments for the existence of a disagreement. We have only the Mathers' denials. Let us consider them now.

Increase Mather had read his manuscript to the ministers on October 3, but by the time his book was published several weeks later, he already knew about rumors, presumably started by the publication of Cotton's *Wonders,* of a rift between himself and his son. Increase added a postscript to the first edition of his own book, and near the end of that addition he said: "Some I hear have taken up a Notion, that the Book newly published by my Son, is contradictory to this of mine. 'Tis strange that such Imaginations should enter into the Minds of Men: I perused and approved of that book before it was printed, and nothing but my Relation to him hindered me from recommending it to the World: But myself and Son agreed unto the humble advice . . . which twelve Ministers concurringly presented . . . which let the World judge, whether there be anything in it dissentany from what is attested by either of us" ([73]). Increase then concluded his book by reprinting the entire eight articles of the Ministers' Return.

Cotton Mather's allusions to the rumors of disagreement appear in a letter and in his diary (or "Reserved Memorials"), and his tone plainly indicates that he considers the minds of the rumormongers just as strange as his father says they were. When *The Wonders of the Invisible World* was printed, he writes in his dairy at the end of the year, "Many besotted People would not imagine any other, but that my Father's, *Cases of Conscience, about Witchcraft,* which came abroad just after it, were in opposition to it." [10] Indeed, we have clear evidence that those besotted minds had put Cotton Mather on the defensive before either of these books had been written. At the outset, in his preface to *Wonders* (which he calls "The Author's Defense"), he says that he has been "driven" to defend himself "by taking off the false Reports, and hard Censures about my Opinion in these Matters"—as if he had been trying to divide rather than reconcile the ministers, the court, and the people. He insists, too, that his "unvaried Thoughts" about witchcraft trials "will be owned by most of the Ministers of God in these Colonies; nor can amends be well made me, for the wrong done me, by other sorts of *Representations*" ([vi]).

But if Cotton Mather agreed with his father and the other ministers, why didn't he sign their preface endorsing his father's *Cases of Conscience?* Perry Miller and Kenneth Silverman have chosen to read the Mathers' protestations of agreement as insincere. In this reading of the evidence, Increase Mather's declaration that he had read and approved his son's manuscript is simply rejected as a polite lie—because neither one signed the preface to the other's book, because the two books differ in tone and emphasis, and because of a letter Cotton Mather wrote to his maternal uncle, John Cotton, a minister in Plymouth.[11] A close examination of that letter may yield a different interpretation.

The letter is dated October 20, 1692. Here Cotton Mather is evidently distressed, only a few days after the publication of his *Wonders,* by both the unfavorable response to his book and the claim that his book contradicts his father's. He begins by saying that he has never needed his favorite uncle's comforting thoughts more than he needs them now, but then he begs his uncle to read the book "critically" and "Lett mee know whether You think, I have served, as you know I have designed there in to serve, God and my generation." The central issue is in the next three paragraphs, which I must quote in full:

There are fourteen Worthy Ministers, that have newly sett their Hands, unto a Book now in the press, Containing, *Cases of Conscience* about Witchcrafts. I did, in *my* Conscience think, that as the Humours of this people now run, Such a Discorse going Alone, would not only Enable our Witch-Advocates, very Learnedly to Cavil & Nibble at the Late proceedings against the Witches, considered in parcels whilst things as they Lay in Bulk, with their whole Dependences, were not exposed. but also everlastingly Stiffle any further proceedings of justice & more than so produce a public & open contest with the judges, who would (tho beyond the intention of the Worthy Author & subscribers) find themselves brought unto the Bar before the Rashest *Mobile*[.] For such cause, & for one more, I did with all the modesty I could use, decline, Setting my Hand unto the Book: assigning the Reason, that I had already a Book in the press, which would sufficiently declare my opinion: and such a Book too, as had already passed the censure of the Hand which wrote what was then before us.

With what Sinful & Raging Asperity, I have been since Treated, I had rather Forgett than Relate. Altho' I challeng'd the Fiercest of my Accusers, to find the Thousandth part of One wrong step taken by mee, in all these matters, Except it were my use of all Humble & Sober Endeavor, to prevent Such a bloody Quarrel between *Moses* and *Aaron,* as would bee *Bitterness in the Latter End;* no other Fault has yett been Laid before mee. At Last I have been driven to say *I will yett bee more vile!* and quoting, Math. 5.9. I have concluded, *So, I shall not want a Father!*

> Since the Trial of these unworthy Treats, the persons that have used them, have Endeavoured such Expressions of sweetness towards mee, as may make mee satisfaction. But for the Great Slander, with which they have now fill'd the country against mee, *That I Run Against my own Father, & all the Ministers in the countrey,* merely because I Run Between them, when they are Like mad men Running Against one another; they can make mee no Reparacion; However my God will!

It is easy to see why modern readers of this extraordinary letter would emphasize evidence of disagreement between the Mathers. Cotton Mather's allusions to the uses that "Witch-Advocates" might make of his father's book, and his concern for what a mob might do to the judges—these combine with the tone of *Wonders,* the rumors of a rift, and the failure of either Mather to sign the other's book. Small wonder, then, that Miller and Silverman, though each in his own way, represent the postscript to *Cases of Conscience* as a belated, perfunctory gesture.

At least for the sake of argument, however, let us look at other language in the letter, and then at the corroborating evidence to which it leads us. Notice first that both father and son say explicitly not merely that Increase Mather failed to condemn his son's book, but that he had read the manuscript and approved it before it was published. Even if one believes that Increase Mather would lie publicly about such a question, we have no reason to believe that Cotton Mather would lie about it in a private letter to his uncle.

Look, too, at the second sentence in the first paragraph, in which Cotton Mather worries about the effects of Increase's book: "I did, in *my* Conscience think, that as the Humours of this people now run, Such a Discorse going Alone" would have dire effects. If published in company with *The Wonders of the Invisible World,* however, Increase Mather's book would not bring a mob's wrath against the court that had tried the witches, nor would it necessarily "Stiffle any further proceedings of justice."

Precisely because historians have credited Increase Mather's book with everlastingly stifling further witchcraft proceedings, they have found it too easy to overlook the evidence that *Cases of Conscience* and *The Wonders of the Invisible World* concur. I have no doubt that Increase Mather's attack on spectral evidence did help to prevent further executions and convictions in Massachusetts and elsewhere. Yet no scholar known to me has met Increase Mather's challenge to find any disagreement between the Ministers' Return and his book. And in *Cases of Conscience* itself we find unmistakable declarations that it is still possible to convict a person justly of witchcraft. Even before the notorious postscript, which Miller and Silverman dismiss as a sop to Cotton Mather, *Cases of Conscience* describes two grounds for conviction: The first is "a free and Voluntary Confession" (59); the second, the sworn testimony of "two Credible Persons . . . that they have seen the Person accused doing things which none but such as have Familiarity with the Devil ever did or can do." That testimony, Increase Mather declares, is "a sufficient Ground of Conviction" (65). He then offers a list of rhetorical questions to show that "Wizzards . . . have very often been known to do" supernatural tricks "in the presence of credible witnesses." "How often," he exclaims, have wizards "been seen by others using Inchantments? Conjuring to raise Storms? . . . And to shew in a Glass or a Shew-stone persons absent? And to reveal Secrets which could not be discovered but by the Devil? And have not men been seen to do things which are above humane Strength that no man living could do, without Diabollical Assistances?" When two real, credible people—not specters—testify that a defendant has done such things, Mather says, "it is proof enough" of witchcraft, and "he or she, whoever they may be, ought to be exterminated from amongst men" (66–67).

Of course it is right here, just after his strongest endorsement of convictions and executions for witchcraft, that Increase Mather says, "It were better that Ten Suspected Witches should escape, than that one Innocent Person should be Condemned." He even declares that he "had rather judge a Witch to be an honest woman, than judge an honest woman as a Witch" (67). But even in the main text of his book, before the postscript, his scruples concerning reasonable doubt do not cancel his plain rule that the sworn testimony of two credible witnesses to feats of superhuman strength or magic should suffice to justify the extermination of a defendant.

I have insisted that Increase Mather propounded this rule in the body of his text, before adding the postscript. The location is not merely academic, for the specific cases cited in the postscript satisfy the rules that he had prescribed and his fourteen colleagues had endorsed. Echoing his son's words, Mather begins the postscript by denying that he has ever wished to appear as "an Advocate for Witches," and he says he has written another essay, which he may well publish later, "proving that there are such horrid Creatures as Witches in the World; and that they are to be extirpated and cut off from amongst the People of God." He declares himself "abundantly satisfied that there are still most cursed Witches in the Land," for several persons "now in prison have freely and credibly acknowledged" their guilt directly to him, including "the Time and Occasion, with the particular circumstances of their Hellish Obligations and Abominations" ([70]).

But it is in the second paragraph of the postscript, disclaiming an intent to criticize the judges, that Increase Mather persuades me most conclusively of his agreement with his son. Here Increase Mather calls the judges "wise and good men" who "have acted with all Fidelity according to their Light, and have out of tenderness declined the doing of some things, which in their own Judgments they were satisfied about." Because the cases were so difficult, Mather says, they deserve our "Pity and Prayers rather than Censure. . . . On which Account I am glad that there is Published to the World (by my Son) a Breviate of the Trials of some who were lately Executed, whereby I hope the thinking part of mankind will be satisfied, that there was more than that which is called *Spectre Evidence* for the Conviction of the persons Condemned" ([71]). Whether or not Increase Mather really believed that the convictions were based on better evidence than the spectral, he at least says here that he hopes his son's book will persuade the thinking part of mankind to the belief.[12] That statement in itself would suffice to endorse one major purpose, however insincere, of Cotton Mather's *Wonders:* to avoid attacks upon the court. But in my judgment Increase Mather's very next sentences, in the same paragraph, clinch the case. From the mere hope that we will see more than spectral evidence in Cotton Mather's narrative, Increase turns immediately to his own judgment of the one trial that he himself attended, the trial of George Burroughs, the only minister convicted of witchcraft and the first convict whose trial is summarized in *The Wonders of the Invisible World*. Even more important here than Increase Mather's statement that if he had been one of Burroughs's judges, "I could not have acquitted him," is the reason that he gives. It is precisely the same kind of evidence endorsed in the body of *Cases of Conscience:* "For several persons did upon

Oath Testify, that they saw him do such things as no Man that has not a Devil to be his Familiar could perform" ([71]). Not until two pages later, after more discussion of unacceptable ways of fighting the devils, does Increase Mather answer the rumor of disagreement between himself and his son.

When Increase Mather wrote his version of his own part in these events, several weeks or months after both books had been published, he retained for his autobiography only five or six lines, which condense everything into one entry, dated May 14, 1692—the day of his return from England with a copy of the new Massachusetts charter in one pocket and the new governor, nominated by himself, in another. [13] Here Increase Mather says not a word about having approved the extermination of every defendant whom two credible persons swear that they have seen doing things which only witches ever did or can do. He says nothing about having heard free and credible confessions in the prison, nothing about his belief in George Burroughs's guilt, nothing about having written another discourse to prove that witches exist and that they ought to be extirpated. Instead he remembers only his doubts and the humanitarian influence for which some contemporaries and many historians have justly given him credit. Increase Mather's selective memory has its counterpart in the selective narratives of Perry Miller and Kenneth Silverman. Miller does at least chide Increase Mather for neglecting to mention his endorsement of George Burroughs's conviction. Silverman not only fails to mention that endorsement but actually declares that Increase Mather would not have approved of Burroughs's conviction. And then he declares that the Mathers "undeniably" disagreed. [14]

Several lesser items remain to be examined before we turn to the significance of these recondite details. Cotton Mather's refusal to sign the fourteen ministers' preface to his father's book would be more important if the Mathers had been in the habit of endorsing each other's books. I see no reason to doubt Increase Mather's statement that only his relation to the author kept him from endorsing Cotton's *Wonders,* for (so far as I know) he endorsed none of Cotton's many other books in the 1690s, and he did not even join the other ministers who wrote testimonials to introduce Cotton's church history of New England, *Magnalia Christi Americana.* In 1693, meanwhile, both Mathers endorsed Charles Morton's *Spirit of Man*, for which Cotton Mather wrote the preface.[15]

If the Mathers were cooperating in the late summer and autumn of 1692, they wrote their books to serve complementary purposes. Although I admire Increase Mather's eloquent statements in *Cases of Conscience*, it seems clear to me that the book deliberately left room for further trials and convictions of witches. I cannot agree with Perry Miller that Increase Mather, "and he alone," stopped the executions (195), or that by merely adding the postscript Increase Mather betrayed his conscience and the body of his book, turning what might have been "a bold stroke" into "a miserable species of double-talk" (199). Before either of the two Mathers' books was completed, a strong popular revulsion against the executions and the spreading accusations had alarmed the authorities. I agree with Robert Middlekauff that both father and son wanted to protect the innocent, slow down the rate of accusations and convictions, and yet give no comfort to the Devil, to scientific rationalists, or to political opponents of the court and the incumbent administration. Instead of doubletalk, I hear genuine perplexity.[16]

Just as overstating Increase Mather's criticism of the court makes him either too nearly heroic or at last too hypocritical, so overstating Cotton Mather's submission to William Stoughton and the other judges makes *The Wonders of the Invisible World* seem too simply obsequious. If the Mathers were cooperating with each other, the son certainly drew the nastier assignment. I do not mean to defend him. A wiser man would have argued at least that no sound basis for conviction could be found, and a better man would have written less defensively about himself, less fulsomely about the court, more charitably about the defendants, less shrilly about the Devil's threats. Yet insistence that the two Mathers disagreed, or that the two books about the witchcraft trials were both dishonest as they argued, respectively, for opposite conclusions, may neglect the complexity of Cotton Mather's *Wonders*.

The wonder about Cotton Mather's political achievement here, costly as it was to his later reputation, is not in his submission to William Stoughton but in his acquisition of Stoughton's support. Everybody who has looked into the story of the trials knows that

Stoughton insisted on the value of spectral evidence, and that he even stormed out of the court one day in the winter of 1692–93 after his death sentence against three confessed witches had been overturned by Governor Phips.[17] Yet here is Stoughton in October 1692, less than three weeks after the last executions—and while he still hopes to send other convicts to the gallows—here is Stoughton endorsing a book that repeatedly admits to grave doubts about the value of both spectral evidence and the confessions of accused witches. In "Enchantments Encountered," the first section of the book after the "Author's Defense," Cotton Mather concedes that "the Delusions of Satan" may well be mixed into some of the many confessions, even as he argues that we have little choice but to believe "the *main Strokes* wherein" the "many Voluntary Harmonious Confessions, made by Intelligent Persons of all Ages, in sundry Towns, at several Times, . . . all agree" (7). Cotton Mather admits that some of the witches have actually confessed that they conspired to project spectral representations of innocent persons in order to save themselves (9). And he insists that since "the best man that ever lived" was denounced as a witch, specters must sometimes appear in the shape of "a person that shall be none of the worst" (9). Cotton Mather admits in a backhanded way that "disputed Methods" have been used in the witch-hunt, and that "there are very worthy Men, who are not a little dissatisfied at the Proceedings."[18] He insists that the Devil's chief purpose is to inflame us "one against another" (13), and that hereafter the methods of trying the defendants must be "unquestionably safe, *lest the latter end be worse than the beginning*" (13).

Cotton Mather's success in gaining the endorsement of Stoughton and Sewall may well be connected to his decision not to join the other ministers in signing the preface to his father's book. Cotton Mather had been seeking Stoughton's approval for such a book ever since September 2, 1692, three weeks earlier than the date on which Thomas J. Holmes and Perry Miller say that Mather began to slap the book together. And the outline that Mather sent to Stoughton says plainly that the first part of the book had already been written more than a month before Increase Mather read *Cases of Conscience* to the ministers. Perry Miller is therefore mistaken in attributing the opening section to Cotton Mather's compulsive need to fill up pages while waiting for the transcripts of trials (promised around September 20) to arrive in Boston

(201). In the letter of September 2, Cotton Mather admits privately to Stoughton that in the manuscript "I have Lett fall, . . . once or Twice, the Jealousies among us, of Innocent people being Accused." But of course he promises "humbly [to] Submitt all those Expressions unto your Honours Correction; that so there may not bee one word out of Joint." [19]

After all this analysis, one may well ask the implicit question with which we began: What difference does it make whether the Mathers agreed or disagreed? Aside from ironing out one wrinkle in the record, this little study may remind us that there were no heroes in 1692, except for Mary Easty and several of the other people who were executed—convicts who went to the gallows protesting their innocence, praying for the judges, and pleading for more charitable procedures that might save the lives of others who were wrongly accused. Increase Mather not only read and approved of his son's book but prescribed two explicit and unqualified ways by which the court could still justly condemn witches. I believe Perry Miller is correct when he declares that the ministers who did not condemn the executions were betraying the best principles of Puritan tradition in their own time; they fell short of their own best standards. But Perry Miller does not advance our understanding of the characters or the time, then, when he proceeds on the assumption that both Mathers knew they were justifying "murders" (204). I see no reason to disbelieve Increase Mather's statement that he considered George Burroughs guilty and justly convicted. I see no reason to ignore Increase Mather's vehement denunciations of the Devil, no reason to ignore Increase Mather's participation in his son's examination of a bewitched young woman in Boston in the autumn of 1693, long after the last execution had taken place in Salem. Even if we reject Robert Calef's libelous claim that he saw both Mathers fumbling under that young woman's bedclothes in search of demons (and the pleasure of fondling her breast and belly),[20] and even if we reject the tradition that President Increase Mather had Calef's book burned in the Harvard College Yard, we should hesitate to portray Increase Mather as the voice of unqualified reason and charity. We should applaud Robert Middlekauff's perceptive reminder that Increase Mather continued to insist on the limits of human reason and the power of the supernatural.

If we recognize the major points of agreement in the two Mathers' books about the Salem trials, we may not only avoid the temptation to find heroes and villains. We may reimagine minds that believed simultaneously in strengthening the Congregational ministers' power, in resisting the Devil during his last assault upon the people of God, in protecting the rights of the accused, in deploring the witchcraft court's unjust procedures, in the justice of many of the convictions, in sympathetic appreciation of the judges' difficulties, and in the grave necessity of maintaining popular respect for the newly established government. We cannot avoid judging those minds for the choices they made. We will judge them more fairly as we come closer to perceiving their full complexity.

Notes

1. See John Hope Franklin, *From Slavery to Freedom: A History of Negro Americans,* 3d ed. (New York: Vintage Books, 1969), pp. 93–94.

2. Mark Twain, *Adventures of Huckleberry Finn,* ed. Leo Marx (Indianapolis: Bobbs-Merrill, 1967), p. 82.

3. Perry Miller, *The New England Mind: From Colony to Province* (Cambridge: Harvard Univ. Press, 1953), and Kenneth Silverman, *The Life and Times of Cotton Mather* (New York: Harper and Row, 1984).

4. It was Samuel Eliot Morison who wrote that Robert Calef had tied to Cotton Mather's tail a can that has rattled through the pages of popular history for three centuries. Perry Miller declares that "the right can was tied to the proper tail, and through the pages of this volume it shall rattle and bang" (*From Colony to Province,* p. 204).

5. One of the most sympathetic versions of this judgment is that of Chadwick Hansen, *Witchcraft at Salem* (New York: George Braziller, 1969).

6. Cotton Mather to John Richards, May 31, 1692, *Collections of the Massachusetts Historical Society,* 4th ser., 8 (1868): 391–97. My quotations from *The Return of Several Ministers Consulted . . . by His Excellency . . . upon the Present Witchcrafts in Salem Village* are taken from Thomas J. Holmes, *Cotton Mather: A Bibliography of His Works,* 3 vols. (Cambridge: Harvard Univ. Press, 1940), 3:913.

7. Increase Mather, *Cases of Conscience concerning Evil Spirits Personating Men, Witchcrafts, Infallible Proofs of Guilt in Such As Are Accused with That Crime* (Boston, 1693), p. 6.

8. Cotton Mather, *The Wonders of the Invisible World* (London, 1693). On the dates of publication, see Holmes, *Cotton Mather* 3:1257–58, and *Increase Mather: A Bibliography of His Works,* 2 vols. (Cleveland: n.p., 1931), 1:106, 123.

9. Stoughton's letter is printed on p. [vii] of Mather's *Wonders of the Invisible World,* and the brief endorsement of factual accuracy, subscribed by Stoughton and Sewall, appears on p. 48.

10. *The Diary of Cotton Mather,* ed. Worthington C. Ford, 2 vols. (Boston: Massachusetts Historical Society, 1912; rept. New York: Ungar, n.d.), 1:153.

11. The letter from Cotton Mather to his uncle, held in the Boston Public Library, is printed in Holmes, *Cotton Mather* 2:551–52.

12. Increase Mather's language here does not prove that he, rather than his son Cotton, is the person referred to as "Mr. Mather" in an important entry (dated Aug. 19) in *The Diary of Samuel Sewall,* ed. M. Halsey Thomas, 2 vols. (New York: Farrar, Straus, and Giroux, 1973), 1:294. But the diction is strikingly similar. Recording the execution of George Burroughs and others in Salem on a day when Sewall himself was in Watertown, Sewall says: "All of them said they were innocent, [Martha] Carrier and all. Mr. Mather says they all died by a Righteous Sentence. Mr. Burrough by his Speech, Prayer, protestation of his Innocence, did much move unthinking persons, which occasions their speaking hardly concerning his being executed."

Scholars have usually treated Sewall's entry as corroboration for Robert Calef's report (eight years later) that Cotton Mather, mounted on a horse, made an impromptu speech that prevented the unthinking persons from blocking the execution. Calef himself says that Mather spoke after the execution. Increase Mather's appeal to the thinking part of mankind may combine with Sewall's absence from Salem and Sewall's use of the past tense ("died") to undermine the corroborative value of Sewall's report as evidence that Cotton Mather caused Burroughs's death.

13. This entry, taken from *The Autobiography of Increase Mather,* ed. M. G. Hall (Worcester: American Antiquarian Society, 1962), p. 344, reads: "I found the Countrey in a sad condition by reason of witchcrafts and possessed persons. The Judges and many of the people has espoused a notion, that the devil could not Represent Innocent persons as afflicting others. I doubt that Innocent blood was shed by mistakes of that nature. I therefore published my Cases of Conscience dé Witchcrafts etc—by which (it is sayed) many were enlightened, Juries convinced, and the shedding of more Innocent blood prevented."

14. See Miller, *From Colony to Province,* p. 200; Silverman, *Life and Times,* pp. 110, 113–14, 117.

15. See Holmes, *Cotton Mather* 2:834.

16. Robert Middlekauff, *The Mathers: Three Generations of Puritan Intellectuals, 1596–1728* (New York: Oxford Univ. Press, 1971), pp. 153–55.

17. Sir William Phips to the Earl of Nottingham, Feb. 21, 1693, in David Levin, ed., *What Happened in Salem?,* 2d ed. (New York: Harcourt Brace Jovanovich, 1960), p. 94.

18. Here Mather quotes from the Ministers' Return. See Mather, *Wonders,* p. 12.

19. This letter was available only in typescript when Kenneth Silverman edited *Selected Letters of Cotton Mather* (Baton Rouge: Louisiana State Univ. Press, 1971) and when I wrote *Cotton Mather: The Young Life of the Lord's Remembrancer, 1663–1703* (Cambridge: Harvard Univ. Press, 1978). But the original holograph has since been acquired by Boston College. The last word that I have quoted is misprinted as "Point" in Silverman, *Letters,* p. 44. I am grateful to Boston College for permission to read a photocopy of the manuscript, and for permission to quote it here.

20. Robert Calef, coll., *Salem Witchcraft: Comprising More Wonders of the Invisible World* [London, 1700], in Samuel G. Drake, comp., *The Witchcraft Delusion in New England,* 3 vols. (Boston, 1866; rept. New York: B. Franklin, 1970), 2:49.

5.

Body and Soul in *The Angel of Bethesda*

Practical Advice with Literary and Spiritual Entertainment

Cotton Mather designed his medical book, *The Angel of Bethesda,* to serve as both a guide to practical care and a homiletic work of literature. He chose for his subtitle "An Essay upon the Common Maladies of Mankind," and he promised that his "Rich Collection of *plain* but *potent* and *Approved* REMEDIES" would appear only after he had used the *"Bodily Maladies"* as Providence had surely intended them: to awaken "invalids" to "the Sentiments of Piety." He would also give "practicable directions" to others "for THE PRESERVATION OF HEALTH" and would "occasionally intermix" with all these matters "many other curious, and grateful and useful entertainments."[1] If we read Mather's book according to these declared intentions, we may deepen our understanding of how he thought about the relationship between body and soul.

How shall we account for the apparent inconsistencies in Mather's attitude toward the body? Throughout *The Angel of Bethesda* we can find conventionally Calvinist declarations that the body is "vile" and that illness represents divine retribution for human sins. Mather had resolved in his youth to emulate "the *silkworm,*" to spin sermons "out of the bowels of [his] own *experience,*" and in the winter of 1697–98 he had published anonymously a sermon celebrating his recovery from an illness that had been "Breaking him" for nearly a month, during an epidemic that laid low "a great part of" Boston. *Mens Sana in Corpore Sano. A Discourse upon Recovery from Sickness. Directing How Natural*

A paper presented to the conference on "The Body and the American Imagination" at the University of Paris, May 1990.

Health May Be Improved into Spiritual . . . identifies "*Sin* as the *Cause* of *Sickness.*" Of the two thousand separate human maladies—"*any one of them, able to Crush us!*"—Mather declared that the primary cause was the Original Sin, "which First brought *Sickness* upon a Sinful World, and which yet continues to *Sicken* the World, with a World of Diseases. Our *Sickness* is in short, *Flagellum Dei, pro Peccatis Mundi.*"[2]

Under this conviction, both the author and the suffering patient who might consult his work were obliged to look for the hand and the concealed intention of Providence in any affliction. In *The Angel of Bethesda* most of Mather's sixty-six chapters[3] on the various diseases set his collection of medical remedies between exhortations and ingenious ways to get the best spiritual good out of one's misery. Consider, for example, Mather's elaborate appeal to sufferers from"*Flagellum,* or the Stone":

In you, as much as in any, there is an Opportunity for *Patience to have its perfect Work.* Tis by a Consummate *Patience,* that you are to *Glorify* God.

You are a *Spectacle to Angels,* as well as to *Neighbours,* in all your Sufferings. And when you are Suffering of *Terrible Things, Now* for you to whisper not One Word, that shall have in it, the least murmur against the *Justice* and *Goodness* of the Glorious God, but on the Contrary, to keep Admiring and Adoring of Him, as a God infinitely worthy to be Loved and Served and Praised forever; To Express nothing but such a *Faith* as this; *Tho' my God slay me, yett will I trust in Him;* And, *I will believe Him a GOD of unfailing Mercies and Compassions, Even tho' I am Consumed:* Verily, This will be to the *Angels,* as well as to the *Neighbours,* a most Lovely *Spectacle. God will be glorified* in you. Yea, the Infinite God Himself, who is infinitely more than all the Spectators in the World, will with Delight behold the *Spectacle.* And you are all this while but under a Præparation for *Astonishing Fœlicities* which are prepared for you in a *Future State;* where your *Stone* shall be turned into a *Radiant Jewel* of the *Crown* which is laid up for you; and the *Trial of your Faith, shall be found unto Praise and Honour and Glory at the Appearing of JESUS CHRIST.*

To Engage your *Patience,* Consider what an *Holy* and *Righteous* GOD, He is, who is now smiting of you. Tis true, You are now *Stoning to Death.* But humbly say, *Lord, Thou hast been so Blasphemed by my Sins, that I deserve thus to dy for my Blasphemies!*

I have known an Excellent Person, marvellously *Patient,* when dying of the *Stone;* who, being asked, How he could bear so much *Dolour* with so much *Patience,* replied, *The Thought of my Sins, I find Enough to work Patience in me!* (It was my Grandfather.) [84]

The comfort offered by such an ecstatic passage is the comfort of transcendent exhilaration. Even before he cites the example of his "excellent" grandfather, it is clear that Mather is not berating the sinful sufferer but calling him to accept his opportunity to serve as a glorious spectacle. Here the afflicted body has been stricken by Providence without consultation of the human will. But Mather calls on the sufferer's gracious will to subject the body to spiritual discipline. He even tells him how to engage his patience by thinking of God's holiness and righteousness. If the body can be restrained from uttering "the least murmur," the transcendent individual will may function in harmony with God's hidden purposes. If not, the prayers offered up out of noisier suffering may still be rewarded on the very border between this world and the next: "I know One," Mather says, who prayed, *"Lord, lett us not go Roaring to Heaven!* He had *Roar'd* under the *Stone.* But soon after this, applying himself to the *Urinary Excretion,* he fell at once into a Swoon, and Suddenly went away to a *Better World"* (85).

Only after such powerful injunctions to remember one's sins does Mather concentrate on remedies. As kidney stones offer one the chance to serve as a spectacle of faithful resignation, so the sufferer of intolerable pain in the teeth ought to exclaim, "How much have I *Sinned* with them!" And again: "How often have I dug my *Grave* with my *Teeth.*" Mather acknowledges that a person suffering toothache will not pay much attention to a preacher's "Lecture on our Philosophy of his Distemper." Instead the patient "will cry out *Rather tell me What shall be done to give some Ease unto me.*"

"But," Mather insists, in a sentence that stands alone as a paragraph, "I will first Advise him, how to *gett Good* by his Pain, before I direct him, how to *gett Out* of it" (62).

The meditation that intervenes between this frank declaration and the remedies is the more impressive because Mather has begun this chapter with a brief description of the jaws, the circulatory system, and "the Seeds of all the *Teeth*" hidden "in the Socketts of the Gums, or Jaws, of a *Fœtus*"—a total of "*Fifty-Two* Tormentors in thy Gums alone, O Man, to which thy Sin has made thee liable, as in the Course of thy Life, they may Arise and Appear and Corrupt; and the Nerve at the Bottom of each becomes uneasy" (62). Mather prescribes a meditation that recalls the sufferings of Jesus when "the *Fist of Wickedness*" struck him on the cheekbone, and besides the expiation won by Christ's sacrifice, this meditation asks for the grace "always to *Eat,* and *Speak,* in the *Fear of God!*" Just as the intolerable pain of toothache should remind one of the *"Weeping and Wailing and Gnashing of Teeth"* in Hell, so our *"Perishing Teeth, . . . the Hardest and Strongest Things thou hast about thee,"* should remind us that our bones as well as our flesh will *"soon Moulder into Dust"* (63).

Mather places a buffer between that solemn truth and the beginning of his practical advice about dental care. He quotes a passage from Augustine's *Confessions* in which Augustine, too much in pain to be able to speak, writes out a prayer for his friends to utter for him, whereupon Augustine is "amazed" to find that his toothache disappears as soon as they kneel down (63).

Under the rod of affliction, then, the sinner is obliged to get what good Providence may grant in response to meditation, spiritual self-examination, and prayer. In this context we may be amazed by Mather's abrupt switch to practical advice that seems to be based on a totally different premise about both human ability and the human body. When he begins suggesting practical care of the teeth, for example, just after his account of Augustine's amazing cure through prayer, Mather writes as if people had complete control of their health. Of course he counts on believers to share his conviction about the use of means; it was a commonplace among Puritans that Providence, which controls human affairs, requires saints and sinners alike to use all the good means that it provides for their benefit. But when Mather regrets people's failure to be "more Careful of Præserving a *Good Sett of Teeth*," he writes as if the body were not the corrupt seat of our lusts but a beautiful mechanism "in the Contrivance whereof the Wise Design of the Glorious Creator has been so Conspicuous!" In the maintenance of good teeth, Mather insists, "the *Speech* is much Concerned; the *Breath* kept Sweet; the *Beauty* sett off; and insupportable *Pains* prevented." Washing the teeth "with *fair Water* every Day," washing behind the ears and about the temples, and bathing the entire head in cold water may preserve one's teeth throughout life, and even those who have suffered much from neglecting their teeth may benefit from the proposed care for "the rest of their Days" (64–65). Excessive self-reliance and excessive concern for one's appearance and comfort may be sinful, but Mather apparently sees nothing wrong with homiletic appeals to self-help, vanity, and the desire to avoid pain.

Reading the chapters as homiletic essays reminds us that attention to the context is essential, and that the rhetoric of spiritual comfort forms a major part of the entertainment. The most celebrated instance of Mather's endorsement of practical care is the one for which he suffered the most abuse from his contemporaries: inoculation for smallpox. In Mather's youth, during an epidemic in 1678, his father's household had benefited from the Reverend Thomas Thacher's broadside concerning the treatment of smallpox. Thacher had offered a pithy summary of the famous Dr. Thomas Sydenham's common sense—*Don't make things worse,* for example, *by overheating an already feverish patient*—and Mather repeats that kind of sound practical advice in *The Angel of Bethesda.* Before recommending inoculation in this chapter, moreover, Mather speculates on the history of the disease, pointing out that it was apparently unknown to the ancients. He also suggests that germs may well be the cause, for millions of them have been discovered when microscopes have studied the pustules. Such observations, he says, have drawn us "insensibly . . . into *New Sentiments,* about the *Way* of its *Conveyance,* and the *Cause* why 'tis convey'd but once" (94). Even in this critical chapter, however, written no more than two years after the worst epidemic since the founding of Boston, Mather's essay insists on bringing spiritual help out of physical observation and affliction before he offers remedies or preventatives. The "nasty *Pustules,*" which make the invalid "*Loathsome* even to Thyself as well as to all that are about thee," must be seen as nothing more than "Little Emblems of the *Errors* which thy *Life* had been filled Withal" (96). And acquired physical immunity itself, the very phenomenon that leads to the discovery of inoculation, serves first as another emblem: "*O Man,*" Mather pleads, let the observation that almost nobody ever suffers smallpox a second time "be verified in thy *Moral Experience,*" so that "thou wilt *Never again* fall into" the "*Grosser Sins,* which thou hast once *Repented of*" (97). In this chapter once again, he makes the transition clarify explicitly the proper relationship between spiritual therapy and physical measures: "But thus having *Sought First,* what is *most* of all to be Sought for, and Serv'd the *Kingdome of God and His Righteousness,* from the *Calamity* that is come upon us, we may the more hopefully proceed unto the Work of Encountring and Conquering the *Adversary"* (97).

Here the transition to physical care uses Mather's most stirring rhythmic and biblical rhetoric to summon the reader to action against the Adversary. Mather's thrilling evocation of the flaming dragon makes his rhetoric part of the therapy when he rises into a fervent plea for courage and joins with the afflicted reader by shifting into the first person for that appeal. I have used slash marks to show the metrical lines:

> *wilt thou play with him as with a Bird?* / No, He will *fill* thy *skin* as with *barbed Irons.* / And *shall not one be cast down at the Sight* / *of him?* *Who can come to him with his double Bridle?* / *Sparks of Fire Leap out of his Mouth:* / *His Breath kindles Coals.* / *When he raises up himself* / *the mighty are afraid, He Spreadeth* / *Sharp pointed Things, upon* our Clay. / He makes our Blood to *boil as a Pott:* / He makes our Humours *Like a Pott of Ointment.* /
>
> Yet lett us be of *good Courage;* yea, be *Very courageous.* There is a way to Manage him! [97]

The division between physical self-help and dependence on repentance and Providential mercy may seem narrower still when we remember two obvious facts which the strangeness of Mather's religious and medical world tempts modern readers to overlook. For a number of the maladies—most notably consumption, the stone, smallpox, apoplexy, puerperal fever, dysentery—no reliable cure was available. Death was so likely that emphasis on meditation, repentance, and prayer may well have been considered practical advice, not only in the desire for recovery but also in preparation for imminent Judgment.

Surely, moreover, Mather did not intend this book to be read as curious or skeptical modern scholars read it, from beginning to end. In an eighteenth-century household the book (had it been published) would have been used as it was needed for particular ailments. It is hard to imagine a contemporary of Mather's (except for a medical practitioner) reading through all the catalogues of purported remedies in chapter after chapter. The homiletic frames, too, would have been read separately as one consulted the book for help in responding to a specific ailment, or as one sought spiritual entertainment in some of Mather's meditations on the maladies of mankind.

Mather's credulity in recommending or reporting various kinds of treatment has elicited indignant ridicule or defensive explanation from a number of nineteenth- and twentieth-century commentators. Ever since Dr. Oliver Wendell Holmes deplored both Mather's superstition and some of Mather's loathsome prescriptions more than a century ago, commentators on *The Angel of Bethesda* have assessed Mather's credulity. Holmes had deplored as early as 1860 the almost universal belief "that sick persons should feed on noxious substances."[4] In an essay called "Homeopathy and Its Kindred Delusions," he had excoriated "the saintly Bishop Berkeley" for claiming that tar water ("stirring a gallon of water with a quart of tar, leaving it 48 hours, and pouring off the clear water," then drinking it) was a "panacea" for gout, fever, coughs, pleurisy, indigestion, scurvy, and hypochondria (12–13). Holmes did not call Cotton Mather saintly, but Mather's complicity in "the miserable delusion of witchcraft" (357) and Holmes's horror of clerical interference in medical questions led him to speak occasionally of Mather's remedies as if they had issued from Mather's twisted imagination rather than from the medical writings of Robert Boyle or Giorgio Baglivi. When Mather arrives at "the odious class of remedies," Holmes protests, "he revels in them like a *scarabeus.*" That allusion to beetles flourishing in excremental remedies would suffice, Holmes said, to suggest "the inconceivable abominations with which [Mather] proposed to outrage the sinful stomachs of the unhappy confederates and accomplices of Adam" (360).

For our purposes such amusing judgments are beside the point. Just as we remember that the pious frames of Mather's chapters were intended to put soul and body in proper relation, so we should view the proposed remedies in Mather's book as a varied collection with which Mather chose to offer patients the full range of what respectable authorities and popular lore had tried or recommended, often with testimony that they had been remarkably effective. Holmes knew long ago, of course, that remedies ranging from the "Pizzle of a Green Turtle" (pulverized and swallowed with beer, ale, or white wine) to mixtures that included the urine or dung of mice, horses, goats, sheep, cows, and human beings—Holmes knew that for centuries such "odious" remedies had been prescribed throughout Europe by both the learned and the folk. Few modern readers will be able to peruse Mather's lists of such remedies without wondering why he was not more skeptical of them, but I don't find Mather reveling in them. I find myself drawn as irresistibly as any modern reader must be to contemplate the substance itself rather than the form or the context in which Mather recommends it. Yet we ought to look at some of Mather's language before we accept Holmes's complaint that Mather throws into his text, "or squeezes into his margin," everything that his seventy or eighty learned authors "or the old women of both sexes had ever told him of" (359).

Consider, for example, a few of Mather's proposals for relieving the stone. I will overemphasize certain qualifying words by setting them in uppercase:

> If there be an Inflammation of the Parts, *Bleeding* MAY be proper.
> A Cold, Thin, Spare Diet MAY be proper. . . .
> SOME had a *Suppression of Urine* releeved by powdered *Mouse-dung,* when other means failed.
> *Etmuller* MENTIONS One who on drinking Wine always fell into a *Dysury,* and made Bloody Urine; but was always Cured by taking *Oil of Sweet Almonds.*[91]

For the toothache and other ailments, moreover, the suggestion may take the form of a noncommittal question (65), as in: "What shall one think of [rose] *Hipps* gathered in the Wane of the Moon, in *August,* and worn on the Arm of the same Side with the *aking-Tooth?*" Or again: "THEY PRÆSCRIBE a Thousand Things, to be held in the Mouth, Especially, to chew *Pellitory* of *Spain.*" And finally: "Thrust the Eye of a Needle into the Bowels of a *Sow-bug;* and the Matter which it fetches out, putt in the *Hollow Tooth,* if it be such an one that akes: *This* I HAVE HEARD cried up, as an *Infallible* for the *Tooth-ache,* and I have seen SOME Success of it" (64).

Mather's careful wording in at least some of these reports is reinforced by explicit skepticism concerning others. He warns against giving "pretended *Cordials,* and *Expellers*" or emetics as a treatment for smallpox. He calls them "Vile *Expellers*," for they have "Millions of times *driven* the poor *Souls* out of their *Fired Mansions!* . . . Don't lett 'em Swallow *Fire-brands!* Leave *Nature* undisturbed. It is hardly known, that *Nature* fails of doing its Part for Thrusting out the *Small-Pox. Forcing* it, is the most likely way of *Hindring* it" (99). Of course he follows Sydenham here, just before recommending inoculation, as elsewhere he will paradoxically recommend procedures according to both Galen and Paracelsus. But he is so acutely aware of perplexity at least some of the time that he devotes an entire chapter to the conflicting theories and prescriptions of physicians. On the one hand, "a *Skilful* and *Thoughtful* PHYSICIAN must be always near" the smallpox patient (98). Chapter 40, on the other hand, exposes "The Uncertainties of Physicians" in an elaborately varied series of antitheses. Consider a small sample of four:

> Many hold, that no Good is to be done in a *Consumption*, without *Opiates*. It is held by others, that they are Pernicious Things, and no better than an Halter. . . .
>
> *Conserve of Roses*, has been in high Esteem for many Ages; And an Army of Advocates, besides the great Names of *Platerus*, and *Forestus*, and *Riverius*, might be mustered for the Defending of it. But *Sylvius* decries it as an useless thing, and *Harvey* asserts the Patients to be rather the Worse than the Better for it. . . .
>
> Have not *Snails*, gott as *Early* as any Remedies, into general Esteem and Practice? *Cardan* sais, he has made a Cure of *Desperate Consumptions* with them. Harvey despises them. *Salins* reproaches them.
>
> Lett *Weikard* and *Harvey* Engage one another upon the *Juice of Turnips;* The former with *Panegyricks*, the Latter with *Invectives*. [187]

"Alas, what a *Blindman's Buffet* [is] carried on among these learned physicians!" (188). We must try to choose among them as well as we can, but the lesson is nonetheless moving for being predictable: "O *Thou afflicted*, and under *Distemper*, Go to *Physicians*, in *Obedience* to God, who has Commanded the *Use of Means*. But place thy *Dependence* on God alone to Direct and Prosper them. And know, That they are all *Physicians of no Value*, if *He* do not so" (189).

To such an old Puritan as Mather, then, it was no surprise that we should find "*Darkness* . . . *Sett in our Pathes*" (188). We are commanded, he knew, to use means but not to rely too much on them or on our own resources; to consult physicians and yet to remember (in words that anticipate some of the medical admonitions of our own time) that *"Moderate Abstinence,* and Convenient *Exercise,* and Some Guard against injurious *Changes of the Weather,* with an HOLY and EASY MIND, will go as far" toward preserving us "as all the *Præscriptions* with which all the *Physicians* under Heaven, have ever yett obliged us" (37–38).

In his celebrated chapter on the *"Nishmath-Chajim"* (which he translates from the Hebrew as the breath or spirit of life), Mather follows "the Sagacious Dr. *Sydenham"* (though of course with more emphasis on piety) in declaring that about one-sixth of all diseases are "unjustly" blamed on the spleen in men and the womb in women. And he also follows Baglivi (as well, Mather declares, as ten thousand others!) in perceiving "that a great part of our *Diseases,* either do Rise from, or are Fed by, a Weight of *Cares,* Lying on [our] Minds." Some *"Diseases* that seem Incurable, are easily cured by agreeable *Conversation"* (35). The true origin of the so-called *"Splenetic* and *Hysteric* Ataxy in the Body,"* Mather insists, "is a *Feeble Constitution* of the *Spirits,* and the breaking of their *System,* so that they are Easily Dissipated, or have an unaequal Distribution" (36).

The concept of *Nishmath Chajim* helps us to solve several problems in Mather's thoughts about the body. Here we see quite clearly that although capable of writing about women as if gender had made them peculiarly susceptible to some kinds of sin, he could write evenhandedly about so-called splenetic and hysteric disorders—without the slightest condescension toward women. When discussing the *Nishmath Chajim,* as when writing in his diary in his youth that he hoped to emulate the biblical Isaac by having a mate brought to his bed, he can write about procreation without a hint of allusion to sin. Because he attributes to the *Nishmath Chajim* all those nonrational impulses toward self-preservation or health, from the sucking of an infant to the nursing by the mother, he includes "the Acts requisite in *Generation"* (30) among "the Very Needful and Proper Things" that we do "without Consulting of Reason for the doing of them" (32). The spirit that "Leads to" those acts is also the "Spirit, whose *Way we know not, for Shaping the Bones,* and other Parts, *in the Womb of her that is with Child"* (30–31).

Mather also expresses in this chapter his strong faith in intellectual progress. He knows that the *Nishmath Chajim* "may be of a *Middle Nature*, between the *Rational Soul* and the *Corporeal Mass*"; that it "may be the *Medium of Communication*, by which they work upon One another"; that "It wonderfully receives . . . *Impressions* from *Both* of them" (28); and that it "seems to be commensurate unto our Bodies." But he confesses that we don't yet know "by what *Principle* the Particles" of this "*plastic Spirit*," particles "which may be finer than those of the *Light* itself, are kept in their *Cohæsion* to one another" (30). One day, he implies, we may know much more.

In the meantime, the idea of this mediating spirit reconciles mechanism and soul for Mather, and it allows him to continue calling the body a machine while distinguishing it from all others. "If anything be out of Order" in the human machine, he says, "presently the *Whole Engine*, as under an Alarum, is awakened for the helping of what is amiss, and other Parts of the Engine Strangely putt themselves out of their Way that they may send in Help unto it." A malfunctioning part in any other machine "will remain so," Mather claims, "till some Hand from Abroad shall rectify it" (32).

That reconciliation liberates the faithful Christian writer's imagination. He can use the *Nishmath Chajim* to speculate on supernatural questions such as the resurrection of the dead and the existence of diabolical specters. He can use it to argue for therapy directed at anxiety, rather than any physical defect, as the cause of some illnesses. Quoting his own *Bonifacius* in this chapter, Mather urges physicians to practice "*The Art of Curing by Consolation . . . . :* Lett the *Physician* with all possible Ingenuity of *Conversation*, find out, what matter of *Anxiety* there may have been upon the Mind of the *Patient;* what there is that has made his Life uneasy to him. Having discovered the *Burden*, Lett him use all the ways he can devise, to take it off" (35–36).[5] And Mather can use the *Nishmath Chajim* to justify his insistence that "after all, tis time to have done with the *Metaphysical Jargon*, which for a Long Time has passed for the *Rationale* of Medicine." He can now demand that physicians acquire mathematical skill so that they may go to work "*Mathematically*, and by the *Laws* of *Matter* and *Motion*, to find out the *Cause* and *Cure* of *Diseases*" (47).

Mather's literary imagination amuses him, if not every modern reader, with characteristically playful language, much of it related to the physical body. He calls his chapters "capsulae." He may sometimes play with words in his most elevated passages, as when he promises that in Heaven a sufferer's kidney stone will be converted into a jewel for his crown. But more often he will ask victims of the toothache, for example, to "chew upon" his advice (62), or he will predict that his chapter on the gout will be "*Swol'n*" because the gout gives the patient plenty of time to read, and because diversion should "always be prescribed under this Malady" (66). His chapter on "*Slavery* to the *Custome* of *Smoking Tobacco*" (303) puts "a *Pinch* upon the *Snuff-box*" (301).

In 1724, as in the 1680s and 1690s, Mather tries to steer a course between what he considered the utter skepticism of Sadducees and the superstitions of "our Common People" (297). The false teachings of astrology (301) are no better than those of "*Popery*" (299). "A Skilful and Faithful Physician will do more for a poor Patient than all the *Saints* in the *Romish Kalender*" (301). Toward the end of *The Angel of Bethesda* he warns against relying on demonic cures by telling several catastrophic narratives about people who foolishly trusted to charms for their relief (296–97), and he bears down hard with his own skeptical questions to dispel the common belief that the seventh consecutive son can heal with the touch of his hand (297): "Why should the Intervening of a *Sister* deprive him of this *Distinguishing Prærogative?* Why should the seventh have it any more than the *First-born . . . ?* Is it requisite that all the *Seven* have the Same Father and Mother? Or, may the Father have the *Seven Sons* by different Wives? Or, The Mother of these *Maccabees,* by different Husbands?" People would do just as well, Mather concludes, to "take up the Fashion of applying to a *Sixth Son*" (299).

Mather titles his last chapter "EUTHANASIA. or, A DEATH Happy and Easy." Having armed readers "against the *Approaches of Death,*" his *The Angel of Bethesda* must concede that it cannot by any means redeem them or show them how to live forever in this world. This final application of the word, therefore, assumes that the reader's body has survived into an old age and that he reads as "a *Dying Man*" who wants to die with "those *Dispositions* of, *An Healed Soul,* which all your *Sickness,* as well as this Treatise, has come to bring you to" (318). Through a perfect repentance, total surrender of one's will to God, owning the Covenant, and accepting the spirit of Christ "acting as a *Living Principle*" inside oneself, the Christian may have visions of Heaven—here Mather quotes his first wife's dying words (321)—and may attain an ecstasy that paradoxically releases the body and glories in the prospect of resurrection. Here again I mark the metrical lines:

O my BODY, I am now *dropping* of thee. / Such *Flesh and Blood* as thou art, is not fitt / for the *Kingdome of God*. / But thou art the *Outworks* of a *Temple*, / which God in His Free and Rich *Grace* / has *Chosen* for His *Habitation*: / and tho' thou art now Ruin'd by Sin, / the God who can and will *Raise the Dead*, / will fetch thee out of the *Ruines*; / and thou shalt be Rebuilt / into a much more splendid Edifice. / I *do not fear* to let thee go down / into the *Land of Darkness*; For my God, / who has *Baptised* Thee, and *Employed* Thee, / will surely bring thee up again. Go, / my BODY; Thou shalt Enter into a *Chamber*, / where the *Doors* will be *shut about thee*, / and thou shalt *be hidden as it were* / for a little *Moment*; But the *Resurrection* / of thy SAVIOURS *Dead Body*, has assured me, / that thou shalt *Rise again*. . . . Ah, my *Vile Body*, I now lett thee go / down into the *Pitt of Corruption*, / full of Assurance, / that I shall shortly receive thee again, / marvellously changed; Vigorous, / Luminous, *Incorruptible* / . . . "But One Word more." [321–22]

Mather calls the body and spirit back, to utter last words for the survivors. Having told the reader how to survive and how to die, Mather's angel takes his leave.

Notes

1. Cotton Mather, *The Angel of Bethesda*, ed. Gordon W. Jones, M.D. (Barre, Mass.: American Antiquarian Society, 1972), p. 1.

2. In the first chapter of *The Angel of Bethesda* (p. 5), Mather quotes this passage from *Mens Sana in Corpore Sano*, identifying that anonymous publication as his own work. For the silkworm, see Mather's manuscript "Paterna," University of Virginia Library, p. 20. On the illness, see *The Diary of Cotton Mather*, ed. Worthington C. Ford, 2 vols. (Boston: Massachusetts Historical Society, 1912; rept. New York: Ungar, n.d.), 1:254.

3. Five chapters, numbered 15–19, are missing.

4. Oliver Wendell Holmes, *Medical Essays, 1842–1882* (Boston, 1883), p. 186. Compare Gordon Jones's introduction and notes to *The Angel of Be-*

thesda and Otho T. Beall, Jr., and Richard H. Shryock, *Cotton Mather: First Significant Figure in American Medicine* (Baltimore: Johns Hopkins Univ. Press, 1954), pp. 19–126.

5. Dr. Jones's note (p. 333) speculates on the identity of a particular pope among many named Bonifacius. But Mather clearly alludes here to his own book, published in 1710. See *Bonifacius: An Essay upon the Good,* ed. David Levin (Cambridge: Harvard Univ. Press, 1966), pp. 103–4.

6.

A Historical Reconsideration of
Maule's Curse

John Updike's strategy in a recent essay, "On Hawthorne's Mind," reminds us forty-three years after the publication of *Maule's Curse* that
although major scholarly works have transformed Anglo-American literary history they have not invalidated Yvor Winters's central insight
or his most important judgment. Updike does not mention Winters or
any other critic, but his essay in the *New York Review of Books* studies
the paradox of Hawthorne's relation to Christian faith, the plethora of
religious symbols and ideas in the work of a skeptic.[1]

In all three of the controversial books that Winters republished
together as *In Defense of Reason,* he aimed his strongest rhetoric at contemporary targets: the primitivism, decadence, and nonsense that the
titles of his books had held up as reason's enemies in modern letters.[2]
Yet his campaign was emphatically historical. Historical scholarship
itself expressed the disciplined intelligence that Winters considered
essential to rescuing literature from destructive romanticism. And before they could be free, Winters believed, poets and critics would have
to recognize the historical circumstances that had brought literature
into its modern crisis. Maule's curse was a historical reality. It might
be lifted by careful study of American literary and cultural history.

Winters chose his title shrewdly. He knew that Hawthorne had
borrowed Matthew Maule's curse on the Pyncheon family from a cry
that one of the Salem witches had flung at her accusers: "God will give
you blood to drink!" Blood suggests the emotion whose dominance,
untempered by a sound metaphysics or ethics, Winters laments. And
Maule's curse on the Pyncheons anticipates the choking influence that

Reprinted from an Yvor Winters issue of the *Southern Review* 17 (1981): 803–13.

Winters believed New England Puritanism had had on American literature. To give that influence, while tracing it, an appropriate prominence in this book, Winters took Hawthorne out of his chronological place and set him at the beginning, ahead of Cooper and Emerson.

So much has been written since 1938 about connections between seventeenth-century Puritanism and the literature of the American Renaissance that we need to make a special effort to remember how little of the best scholarship was available to Winters. Not until the year after Winters published these "Seven Studies in the History of American Obscurantism" did the first volume of Perry Miller's *The New England Mind* appear. F. O. Matthiessen's *American Renaissance* (1941), M. H. Abrams's *The Mirror and the Lamp* (which Winters read with admiration in 1953), Miller and Johnson's *The Puritans* (1938)—none had been published before Winters wrote *Maule's Curse*. The best historical works he could use were Charles M. Andrews's history of the American colonies (1934–38) and H. W. Schneider's *The Puritan Mind* (1930). Samuel Eliot Morison's *Builders of the Bay Colony* (1930) and *Harvard College in the Seventeenth Century* (1936) might have helped, but Winters relied most heavily on H. B. Parkes for his account of New England Puritanism and its limitations. The critics whose interpretations *Maule's Curse* either follows or tries to correct are Van Wyck Brooks, Lewis Mumford, Joseph Warren Beach, and Edmund Wilson. Very little of the best work on Henry James had been written.

Without blaming Winters, therefore, anyone who has read widely in the scholarship of the last forty years will consider the version of New England's intellectual history in *Maule's Curse* too simple and too abstract. Fairness obliges us to notice that in a devastating passage on Vernon L. Parrington in 1943 Winters held up as models Perry Miller's *The New England Mind* and "Jonathan Edwards to Emerson" (1940), and that he deplored oversimplification. Parrington, he complains, believed "that one can write the history of a culture with reference only to one intellectual tradition." Winters ridicules Parrington's request that we "put aside the [Puritans'] theology and fasten attention on the politics and economics of the struggle": "In other words," Winters says, "if we will resolutely neglect ninety-nine hundredths of what the Puritans wrote during their first century and a half, we shall arrive at a true understanding of what they were trying to say, and we shall have made a clear and undeceptive beginning to a history of American literature" (558). Even before he had read *The New England Mind,* Winters knew that his version of the connection between Puritanism and nineteenth-century New England literature was "speculative" (158). He knew it was impossible to demonstrate "that New England predisposed Hawthorne to allegory . . . ; yet the disposition in both is obvious. And it can easily be shown that New England provided the material for one great allegory, and that, in all likelihood, she was largely to blame for [Hawthorne's] later failures" (158). The scholarship on which Winters relied in the 1930s, and his own preoccupation with intelligent moral judgment, led him to base his speculative account on a narrow version of Puritan thought. He was looking for tendencies toward obscurantism as well as allegory, and he found them in the Puritan versions of predestination and free will.

Winters's speculative reasoning is powerful. Because Puritans denied that good works could influence a sinner's salvation, he says, New England ethics tended to discourage complex moral thought but at the same time to give cosmic significance to trivial acts. Salvation depended on the arbitrary will of a sovereign deity, but in practice good conduct in this world was taken as a sign of election. Puritanism aggravated the moral plight of New Englanders by requiring intense self-examination for signs of repentance or recalcitrance, even as it denied the possibility of ultimately effective moral choice. In the allegorical world of seventeenth-century New England, sin was sin. One small transgression had the same moral significance as an atrocity. Hawthorne's own clearest statement of the view that Winters thought characteristic of New England tradition declared that "a thumb's bigness" of evil would outweigh whatever good a sinner's whole lifetime could throw onto the balance.[3]

This attitude toward sin persisted, Winters argues, long after Calvinism had lost its doctrinal hold on New England. Hawthorne, who began to write two centuries after the founding, had in Winters's view only one great story—he calls it "pure allegory"—to tell. Having written it flawlessly in *The Scarlet Letter* (which Winters concedes might be read as a fine historical novel of Puritan New England), Hawthorne was left by his tradition with an intense moral consciousness and the habit of allegory, a habit that denied him the complex moral philosophy appropriate for so intense an awareness. In a similarly pathetic discrepancy, Winters says, Hawthorne developed a plethora of symbols, along with techniques of evasion and ambiguity, without rigorously derived social and philosophical meanings to give them substantive value. Indeed, the evasions may well have constituted Hawthorne's strategy for masking the hollowness. In this context the picture of Hawthorne in his last years, writing the four abortive romances, failing repeatedly to find an adequate story or theme, is just as sad as it is in a more psychological perspective, and here it has a historical importance that connects Hawthorne not only to the Puritans but to Melville, James, and Henry Adams.

Winters was so clearly preoccupied with logical and historical tendencies that his inaccuracy on Puritan ethics is of relatively minor significance to the larger argument. It is certainly reasonable to notice the heavily allegorical tone in the histories of William Bradford, Edward Johnson, and Cotton Mather. Yet Winters might have noticed that Bradford, John Winthrop, and Mather often portray historical saints who have to make exquisitely difficult moral choices even as both the saints and the historian recognize that the source of their predicament is the very Providence to whom they owe their election and their covenanted mission. Following Parkes and Andrews,[4] Winters assumes too easily that the seventeenth-century Puritan's moral life was defined by the question of salvation or damnation. And he assumes that the Puritans' Providential mission led them to act without doubt or perplexity against the forces of error.

Except for the tendency toward allegory that was encouraged by Calvinist doctrine, Winters gives no evidence that Puritan leaders were really free of self-doubt, or that in their preference for "a very broad abstraction" they had actually abandoned "the patient study of the minutiae of moral behavior long encouraged by Catholic tradition" (158). When he deplores "the imperceptive, unwavering brutality" that Puritan leaders often "committed in the name of piety" (168), he neglects to point out that if judged by what was done in the name of piety Catholic tradition would have to be pronounced equally imperceptive and brutal. In their actual life and in their histories and tracts, many New England saints struggled to use their best intelligence to understand the baffling behavior of their fellow communicants, to define the limits of their covenanted elders' and magistrates' authority, to interpret ambiguous Providential "callings," to define the just price, to test the validity of owning slaves and the limits of obedience to the crown. Cotton Mather even preached a sermon to the Artillery Company on distinguishing between just and unjust wars. Puritans knew that their historical mission required them to make careful judgments at the risk of grave error. If Winters had known Stephen Foster's *Their Solitary Way* (1971) or Norman Fiering's splendid *Moral Philosophy at Seventeenth-Century Harvard* (1981), he might have revised his sketch of Puritan thought, but he would probably have retained his judgment of allegorical tendency.[5]

Hawthorne's achievement, too, seems today to be much more varied and deep than *Maule's Curse* recognizes. Except for "Young Goodman Brown" and one or two others, Winters dismisses Hawthorne's best short stories as "slight performances" (157), and he gives only a single sentence to *The Blithedale Romance,* a failure (he says) in which Hawthorne "began as a novelist, but lost himself toward the close in an unsuccessful effort to achieve allegory" (170). In the perspective of Winters's concern with moral choice, neither the astonishing psychological insight of "Roger Malvin's Burial" and "The Birthmark" nor the shrewd historical intelligence of "The Maypole of Merrymount," "Roger Malvin's Burial," "Main Street," and "My Kinsman, Major Molineux," seems to be relevant. It is the line from Puritanism to romanticism that Winters wants to trace, and in Hawthorne's own career a corresponding line from the great allegory to the "intense inane" surface that frustrated Hawthorne's groping for significance in the unfinished romances (175). The historical line from Puritanism to Unitarianism moves in *Maule's Curse,* as it had moved in Hawthorne's "Main Street" and Cooper's *The Wept of Wish-ton-Wish* and *Satanstoe,* from the founders' ardor, through the counterfeit of their children's moralizing and persecuting, toward the spiritual deprivation of the Unitarians, who in Winters's view removed from "the ethical life . . . the more impressive aspects of its supernatural sanction" and offered "nothing to take the place of that sanction" (164). The moral conviction "exemplified in the lucid and classical prose of W. E. Channing" had "the greatest firmness and dignity," Winters concedes, but in rejecting the pale negations of Unitarian theology "Emerson eliminated the need of moral conviction and moral understanding alike. . . . In an Emersonian universe there is equally no need and no possibility of judgment" (164). And although Winters perceives that *The Scarlet Letter* embodies a fine allegorical critique of Puritan morality, he concludes from sketches like "The New Adam and Eve" that Hawthorne's own moral sentiments "were much closer to the ideas of Emerson than to those of [Jonathan] Edwards" (164). Except in "the very general notion of regeneration through repentance," Winters complains, Hawthorne never "establishes the nature of the intelligence which might exceed the intelligence of the Puritans, but rather hints at the existence of a richer and more detailed understanding than the Puritan scheme of life is able to contain" (168). Citing three wildly diverse standards of judgment to which Hawthorne appealed at different times in his life, Winters suggests that *The Scarlet Letter* might have been ruined if Hawthorne had not prudently refused there to "explore the [ideal] understanding; the man who was able in the same lifetime to write 'The New Adam and Eve,' to conceive the art-colony described in *The Marble Faun,* and to be shocked at the nude statues of antiquity, was scarcely the man to cast a clear and steady light upon the finer details of the soul" (168).

The evident harshness of this judgment and others in *Maule's Curse* can easily lead one to overlook a major part of Winters's intention. He sounds his monitory theme so powerfully that an offended or unaccustomed ear may miss the intensity of his praise. Winters wrote these essays in the mid-1930s, when neither the critic nor the scholar who specialized in American literature had great standing in departments of English. The very essays that deplore the effect of Maule's curse in American literature celebrate the genius of all six writers except Edgar Allan Poe, and even a few of Poe's poems are allowed "some excellent passages," some "admirable description" (251). Despite Melville's occasional lapses into the "confusion" of "New England mysticism and Romantic amoralism," Winters calls him "the greatest man of his era and of his nation" (173). If Winters's recoil from evasiveness kept him from appreciating some of Hawthorne's best psychological portraits, his focus on allegory and historical intelligence enabled his acute eye to perceive some of the best formal qualities in *The Scarlet Letter:* the importance of Hawthorne's exposition and the use of Puritan symbols to criticize Puritan society. In the setting Hawthorne chose, Winters sees, "allegory was realism, the idea was life itself; and [Hawthorne's] prose, always remarkable for its polish and flexibility, and stripped for once of all superfluity, was reduced to the living idea" (165). Here at last, then, Hawthorne "intensified pure exposition to a quality comparable in its way to that of great poetry" (165). The one example Winters selects to show that Hawthorne had "brought his allegory to perfect literary form" is "the suit of mail" in Governor Bellingham's hall, the breastplate and headpiece in which Pearl and then Hester see themselves reflected, the mother seeming to be "absolutely hidden behind" the "gigantic" scarlet letter, just as the Puritan society often hid the human sinner behind an enormously magnified conception of sin (165–66).

The same formal acuteness leads Winters to praise similar achievements in his essays on Cooper, Melville, Jones Very, Emily Dickinson, and Henry James. He calls Dickinson "one of the greatest lyric poets of all time" (299) and James "the greatest novelist in English" (336). Of the eight writers studied in the book (Emerson chiefly as a foil to Jones Very), only Poe is denied the highest praise as a stylist. Maule's curse is a blight on a distinguished literary tradition. When Winters later deplored Parrington's *Main Currents in American Thought,* he charged Parrington with one offense even greater than the historical oversimplification we have already noticed: ignoring formal values in literature in order to lift economic and political ideas from it. That offense, Winters protested, closes Parrington's literary history not only to the best prose of Cotton Mather but also to the genius of Melville and Henry James (560).

The formal counterpart to Winters's moral version of Maule's curse is a reversal of the logic of literary representation. Winters finds damaging reversals in Hawthorne's unfinished romances, in Poe's criticism, and even in James's last three masterpieces. Hawthorne developed early "the formula of alternative possibilities" (170), a way of disclaiming implausible allegorical or supernatural interpretations of the action even as he describes them—the comet in the shape of an A, the wolf that ("it is said") offers its head to be petted by little Pearl as she plays alone in the forest. In these passages, Winters argues, "the idea conveyed is clear enough, but the embodiment of the idea appears far-fetched" (171). He considers the device harmless in *The Scarlet Letter* but disastrous when Hawthorne, having given perfect form to his allegory, has nothing left but to turn "toward the specific, . . . the art of the novelist" (169), for which Winters (who ignores Hawthorne's theory of the romance) considers him ill-equipped. In this judgment of his declining work, Hawthorne "reverse[s] the formula, so as to make the physical representation perfectly clear but the meaning uncertain" (172). The last sections of *The Blithedale Romance,* and all the unfinished romances, give us "the symbolic footprint, the symbolic spider, the symbolic elixirs and poisons, but we have not that of which they are symbolic; we have the hushed, the tense and confidential manner . . . of one who imparts a grave secret, but the words are inaudible" (172).

Thus questions of literary form and moral judgment come together, as they eventually do in all seven of the essays. Winters concludes the study of Hawthorne himself, and foreshadows his evaluation of Emerson, Poe, and Melville, with a quotation from the unfinished *Septimius Felton.* Percy Boynton had called the passage a self-portrait of Hawthorne, but it could apply as well to the later Thoreau or the Melville of the 1860s, walking "with his head bent down, brooding, brooding, his eyes fixed on some chip, some stone, some common plant, any commonest thing, as if it were the clew and index to some mystery; and when, by chance, startled out of these meditations, he lifted his eyes, there would be a kind of perplexity, a dissatisfied, foiled look in them, as if of his speculations he found no end" (172–73).

The reversals that Winters finds in Poe and James are sometimes close to the process he attributes to Hawthorne, but each is sufficiently different to deserve a brief review here. Poe's best poem conveys "an intense feeling of meaning withheld," so that we have once again "all of the paraphernalia of allegory except the significance" (251). But a major document in Poe's critical theory culminates in a reversal that Winters considers much more pernicious even than Poe's ignorant exclusion of quantity from the scansion of English verse. No longer "an accident of inadequate understanding," as in Hawthorne, obscurantism becomes in Poe "the explicit aim of writing" and the generator "of a method" (246). Having decided that the knowledge of perfect Beauty is unattainable and that the best poets are saddened by the impermanence of their occasional "glimpses" of "the Supernal Beauty," Poe contends that the best expression of Beauty will always have a sad tone. And since "the supreme development" of every kind of beauty "invariably excites the sensitive soul to tears[,] melancholy is . . . the most legitimate of all the poetic tones" (248).

Winters finds Poe's "reversal of motivation" here "singularly shocking," for it seems to say clearly that "since Beauty excites to tears (let us assume with Poe, for the moment, that it does), if we begin with tears, we may believe ourselves moved for a moment by Beauty" (248). Poe's "willful dislocation of feeling from understanding" (246) is thus connected, however playfully in his account of composing *The Raven,* with a method that both calculates an effect on the reader and deliberately substitutes that effect for the genuine experience.

For the reversal in James, Winters relies on the master himself. In James and his characters, Winters says, the traditional moral sense that had developed in the best of New England culture "was a fine but very delicate perception, unsupported by any clear set of ideas, and functioning, not only in minds of very subtle construction, but at the very crisis in history at which it was doomed . . . to be almost infinitely rarefied [and] finally to be dissolved in air" (306). Winters finds in James's preface to the New York edition of *The American* a clear recognition of moral obscurity. Disclaiming knowledge of how to draw the precise line between "the real and the romantic," James suggests that a sure sign of the romantic is "this rank vegetation of the 'power' of bad people that good get into, or vice-versa. It is so rarely, alas, into our *power* that anyone gets!"[6] Winters perceives that rank vegetation as the specific form of James's moral obscurity in several of the novels, including *The Portrait of a Lady,* and he cites James's own recognition of obscurity or evasion in the characterization of Claire de Cintré: in that heroine, James confesses, "a light plank, too light a plank, is laid for the reader over a dark 'psychological' abyss. The delicate clue to her conduct is never definitely placed in his hand: I must have liked to think verily it *was* delicate and to flatter myself that it was to be felt with the finger-tips rather than heavily tugged at."[7] Sometimes, Winters concedes, the obscurity of a plot may be partly justified by the subject of the novel, but in *The American* and several other works James and his characters "alike . . . read into situations more than can be justified by the facts as given"; and they "build up intense states of feeling on the basis of such reading, and . . . judge or act as a result of that feeling" (331). James's effort to portray characters in a setting that allows them and himself "to understand ethical problems in a pure state" (338) alienates them from the particular social world in which moral choices are actually made, so that even in some of the great novels a "supersubtle" moral consciousness struggles toward a choice that Winters considers "strained and unjustifiable" (338). Sometimes, if pushed far enough, the supersubtlety produces an "obscurantism" that amounts to "hallucination" (338). To show that James at least occasionally recognized the difficulty, Winters cites James's description of a wife and husband in *The Bostonians.* The wife insistently tries "to express the inexpressible, which turned out, after all, to be nothing"; the husband is "a moralist without a moral sense." Winters concludes that James "had too much moral sense, but was insufficiently a moralist" (336).

Here again preoccupation with Maule's curse should not lead us to neglect Winters's great admiration for James or for James's subject. Anticipating one argument in Wayne Booth's *The Rhetoric of Fiction,* Winters rejects Joseph Warren Beach's claim that the form of the novel required a progressive narrowing of James's technical point of view, the elimination of the omniscient author, or what Winters calls "the vitiation of prose as prose." Yet although he deplores James's role in the stylistic development "from *The Golden Bowl* to Dorothy Richardson and Proust," and from them eventually to "the latest Joyce," Winters insists that James's great virtues are indeed separable from the defects of the later style. The virtues are "strongly marked in the early works." He attributes their later growth to an increased "maturity and richness of observation, . . . a result of age and experience," even as James followed "a defective procedure, the result of an error in theory" (339–40). He praises James not merely as the author of many "perfect" minor works but also as the creator of a larger number of vivid characters than Winters can remember in "all the rest of English fiction" (337). These characters, he says, are created with "no exaggeration, yet with an awareness so rich that every essential detail is realized; after the lapse of years they are remembered not like portraits from a book but like persons one has known, yet they are remembered more clearly, for the observation of James is finer than our own would have been" (338).

One historical oversight in *Maule's Curse* resembles the oversimplification of Puritan ethics. Winters persistently writes about Emerson as a pantheist and a relativist who trusted "implicitly to the whimsical turns of his thought" (271) and who "believed that all impulses were of divine origin" (267). Nowhere in *Maule's Curse* does Winters acknowledge Emerson's conception of Reason, the distinction between the faculties of Reason and Understanding, or the discipline Emerson considered necessary to apprehend the spiritual laws accessible to the Reason. The key to Winters's evaluation of Emerson is implicit in an epigrammatic line about Jones Very: we can afford the luxury of such a mind, Winters says, "so long as he refrains from making converts" (278). Emerson's notoriously heady invitations to plant ourselves on our instincts and to do our own thing, even speak as the devil's child, may well be judged "fraudulent" by readers who, like Winters, see that Emerson's personal behavior is "qualified by tradition," by both the line of clergymen from whom he was descended and the very "society which they and their kind had formed" (267). Surely, too, one can see why Winters sees appalling irresponsibility, as Melville did, in Emerson's teaching about both literature and life. If neither the horrified observer nor the self-destructive disciple of Emerson believes Emerson's Reason to be authoritative or even real, then the observer's judgment must at least recognize that Emerson was a very dangerous man. "Submission to emotion" may well seem to be Emerson's central doctrine if one denies the existence of Reason. But *Maule's Curse* would surely have given a more persuasive account of New England's intellectual history if Winters had acknowledged the importance of Reason, the intuitive faculty enthroned above the empirical Understanding, in Emerson's thought.

Here too, however, as in the misapprehension of Puritan ethics, to correct Winters on the particular historical idea is not to invalidate the theme of *Maule's Curse*. He finds in several literary generations— even as the impulse toward moral judgment is intensified and refined—a strong tendency to reduce or deny the importance of reasoning intelligence in moral judgment: in the seventeenth century because of man's absolute dependence on an allegorical drama of salvation; in the nineteenth, because a variety of perspectives (most of them no longer religious) tends to deny the possibility of intelligent moral choice. In sketching a line from Puritanism through James to some "obscurantist" practices in modern letters, Winters repeatedly ventures to connect a writer's philosophical predicament to particular aesthetic or technical defects. And in every essay his celebration of the author's achievement focuses on specific technical qualities in the language. Not even the most vehement dissenter from his general argument should miss his splendid analysis of Emily Dickinson's metrical art or his analysis of the passage in which Cooper's Deerslayer becomes Hawkeye. These observations and a dozen others explicating Melville, Very, Hawthorne, and James remind us that in the very book to whose title this supposed Jeremiah of American criticism affixed a curse, a major source of his enduring strength is his capacity to celebrate our literary blessings.

Notes

1. John Updike, "On Hawthorne's Mind," *New York Review of Books* 28 (1981): 41–42.

2. The three books collected as *In Defense of Reason* are *Primitivism and Decadence* (1937), *Maule's Curse* (1938), and *The Anatomy of Nonsense* (1943). Page numbers refer to the third edition (Denver: Alan Swallow, 1959).

3. Nathaniel Hawthorne, *The House of the Seven Gables,* ed. William A. Charvat et al. (Columbus: Ohio State Univ. Press, 1965), p. 231.

4. H. B. Parkes, *The Pragmatic Temper: Essays on the History of Ideas* (San Francisco: Colt Press, 1941); Charles M. Andrews, *The Colonial Period of American History,* 4 vols. (New Haven: Yale Univ. Press, 1934), vol. 1.

5. Stephen Foster, *Their Solitary Way: The Puritan Social Ethic in the First Century of Settlement in New England* (New Haven: Yale University Press, 1971); Norman Fiering, *Moral Philosophy at Seventeenth-Century Harvard: A Discipline in Transition* (Chapel Hill: Univ. of North Carolina Press, 1981).

6. Henry James, *The Art of the Novel* (New York and London: Charles Scribner's Sons, 1934), pp. 38–39.

7. Ibid., 39.

7.

In the Court of Historical Criticism

I. Alger Hiss's Narrative

*I had rather judge a Witch to be an honest woman,
than judge an honest woman as a Witch.*
                                        —Increase Mather

i

The fall of Richard Nixon accelerated a process that had begun for me
four years earlier. I had taught an undergraduate seminar on American
autobiographies in 1970, and in order to consider at least one book
that makes a central issue of its own veracity I had assigned Whittaker
Chambers's *Witness*.[1] That assignment had drawn me back into the
world of the Hiss case—the Case, Chambers calls it—an irresistible
accumulation of baffling personalities, mysterious evidence both sworn
and circumstantial, questions of civil liberty, major issues of congressional power and ethics, and (for my generation) major problems of
symbolic allegiance. To teach *Witness,* one could not simply read
Chambers. One had also to read Hiss's *In the Court of Public Opinion,*
Nixon's *Six Crises,* and transcripts from the Case.[2]

I have begun autobiographically because a statement of past prejudices and current preferences will clarify my argument about Hiss's
book. I was a Harvard graduate student, a Democrat, and a civil lib-
ertarian when the accusations against Hiss were made public in 1948,
and I was disgusted by the tactics of the House Committee on Un-
American Activities (hereafter HUAC or the Committee), especially
by its attacks upon private citizens through quasi-judicial proceedings

Section I reprinted by permission from the *Virginia Quarterly Review* 52 (1976):
41–78.

and lurid publicity. Because of those tactics and general sneers against his Harvard background and his liberal sponsors (among them Felix Frankfurter and Oliver Wendell Holmes), Alger Hiss became for me what his most vehement detractors wanted to make of him: a representative of liberal education and liberal politics. His detractors wanted to show that that image masked at first a smug dupe and then a traitor; I wanted him to be a hero of reasonable humanity. I wanted his vindication to be a triumph of decency. Following the Case as well as one can ever follow a trial in the daily press, I felt sure that Hiss's conviction after a second trial (the first jury having failed to agree on a verdict) was unjust.

The jury decided that Hiss had twice perjured himself before a grand jury: when he had denied giving State Department documents to Whittaker Chambers and when he had declared that he had not seen Chambers after January 1, 1937. The indictment on these charges in December 1948 had followed nearly five months of secret and public testimony in which Chambers, under subpoena from HUAC, had first accused Hiss and others of membership in a Communist underground group whose goal was not to spy but to "mess up policy." Hiss had appeared voluntarily under oath to deny the charges, and in the first weeks of sensational publicity during August 1948 one major controversy had turned on whether Hiss had ever known Chambers at all, and whether Chambers had been an intimate friend of the Hisses before he had broken with the Communist party at the end of 1937. Once Chambers was actually presented to Hiss without the aliases that he later said he had used during his years in the underground, Hiss admitted having known him for a time as George Crosley, an impecunious journalist to whom Hiss had lent some money, lent or given an old Ford, and sublet an apartment for two or three months, but whose failure to repay any of the loans had led to a complete break in 1936. Hiss had dared Chambers to repeat his 1948 charges outside Congress so that a libel suit might test their validity, and Chambers had done so at the end of August, whereupon Hiss had sued for libel. In November, with attorneys for both sides requesting evidence, Chambers had suddenly produced typewritten copies of some State Department documents and had accused Hiss of espionage after all. A few weeks later Chambers had revealed the so-called pumpkin papers, microfilm of some other State Department documents. Chambers had then confessed that his earlier testimony had been perjured, and for a time the public debate had focused on the prospective indictment not only of Hiss but also of Chambers. Since the statue of limitations prohibited indictments for espionage, the question was one of perjury. Richard Nixon and HUAC worked openly to persuade the grand jury to indict Hiss but not Chambers, and the grand jury (by a majority of one) did indict Hiss on December 15, 1948. The indictment and eventual conviction of this former State Department official, one of the chief men responsible for American policy in the United Nations, had an immeasurable effect on the movement that came to be known as McCarthyism.

By the time Hiss published *In the Court of Public Opinion* in 1957, I was too busy to read his book. I read the reviews, of course, regretted that they were not more conclusively favorable, and wavered slightly in my confidence that Hiss had been falsely accused. I had seen no new evidence. I had merely grown accustomed (more easily, no doubt, than Hiss) to the jail term that Hiss had served and to the lack of any major national effort to continue insisting on his innocence. Then an essay by Herbert Packer made me suspect that I had ignored genuine evidence against Hiss, and I gradually came to accept a cliché: if Hiss hadn't been guilty of the specific charges, he nonetheless had had a deeper intimacy with Chambers and with Communism than he had acknowledged; and although he may have been protecting someone else throughout his ordeal, there had been just too much circumstantial evidence that he had never succeeded in explaining away. Until 1970, then, the Case was filed uncomfortably in my memory as closed.

Reading *Witness* and *In the Court of Public Opinion* shocked me. When I read for the first time what the two antagonists themselves had to say about the evidence, I saw that I had been credulous and inaccurate in my recollection of the trial even while advocating Hiss's exoneration. Although a partisan defender, I had come to believe, for example, that Hiss had begun by denying he had ever known Chambers, and I had even failed to see how completely and how early the burden of proof had been shifted from prosecution to defense.

Six Crises deepened my perplexity and introduced new questions of veracity, which provoke new interest in 1976. A familiar kind of evasion or prevarication occurs, for example, in the first chapter. To explain why he suddenly called an extraordinary executive session of the HUAC subcommittee to meet in a New York hotel on August 17, 1948, so that Hiss might be confronted by Chambers for the first time, Nixon declares that he decided late on the night of the sixteenth to avoid giving Hiss time to "make his story fit the facts" in the eight days before the next scheduled hearing; Hiss and Chambers must be brought together on the seventeenth, because "only the man who was not telling the truth would gain by having additional time to build up his case" (30). Before Nixon wrote his narrative, however, both Chambers (1952) and Hiss (1957) had suggested in their respective books a relationship between the sudden decision to hold this surprise hearing and the death of Harry Dexter White, a former Treasury Department official, on August 16. Nixon says that the subcommittee read the news of White's death during their train ride from Washington to New York on the afternoon of the seventeenth. Then he denies the "plausible" but "completely untrue" allegation that the subcommittee had arranged the Hiss-Chambers meeting for that afternoon "in order to divert attention from White's death" (31).

Chambers's own strange account of that day must arouse the suspicion of any reader who sets it beside Nixon's, because the two reports differ on the telling detail of the newspaper story. En route from his Maryland farm to his office in New York, Chambers has suddenly felt "a curious need to go [to Washington] to see the Committee, as if its members were the only people left in the world with whom I could communicate." He buys a ticket to New York but goes to Washington instead, only to learn that the subcommittee has been "frantically trying to reach me." They will not tell him why they want him, but instead, "as we rolled to Union Station, Appell [an investigator on the staff] wrestled a newspaper out of his pocket and pointed to a headline: Harry Dexter White had died of a heart attack" (600).

Nixon claims that the subcommittee learned of White's death during the train ride to New York, but Chambers, with the same rhetorical skill that was so deadly to Hiss, gives us the memorable picture of Appell graphically answering Chambers's question on the way to Union Station, before Chambers even learns that their destination is New York. In the rest of the paragraph Chambers supplies adequate reason for the subcommittee's dramatic response to White's death: White had made a "gallant" and celebrated defense in his public hearing before the Committee (600). But neither Chambers nor Nixon lists a third relevant fact about the relationship between White's fate and the sudden confrontation of Hiss and Chambers. Of our three autobiographical narrators, only Hiss points out that White's heart condition had become an issue during the hearing itself, and that Congressman Thomas had jeered at White's request (as a medical precaution) for a brief recess every hour. White had testified on Friday the 13th, had been stricken almost immediately after his return to New Hampshire that night, and had died at 5:45 P.M. on the sixteenth. I suspect (as Chambers implies) that before Richard Nixon ordered the surprise hearing he had learned of White's death.

Neither Nixon nor Chambers mentions here the way that Hiss was actually called to that hearing. Hiss was not "summoned," as Nixon's narrative suggests (31). Instead he was told that Congressman McDowell was coming to New York that afternoon and would like to speak to him for a few minutes. Then, just before the appointed time, Hiss was telephoned again and invited to stroll over to the Commodore Hotel for his brief chat with McDowell and—it was now revealed—two or three others. When he arrived, the subcommittee was declared to be in session and he was questioned under oath. Both Nixon and Chambers, moreover, neglect to mention Hiss's request at the very first hearing on August 5 to be allowed to confront Chambers as soon as possible, and both ignore the Committee's concurrence in Hiss's persistent request on the sixteenth that the confrontation scheduled for the twenty-fifth be held in public session. Both therefore leave the reader without any preparation (besides a consciousness of guilt and danger) for the anger and wariness that all three narratives agree Hiss displayed through most of this climactic hearing. Commentators as disparate as Nixon, Hiss, and Leslie Fiedler agree that (in the public mind, at least) this hearing broke the Case—remember Hiss's demand to examine Chambers's teeth—and a recent article by a Cornell University law professor who believes Hiss was guilty quotes more extensively from this transcript than from any other evidence before the testimony at the actual trials.[3]

What I hope to demonstrate here and throughout the essay is the value of historical criticism in both the understanding of factual books and the evaluation of a baffling case. Close comparative reading of the texts and some of the transcripts should help us to understand the books—among which Hiss's has been the most widely misunderstood—and perhaps the issue that unites them. The evidence that we have already considered requires us to remember that all three books are to some extent self-serving, apologetic. Before we agree with Nixon that only the false witness would have been aided by having a week to "make his story fit the facts," we ought to reflect that, as Hiss's narrative plainly demonstrates, a truthful witness might have benefited from having the time to look up the records concerning the sale of his 1929 Ford twelve years earlier—if the Committee (or someone else) had not removed those documents from the Department of Motor Vehicles.

Nor is Hiss the only person with whom Chambers disagrees about the facts. Chambers sometimes remembers quite differently from Nixon, even when Nixon's prudently selective memory has the opportunity to check *Witness* before committing itself to print. Both Chambers and Nixon, moreover, set up the meeting of August 17 in their narratives as a way of forestalling the charge of collusion between them. Both seem to agree with Hiss that Chambers and the Committee needed one another. Chambers's "curious need" to visit the Committee seems as strange to the reader as it does to Chambers. Why would Chambers feel, so early in the Case, before the Committee had accepted his story, "as if its members were the only people left in the world with whom I could communicate"? Remember that Chambers has set out for New York from his Maryland farm but has suddenly decided to go to Washington instead. So remarkable is his encounter with the subcommittee members as they leave the House Office Building by "an entrance that I had never used before" that he himself highlights the coincidence. Robert Stripling, he says, "fixed me with a somewhat birdlike stare and said darkly, 'I believe he must be psychic.' I sensed that he felt that among so many complicating factors that was one too many" (600).

The world of this case abounds in complicating factors, selective remembering, and special pleading, even in books written long after the trials. The issue is not between a truth teller and a liar, but between two sides trying equally hard to persuade us. Nixon's repeated and flagrant lies during the Watergate investigation, Chambers's admitted espionage and his admitted perjury during the early part of the Hiss investigation, and Hiss's conviction on two counts of perjury mean that any reviewer of the Case in 1976 must find his way among the testimony of three writers all of whom now stand impeached of falsehoods. The behavior on both sides includes some actions or circumstances so strange that the advantage in any argument will often lie with the adversary who can ask his antagonist to answer the rhetorical question: Why would anybody have done that? Chambers, Nixon, and the Committee can ask tellingly, Why would Chambers want to risk his own career for petty revenge, and why would he want to ruin Hiss? The burden of answering such questions was put on Hiss throughout the ordeal, and even after he had served his term in prison. It is that burden that I mean to question in my discussion of *In the Court of Public Opinion,* but here we must notice that Hiss and the defense had a number of telling questions which they could ask: Why would a guilty man seek out and turn over to the court an incriminating typewriter? Why would a traitor in the State Department, working with a Communist party member whose last name he didn't even know (Chambers said he was known only as Carl), meet that agent regularly in his own home, give him official notes in his own handwriting, photograph confidential documents bearing his own initials, and have his wife transcribe others on her own typewriter? Since the transfer of documents from Julian Wadleigh, the one government employee who actually admitted giving documents to Chambers, had been accomplished with all the precautions of the most secretive espionage—seemingly casual exchanges on street corners, etc.—Hiss and his attorneys argued in their appeal that Chambers's story of weekly deliveries and typing sessions in Hiss's own home was preposterous. To believe Chambers, one must believe that these spies took better precautions to disguise their transfer of a rug and a Model A Ford than to disguise the espionage itself.

Another of Hiss's unanswered rhetorical questions leads us to consider recent revelations about the FBI. Why, when Hiss was already in prison, did FBI agents follow his attorney and other investigators who sought factual evidence about the incriminating typewriter, and why did FBI agents forewarn prospective witnesses concerning affidavits about the manufacture and sale of that typewriter, forewarn them against cooperating with the Hiss attorneys' inquiries? Imputations of FBI skulduggery have followed the Case ever since Chambers met regularly with FBI agents and interrogated prospective defense witnesses during the weeks before the trial. The defense claimed that the FBI was coaching Chambers about Hiss's earlier life, and Hiss recounts in his book some dubious conduct by FBI agents who interviewed one of his former servants and another witness. Richard Nixon, while of course praising the FBI, gives especial credit to Justice Department "employees in lower echelons" for keeping the Committee informed of confidential Justice Department plans concerning the Case (58). He even declares—along with a surprisingly large number of other writers on the Case—that it was FBI agents, rather than Hiss's investigators, who found the missing typewriter in 1948 (60). Today, however, we don't need the accusations of antagonists or the praise of former allies on the Committee. The FBI itself has now admitted not only entrapment but forgery—most notoriously in its harassment of Martin Luther King, Jr., and in an effort to set the Mafia and the Communist party against one another—in its aggressive program to confound the Left.

ii

My interpretation of Hiss's book asks the reader to assume for the sake of argument that Hiss was not guilty. We must seem to beg the question in order to be prepared to consider the narrator's experience. Many reviewers, some of them sympathetic to Hiss, criticized his restrained tone, and some even used that dispassionate quality as evidence of his guilt: surely a man who had been so unjustly treated would have written a more volatile prose. Surely, moreover, he had erred in writing his book as if it were a lawyer's brief, for now that he was appealing to the court of public opinion it wasn't enough to show that he had not been proved guilty. To convince the public (and the reviewers in question), he was obliged to prove his innocence. If I am correct, the mistake of those readers was to beg the question in the opposite way from the one that I temporarily propose. Knowing of his conviction and his prison term, and knowing much of the evidence, they seem to be looking for revelations that will positively exonerate Hiss. Wherever the burden of proof ought to have rested during the trial, they understandably believe that it now belongs to Hiss. And so, I believe, they misread his book.

In the Court of Public Opinion is both the record of an experience and a demonstration of principle. It teaches in a way that neither *Witness* nor *Six Crises,* both heavily and explicitly didactic, can approach. Chambers begins *Witness* with an impassioned letter to his children about the importance of the Case to their generation and to history, and he draws attention throughout the book to his feelings of anger, misery, loneliness, fright, remorse, compassion as he played his part in a "tragedy of history" (3). Nixon later borrows in his first chapter a version of Chambers's device, narrating the Hiss case in response to a question about it from his daughter and then considering the historical significance of the Case and its political and personal meaning to himself. His introduction announces several hypotheses about successful behavior in crises, and his account of the Case emphasizes the narrator's responses and resources during critical moments of stress and triumph.

In the Court of Public Opinion, however, begins flatly with no preface at all:

> In August 1948 I was living in New York City. For the preceding year and a half I had been president of the Carnegie Endowment for International Peace. To accept that position I had resigned from the State Department, where I was director of the office responsible for proposing and carrying out our policies in the United Nations. [3]

This is a reserved book. Here we find no autobiographical emphasis beyond the Case, none on the narrator's family, none on the lessons of the Case for American democracy, none on how to endure disgrace and misery. The narrator takes us methodically through his intellectual experience of the Case. He does, of course, arrange the record to support his case, but he concentrates for his effect upon the record, including *Witness,* counting on the contrast between Chambers's past and his own public service to return the burden of proof to the accusers. This narrator has served nearly four years in prison. He has seen his respected name become a byword. He will show us how he fell from the position described in his first paragraph, and how he fought to defend himself.

Only at the very end of his book will he write three brief, restrained paragraphs of what he calls "personal comment" (419).

Whatever its deeper psychological significance, I call this quality a demonstration of principle because the style, the form, the tone of the book reinforce the central declaration of a defendant's rights in criminal cases, that he must be presumed innocent until he has been proven guilty. If I am correct, the very form of this book rebukes the reviewers who have declared that Hiss must now "prove his innocence." Even some of the most sympathetic commentators on Hiss's book warn the reader to distinguish between concluding that Hiss had not been proven guilty and concluding that he has been vindicated. Hiss, I believe, was perfectly aware of that distinction when he wrote his book, and we must explicitly recognize it here. But I believe the form and the extent of his argument are limited by more than the difficulty of proving a negative, more than the reserved habits of a legal and diplomatic career.

Our legal principle has an ethical basis which demands more than the negative act of refusing to jail those who have not been proven guilty. Hiss, I believe, calls us by his very restraint to honor principles of charity and trust, to see that in the republic an official ought to be judged according to his public record. Hiss challenges our magnanimity by assuming that if we see how his ruin came about we will understand his premise. If he was not guilty, then he chose the most appropriate form and tone for his book. Discrediting the case against him would mean restoring to him the assumption to which not only our legal traditions but his known public and private life had entitled him before the nightmare began. Cruelly presumptuous are the well-meaning and the skeptical observers who would tell the innocent victim of such horrors not only that he must disclose more of his personal feelings—portray himself as more "human"—but also that he must explain both the motives of his accusers and their partially discredited evidence. If he was innocent, he owes us nothing. If he was innocent, we owe him an unlimited debt.

Elderly readers, of course, cannot erase their memory of the incriminating evidence or their human interest in the general mystery rather than the narrower question of whether Hiss ought to have been convicted or later granted a new trial. Yet before judging his book we ought to respect the premises, the order, and the shape of his narrative and argument as he develops them. Although aware that the narrator may be a guilty man trying to hoodwink me, I shall proceed on the assumption implicit in his opening paragraph: the president of the Carnegie Endowment, who has distinguished himself in public service, returns to New York from his summer vacation and learns that he has been named as a Communist party member who worked in an underground cell while serving in the federal government eleven to fourteen years earlier. How did he reply to the charges? What happened to him?

Hiss's title, as Mark Howe perceived, does more than appeal to the court of public opinion.[4] It suggests that he was tried there. Procedural and chronological questions have great significance throughout his account and especially in the beginning. He first learns of the 1948 charges not from the Committee but from a newspaperman, who telephones him at home the night before Chambers's testimony. Hiss immediately volunteers to appear before the Committee so that he may deny the allegations. The name of Whittaker Chambers, he explains to us, was unknown to him except as that of a person about whom two FBI agents had asked him in 1947. J. Parnell Thomas, the Committee's chairman, later said that the Republican presidential campaign leaders had asked him to "set up the spy hearings, . . . to stay in Washington in August in order to put the heat on Harry Truman" (6). Yet Hiss represents himself as having felt "convinced," despite his mistrust of the Committee, that he could exonerate himself. "I had nothing to hide and, I thought, nothing to fear. A simple statement of facts would surely clear up the whole business" (8).

Vestiges of that faith reappear throughout the book. At the end of the first trial Hiss is astonished to learn that eight of the twelve jurors voted for conviction. Even after his conviction in 1950, he is "confident of obtaining a new trial" (324). When the judge invites him to make a statement before being sentenced, Hiss remains "confident that in the future the full facts of how Whittaker Chambers was able to carry out forgery by typewriter will be disclosed" (323). And in his personal statement at the end of the book, Hiss reaffirms "the democratic ideals which motivated me in government service" (419).

But in the narrative of *In The Court of Public Opinion* the protagonist never has a chance to make "a simple statement of facts." Hiss becomes involved at once in an adversary proceeding which screens his adversary from him. The main conflict sets a believer in traditional procedures against a congressional committee and a mysterious accuser who seem determined to ruin him. Hiss expects to be confronted with Chambers at his first, voluntary appearance before the Committee, but instead he is shown a picture taken—from an odd angle, he says—twelve years after his last admitted meeting with the man he later comes to identify as Chambers. A subcommittee interviews Chambers secretly two days after Hiss's first testimony, and the congressmen, who confide some of Chambers's accusations to the press, do not tell Hiss or the reporters that Chambers himself has positively denied Hiss ever knew him by his real name. Nor do they seem to notice that Hiss has immediately asked to see Chambers in order to determine whether he once knew him. They question Hiss about details of Chambers's secret testimony, but without letting him see the transcripts before replying under oath. Thus Hiss not only risks damaging errors in testifying about events more than a decade in the past, but he is also denied access to the demonstrably false portions of Chambers's testimony. Committee members tell Hiss in his second hearing (August 16) that Chambers has testified in "dazzling" detail about Hiss's personal life in the 1930s (39), but Hiss has access to those details only through their questions. When they ask him about bird-watching, therefore, and he replies in response to a further question that he once saw a prothonotary warbler, the seeming corroboration of Chambers's testimony has much more impact, both on the congressmen and on newspaper readers, than if Hiss were able to corroborate that accurate detail in the context of all the misinformation that Chambers also supplied. Hiss uses the early part of his book to establish that context.

The most damaging evidence against Chambers in this part of Hiss's book is Hiss's refutation of gratuitous details which Chambers must have volunteered either maliciously or self-deceptively. We see Chambers, for example, swear that Hiss regularly paid him dues for the Communist party, and that Hiss transferred his stepson to a less expensive private school so that the tuition money sent by the boy's father could be used for both the new school and the Party dues. Hiss is able, belatedly, to show that the father himself had paid the tuition directly to the schools, and that the new school was not less but more expensive than the preceding one (so that Hiss himself had to add to the father's payments). Chambers says that Hiss walks with a slight mince "if you watch him from behind" (48); Hiss not only denies that quirk but shows that Chambers used a virtually identical description in a novel he translated before he had met Hiss—a novel about forgery and perjury used by one man to convict his innocent friend of a crime. Chambers testifies that Hiss "is deaf in one ear"—probably, Hiss suggests, because a newspaper photograph depicted Hiss cupping one ear during interrogation (48). Hiss later has his hearing checked at Columbia Medical Center, where it is certified as normal.

Almost equally telling at this point is Hiss's list of facts that Chambers did not know, facts that Hiss says any intimate friend in 1937 must have known. In a decade a casual acquaintance might forget—but would an intimate friend forget?—a tall man's stature. Chambers testified that Hiss was five feet, eight or nine inches tall, whereas Hiss, in 1937 and 1948, was six feet tall. Timothy, Hiss's stepson, was nearly killed by an automobile in 1937 and then "was bed-ridden and cast-bound for months in the small house to which we had moved in July 1936" (44), but Chambers does not remember that dominant fact of the household during his own professed intimacy there. Chambers says that Hiss's sister and mother lived at their home in Baltimore during the alleged friendship. Although listed in the telephone directory, which Chambers might easily have consulted twelve years later, Hiss's mother did not live at her Baltimore home during the alleged friendship, and the sister, a professor of physical education, had already been living in Austin, Texas, for some years. (When the Committee asked Chambers if he knew the occupation of Hiss's sister, he twice replied, "I don't think she did anything." Even after a congressman asked whether Hiss had ever mentioned that the sister "was interested in athletics" [50–51], Chambers could not come up with the right answer). Chambers can remember nothing about Hiss's library except that it was "very nondescript," but he claims to have spent as much as a week at a time in the household and to have done much reading there (53). He does not know that the reason the Hisses suddenly moved in the spring of 1936 was that the heating system in their house had collapsed while Hiss was recovering from pneumonia. Intimate friends, Hiss insists, would have remembered that because of the illness the Hisses had moved to a hotel for two weeks while the new house was being renovated.

From Chambers's errors and ignorance Hiss moves to the Committee's decided lack of interest in investigating them. Committee investigators never asked the landlady of the apartment that Chambers had sublet from Hiss whether she remembered any tenant whose name had been unknown to her and to her other tenants. (Chambers, we remember, contended that Hiss had known him only as "Carl," with no last name.) Nor, in considering whether Hiss had paid one-tenth of his salary as Communist dues, did the Committee look into Hiss's withdrawals from his bank account (into which his salary was deposited by the State Department) or the tuition fees of the two schools about which Chambers was so insistent. The Committee did not even challenge Chambers's self-contradictory testimony about the Party dues; he had denied on August 3 that he had collected individual dues from Party members, but on August 7 he swore that Hiss had "devoutly" given the monthly tithe to Chambers himself and that Chambers himself had collected all the individual members' dues (70–72).

By far the strongest example of the Committee's attitude toward Chambers's errors is the Ford roadster that came to dominate the public hearing of August 25, and Hiss saves that troubling subject for his final illustration. In the first months of the Case the car was probably the most damaging evidence against Hiss. Even now it remains the most mysterious of the early obstacles to Hiss's vindication. At the hearing of August 16, Hiss volunteered the surprising information that in 1935 he had given or sold George Crosley a 1929 Ford roadster, then worth about $25, as part of a sublet transaction. Chambers denied that Hiss had given or lent him the Ford. He testified that in 1936 Hiss had insisted on giving the car to "some poor [Communist] organizer in the West or somewhere," and that a small service station or used car lot owned by a Communist had served as intermediary. When the official records revealed that Hiss's apparent signature on the certificate of transfer had been notarized by a Justice Department attorney in 1936 and had transferred title to the largest Ford agency in Washington, the Committee ignored the large inaccuracies in Chambers's account and concentrated instead on Hiss's errors.

The records indicated that Hiss's purchase of a new Plymouth (which would have made the Ford expendable) did not coincide with the sublease of the apartment, and the transfer of title, dated a year later than Hiss's unaided memory had acknowledged, included a resale of the Ford on the same day to a former Communist named William Rosen. The mystery of that transaction remains so inconclusive that the Committee eventually abandoned the issue, but only after great damage had been done to Hiss. A separate article would be necessary to describe the unresolved mystery. Rosen, for example, insisted on invoking the Fifth Amendment when asked about the Ford, even though he was later able to prove that the signature on the document was not his and although there was no other evidence that he had ever owned a Ford. Neither of the notaries involved in the two sales, moreover, had any recollection or record of the transaction; and the Justice Department attorney, who never did get to see the original document but saw only the photocopy that the Committee showed him, would not positively swear that he had notarized Hiss's signature or that he would have refused to notarize it in Hiss's absence. What matters here, however, for both Hiss's narrative and our analysis, is the Committee's failure to investigate Chambers's story with the rigor that it applied to Hiss.

The Committee never asked why, if Hiss had not given or sold the car to Chambers, he would have volunteered the false story on August 16, as soon as he was asked whether George Crosley had owned a car and before he had any indication that Chambers had mentioned the Ford. (A guilty, canny man who had conspired to use a large agency as a cover would presumably have waited to be asked about his own car, and would then have testified that he had sold it to that agency, not that he had given or sold it directly to a member of the Communist underground.) Nor did the Committee cross-examine Chambers on his false testimony about the car. Chambers, after all, had sworn that Hiss had delivered the car to a small service station or used car lot owned by a Communist. Neither the Ford agency nor Rosen could be used to corroborate that story, nor did the Committee find any evidence that Hiss himself had delivered the car. The interrogation of Chambers is consistently gentle, even when he hedges. Sometimes the Committee allows him to go "off the record," even when testifying secretly under oath (*Witness* 570).

Hiss succeeds in demonstrating, then, that in both the congressional investigation and the trials "Chambers was not requested to prove his assertions. I was expected to disprove them" (76). At the second trial, long after the Committee had ceased trying to show a connection between Hiss and Rosen or to corroborate Chambers's version, the prosecutor called Rosen to the stand. When Rosen predictably invoked the Fifth Amendment again, the prosecutor treated his silence as the Committee had treated the absence of other evidence in the matter, as if it were evidence against Hiss. Having made this point in his book, Hiss has the satisfaction of reporting that Robert Stripling, in his own narrative of the Case, abandoned the claim that Chambers's story about the Ford had been corroborated by the evidence.

The lesson for us readers, if we have maintained our hypothetical conjecture that Hiss was not guilty, must be to distinguish between mysteries and positively incriminating evidence. Congressmen reminded Hiss of the rule that courts ought to be skeptical of further testimony by a witness who has testified inaccurately about a material matter. Both *Witness* and *In the Court of Public Opinion* quote Congressman Mundt's declaration about evaluating the testimony of Chambers and Hiss:

> We proceed on the conclusion that if either one of you is telling the truth on the verifiable data, that you are telling the truth on all of it. And if either one of you is concealing the truth from the committee on verifiable data, it points out that you are concealing from us the truth on obviously the points that we cannot prove. [141]

The Committee did persistently act on a modified version of Mundt's simple axiom. It applied his first sentence to Chambers and his second to Hiss.

iii

With the evidence about the car we arrive at the chief horror in Hiss's nightmare. Just as the absence of evidence concerning the Ford was treated as incriminating evidence, so the logic of conspiracy led Hiss's accuser and the Committee to treat positively favorable evidence about Hiss as if that, too, were irrelevant or incriminating. The Committee, Chambers, and the prosecutor applied conspiratorial logic to the entire record of Hiss's fifteen years in government service. At his first inter-rogation, one or two Committee members did ask what position Hiss had taken on issues affecting the USSR—offering the USSR virtually three votes in the United Nations, for example—and Hiss's answers had led Congressman Mundt (no friend to Hiss even in the first hear-ing) to congratulate him for his opposition to Soviet interests. But as the logic of conspiracy takes over, Hiss loses the support that his record ought to give him. At the televised hearing on August 25, he is for-bidden to read a statement concerning his record until after a damag-ing and protracted interrogation (chiefly about the Ford), and when he does ask that his conduct under the supervision of many statesmen and jurists be studied for evidence of disloyalty and that those associates be asked about his conduct, he is rebuked in two ways. Committee mem-bers accuse him of trying to shield himself with eminent names and reputations. (In *Witness* Chambers calls this tactic "drawing the toga of his official career about him" [556]). And when Hiss insists that he means to appeal to his actual conduct, the basis for the confidence those men have had in him, he is rebuffed with pronouncements which close the logical circle. Congressman Mundt concedes that the Committee never believed it could "prove definitely that you were a Communist because . . . we have found that those who are guilty, refused to admit it" (139–40). Congressman Hébert's argument a little later was so ef-fective at the time that Richard Nixon gives it a prominent place in the first chapter of *Six Crises* (43): If you, Mr. Hiss, cannot tell whether the people about whom we have asked you are Communists, how can all these eminent men who trusted you know whether you were a Com-munist?

Hiss does not fail to point out, when his narrative reaches these exchanges, the close resemblance between the congressmen's logic and that of the prosecutors in seventeenth-century witchcraft trials. Irving Younger's article on the Case praises the prosecutor for urging the jury at the second trial to ignore all character witnesses because Benedict Arnold and Satan, respectively, could have received excellent references from George Washington and God. "There is no answer to this [argument]," Younger declares (33). But there is an answer, and Hiss might have found it, had he known the literature of the witchcraft trials, in a statement published belatedly by the ministers of Boston after twenty men and women had been executed in Salem in 1692. The ministers condemned as "very dangerous and unjustifiable" the argument that "a less clear evidence ought to pass in" the obscure crime of witchcraft than in other cases. God, they declared,

> never intended that all persons guilty of Capital Crimes should be discovered and punished by men in this Life, though they be never so curious in searching after Iniquity. It is therefore exceeding necessary that in such a day as this, men may be informed what is Evidence and what is not. It concerns men in point of Charity; for though the most shining Professor [i.e., apparent believer] may be secretly a most abominable Sinner, yet till he be detected, our Charity is bound to judge according to what appears: and notwithstanding that a clear evidence must determine a case, yet presumptions must be weighed against presumptions, and Charity is not to be foregone as long as it has the most preponderating on its side.[5]

The irony of Hiss's futile appeal to his record reaches its sad conclusion in his surprisingly gentle treatment of John Foster Dulles's testimony for the prosecution during the second trial. Dulles was presumably summoned to counteract the effect of Supreme Court justices and other character witnesses. Richard Challener has recently shown that, during the presidential campaign of 1948 and consistently thereafter, Dulles understated both his former commitment to Hiss and his own part in recruiting Hiss as a person "ideally" qualified for the presidency of the Carnegie Endowment. At the second trial, then, while some men who had testified truthfully in the first trial about Hiss's fine record were dissuaded from testifying again, Dulles now testified falsely as a prosecution witness whose chief function was to impeach Hiss's credibility! Using Dulles's recently discovered correspondence in the Princeton University library, Challener proves that Hiss testified truthfully about his recruitment by Dulles.[6] If Hiss had had the Dulles letters as well as one of his own to corroborate his testimony when he wrote his book, he might have expressed more indignation toward Dulles.

Like Hiss's narrative, my discussion has necessarily gone ahead of the chronological account, following into the public hearing of August 25 (and beyond) kinds of argument that had been used by August 16. The extraordinary confrontation of Chambers in the Commodore Hotel on August 17 can be considered more briefly here, now that we have examined the character of Hiss's narrative and the key issues in the first month of the Case. Having volunteered to answer the Committee's questions and to confront Chambers publicly, and having been told that the public confrontation would occur on August 25, Hiss is angry to discover on the seventeenth that the meeting has been arranged deceptively and that it will be held in secret at the Commodore Hotel. Not until his arrival does he learn that the meeting he has been requested to attend is a hearing. He is angered, too, by newspaper accounts not only of Harry Dexter White's death but also about Priscilla Hiss, for Congressman Nixon has promised that she will be interviewed without any publicity. Now, with Chambers at last present, and with Committee members insisting that Hiss has positively denied knowing him, the confrontation is even more rancorous than one might expect it to be. Nixon's account stresses Hiss's evasive and angry testimony: "From the beginning, Hiss dropped all previous pretensions of injured innocence. He was on the defensive—edgy, delaying, belligerent, fighting every inch of the way" (31).

The reader of Hiss's book can see why Hiss had become more indignant and more wary, and that his indignation and defensiveness need not indicate guilt. Hiss's narrative focuses on the Committee's prejudicial behavior before and during the hearing. In both the Hiss and Nixon accounts, as in the commentaries that persuaded me for a time of Hiss's evasiveness, Hiss insists on examining Chambers's teeth—a detail that prompts Congressman Nixon to ask whether Hiss never saw Crosley with his mouth shut. As Hiss insists, however, both in his testimony and in his book, he has made Crosley's teeth a major point of identification in his previous testimony, and both friendly and hostile reports concerning Chambers in the 1930s describe his poor teeth, which have since been replaced. (As late as 1975, Lionel Trilling, who still believed Hiss was guilty, remarked on Chambers's extraordinarily bad teeth.)[7] At the end of the August 17 hearing, Hiss cannot find out whether the Committee plans to publicize the transcript or whether he is obliged to maintain silence about the secret hearing. Only at midnight, after Nixon has told a press conference that Hiss has retracted his alleged denial of knowing Chambers, does Hiss learn (from reporters) that he, too, is free to speak to the press. Nixon, moreover, seems no longer interested in interviewing Mrs. Hiss, who at the Committee's request has already come all the way from northern Vermont to New York on a local train. Nixon alone interviews her for ten minutes the next day. (In *Six Crises,* Nixon regrets his cursory interrogation of Mrs. Hiss as a missed opportunity, missed because of the "letdown" that occurs after one has successfully met a crisis [37–38].)

Again at the televised hearing on August 25, Hiss finds himself caught in a wrangle over the Committee's insistence that he has previously denied knowing Chambers and over his testimony about the Ford. Still unable to see all of Chambers's testimony or his own records for the Ford and various leases during the period in question, Hiss finds himself at a great disadvantage, and in the narrative he admits that his testimony was deliberately much more guarded than at his first two hearings. Near the end of this long session, at which Chambers repeats some of his charges without any hostile questioning from the Committee, three congressmen sum up the case against Hiss's veracity and loyalty, with no evidence of any actions directly indicating Communist allegiance. Only then does Hiss have a chance to reply to what he has read in the newspapers of Chambers's secret testimony and at last to read the statement with which he had hoped to open his testimony. Curiously, although Chambers printed virtually the entire statement in *Witness,* Hiss does not print here that eloquent version of the premise for his entire book: the value of his public record in contrast to Chambers's criminal past and Chambers's admitted and newly discovered false statements; the implausibility of supposing that the men with whom Hiss has worked during fifteen years in government service would have failed to notice at least some sign of his alleged disloyalty.

But in that statement Hiss also poses a number of questions that he wants the Committee to ask Chambers, including one about Chambers's mental health and medical history. Congressman Nixon immediately puts Hiss on the defensive once again, demanding that Hiss substantiate his "charge," and Hiss is caught up in an argument over whether he has indeed made such a charge (144).

One of the most extraordinary qualities in all three of the auto-biographical books about the Case is the certainty with which each of the authors considers himself to have been on the defensive. Chambers writes in *Witness* that the hearing of August 25 ruined his life by turn-ing the power of liberals and Communists publicly against him (626–27), and Nixon focuses on the "smears" against both Chambers and himself. Although both Chambers and Nixon provoked much hostile criticism, no reader of the three books will deny that in this final hearing and thereafter Hiss was made the defendant in a special way. The hearing ended, indeed, as Hiss points out, with a declaration by Mundt that Hiss might "just as well" be the 135th Communist in a State Department that (Mundt claims) has already harbored 134 (149). Throughout the rest of the narrative the Committee continues to pur-sue Hiss both by the release of selected testimony and through the grand jury system.

Whatever Chambers's fantasies, he, too, is really on the defensive, both in the actual world of 1948 and in all three of the books. With help from the Committee and the FBI, all three books agree, it is Chambers's self-defense that ruins Hiss. At the August 25 hearing Hiss challenges him to repeat his allegations outside congressional hearing rooms. A few days later Chambers does repeat the central charges on a radio program, and within a month Hiss sues him for libel. Hiss de-scribes his relief at having the issue at last in the courts, where the rules of evidence apply and attorneys respect them. As the attorneys take depositions, both sides quickly begin to press Chambers for more evidence, for even Chambers's own counsel sees that the case against Hiss is extremely weak. President Harry Truman is reelected in No-vember despite his remark that the Committee's "spy hearings" are a red herring, and in the same election two members of the Committee are defeated. The chairman of the Committee is indicted for accepting "kickbacks." Cross-examination persuades Chambers that he, too, may be ruined by the $75,000 libel suit. His knowledge of Hiss looks less impressive under the criticism of Hiss's attorneys than it seemed when the question was whether Chambers had known Hiss at all.

In November, therefore, Chambers brings forth what he later called "a life preserver" (161), a set of documents which he says he had given to a nephew upon breaking with the Communist party ten or eleven years earlier. Hiss's attorneys immediately give these documents to the Justice Department, but Chambers, like the Committee, suspects the Truman Justice Department of partiality to Hiss, and so he retains some additional documents for the revelation of early December: the notorious pumpkin papers, microfilm which Chambers conceals in a hollowed pumpkin on his farm and which Richard Nixon, summoned dramatically from a Caribbean cruise early in December, comes home to receive, sequester, and manage during a campaign to get Hiss—and not Chambers—indicted for perjury.

That campaign is astonishingly brief. Here again Hiss finds himself nearly overwhelmed by unknown and extremely complex evidence before he can plan a defense, and here again the Committee's methods include brilliant publicity, threats against the Justice Department, and an extraordinarily protective attitude toward Chambers. Only twelve days after the revelation of Chambers's pumpkin, the federal grand jury votes to indict Hiss on two counts of perjury. Hiss calls this chapter of his book "Indictment by Committee," citing not only the prejudicial reports of August and press releases thereafter, but also the aggressive attempts of congressmen to intimidate the Justice Department and influence the grand jury. Congressman Nixon goes beyond insisting that the grand jury let him testify about the microfilm that he has pointedly refused to turn over to the Justice Department. He also demands publicly that Chambers not be indicted. He concedes that Chambers may be guilty of "technical violations of law, particularly technical perjury." Then he declares that if the United States attorneys seek Chambers's indictment they will both ruin the case against Hiss and give "the greatest encouragement to the Communist conspiracy in this country" (184–85).

The "technical perjury" that Nixon concedes in the speech reverses Chambers's testimony on a subject so important that even the Committee cannot ignore the contradiction. Chambers has insisted that Hiss and the others committed no espionage. The Committee, nonetheless, has continued to tell witnesses that their testimony is needed for the inquiry into "espionage activities" during 1936 (150). Hiss begins his chapter on "Indictment by Committee" with a reminder of that language and of Nixon's private exhortation of Chambers late in August. Hiss reminds us that *Witness* says Chambers told

Nixon he "could not go through another public hearing," whereupon Nixon insisted:

> "It is for your own sake [Chambers, Hiss says, 'purports to quote' Nixon here] that the Committee is holding a public hearing. The Department of Justice is all set to move in on you in order to save Hiss. They are planning to indict you at once. The only way to head them off is to let the public judge for itself which one of you is telling the truth. . . .
>
> "If there is anything else that you have not told us about Hiss, now is the time to tell us. Think hard about it. If there is anything else, for your own sake, tell us now." [151–52]

Hiss thus establishes what he calls "the classic elements of motivation for false witness," and he builds his narrative in this chapter to the point at which Chambers at last feels sufficiently endangered to "assume this further extension of the role which the Committee so evidently pressed upon him" (152). Even during the radio broadcast on which the libel suit was based, Hiss shows, Chambers denies that the alleged group planned espionage; its purpose was merely to influence "government policy by getting Communists in key places." Under pressure from the reporters Chambers at last concedes that he has no knowledge of any pro-Communist influence attempted or achieved by Hiss in the State Department (155).

Although we need not consider the new evidence in detail, we should remember that the relevant material Chambers produced in November and December consists of three kinds: (1) four small slips of note paper in Hiss's own handwriting; (2) sixty-five typewritten pages which Hiss says he has "consistently denounced as ingenious forgeries" (160); and (3) microfilm copies of eight State Department documents. Hiss reviews here the conflicting stories that Chambers has told about those documents at various times since 1939. Neither the journalist nor the State Department officer to whom Chambers first told his story in 1939 had been shown the documents then. The journalist had not been told at all about the typewritten documents, and the State Department official testified in 1948 that in 1939 Chambers had explicitly denied knowledge of espionage and had pointedly refrained from claiming that any member of the alleged "study group" had belonged

to the Communist party. Hiss is also able to report here the later testimony of Malcolm Cowley, who swore during Hiss's trial that in 1940
Chambers had accused not Hiss but Assistant Secretary of State Francis
B. Sayre of serving as "the head of a Communist apparatus in the State
Department" (167). Cowley testifies, moreover, that Hiss was not
among the others named in Chambers's fantastic accusation, an accusation so extraordinary that Cowley immediately wrote an account of
it in 1940. Perhaps, Hiss suggests, Sayre was originally the victim
against whom Chambers planned to use the materials he had secreted,
for Sayre was Hiss's superior and all the microfilmed State Department
documents "had some actual or apparent connection with Mr. Sayre's
office" (167). It is hard (but necessary) to remember in 1976 that
Chambers did not single out Alger Hiss for unique significance in his
accusations until after Hiss had publicly challenged his veracity.

Even in *Witness,* Hiss reports, Chambers contends that he had
completely forgotten about the typed documents and about everything
but "two or three scraps of Alger Hiss's handwriting and perhaps something of Harry White's" (162). Yet Isaac Don Levine, the journalist to
whom Chambers had first brought his story in 1939, testified in 1948
that Chambers had emphatically mentioned microfilm to him. Since
Chambers insisted throughout Hiss's trials that Hiss had brought him
official documents every week or ten days, Hiss finds it inconceivable
that Chambers would not have mentioned both the weekly schedule
and those documents to Levine in 1939—unless the "forgotten" typewritten documents or the story of their regular delivery had not been
"concocted" until the fall of 1948 (162–63).

In Chambers's own book, moreover, Hiss finds evidence of the
mental instability that Congressman Nixon scorned as an outrageous
imputation when Hiss proposed to ask questions about Chambers's
medical history. Before delivering the "forgotten" documents to his
attorneys in mid-November, Chambers considers shooting himself,
and later he buys some cyanide. Then, when the microfilm appears
temporarily to be of a kind that was not manufactured until years after
1938, he is so distressed by Nixon's anger that he feels "whipped to
torment" by an "organic revulsion," a "self-revulsion," and he does use
cyanide. He survives, he says in *Witness* (774–75), only because he
misread the directions on the container! (When *Six Crises* reports this

incident, Nixon does not consider its relationship to mental stability but only the close call, his own error in underestimating the effect of his rebuke upon Chambers, and the dramatic though momentary threat to the Case and the Committee [56].)

Before reporting the indictment, Hiss quotes speeches made by congressmen and by Isaac Don Levine at a public hearing on December 8. It is here that Committee members most vociferously oppose the prospective indictment of Chambers, and on December 14, the day before the grand jury's term expires, Congressman Mundt declares that "the crime involved here is definitely a capital crime. It is either treason in wartime or treason in peacetime" (104). The Committee then issues a long statement calling for indictment of "all guilty parties" except Chambers (105). Empaneled eighteen months earlier to investigate espionage, the grand jury has indicted nobody for that crime and has been criticized for its weak record. Now, Hiss points out, it is persuaded not to indict the one admitted spy who has appeared before it. It only charges Hiss with two counts of perjury: first when he denied giving Chambers any State Department documents, and then when he denied having seen Chambers after January 1, 1937.

In the trials themselves it is chiefly the typewriter and the documents that account for Hiss's jeopardy and his eventual conviction. As his narrative proceeds, Hiss does report a surprising number of new moves by the Committee, new contradictions in Chambers's testimony and that of Mrs. Chambers, and new witnesses to controvert Chambers. The Committee publishes several State Department documents and a new espionage report, and it declares explicitly before the first trial what it has implied for some time: that the burden of proof has been shifted from the prosecution to Hiss. It reports erroneously that only Hiss and three other people could have had access to the documents in question, and (also erroneously) that those documents enabled the Russians—and perhaps the Nazis—to break the U.S. State Department's code. These allegations gain force, Hiss notes, from the coincidental criminal trials in the same building of Judith Coplon, convicted of espionage, and several leaders of the Communist party, convicted of advocating violent revolution.

To refute the Chambers story, Hiss's defense finds Claudia Catlett, a former servant, who testifies that when the FBI brought her together with Chambers for a private conference she told him he had never slept overnight in the Hiss house and that he had never come to dinner, either. Where would you have slept, she asks Chambers, for the house had only two bedrooms and two beds, one for the parents and one for Timothy. Hiss's defense also proves (as Chambers himself later conceded in *Witness*) that on the date Chambers specified, Chambers and the Hisses could not possibly have stayed in the lodgings Chambers swore they had occupied during an alleged trip to Peterborough, N.H. But that evidence and further refutations of that kind need not concern us any longer, so long as we notice that Richard Nixon's denunciation of the judge who presided at the first trial preceded the assignment of a different judge, who ruled more favorably for the prosecution, to try the second. What remains to be discussed is the most powerful evidence against Hiss.

Although I have come to believe in Hiss's innocence, I cannot presume to refute all the documentary evidence. I wish only to show that Hiss's book consistently throws enough doubt on the strongest evidence to overturn the case against him by returning the burden of proof to his accusers. If Hiss had been able to prove that the typewritten documents were forged, he would have done so. He believes that it was chiefly the denial of a new trial that prevented that achievement after his attorney had found new evidence. Hiss does show that those documents could have been forged and that Chambers and a confessed collaborator could have had access without Hiss's aid to the handwritten notes in Hiss's office and the microfilmed documents. Hiss also shows that Chambers had to change his story in December 1948 in order to fit the new evidence he then revealed.

The only evidence that comes close to establishing a positive connection between Hiss and the delivery of the documents is the sixty-five typewritten pages. These, an FBI expert testifies, were typed on the same machine as the "Hiss standards," letters which Mrs. Hiss had typed on the Woodstock machine that her father, Thomas Fansler, had given her after it had been used for some years in his insurance office. The mystery of that machine has never been solved. As I have already remarked, Hiss's submission of the typewriter to the court argues in his favor, for he would hardly have submitted it if he had believed that it would incriminate him. Although Nixon and others have said that the FBI found the typewriter, Hiss reports that the defense was led to the typewriter by the son of Claudia Catlett, the servant to whom the Hisses had apparently given the machine. During both trials, Hiss points out, the defense accepted the widely held but inaccurate belief that a typewriter is as unique as a fingerprint, that it cannot be counterfeited. Richard Nixon continued to assert that disproven belief as fact in *Six Crises,* five years after Hiss published *In the Court of Public Opinion,* but Hiss's attorneys found an expert who succeeded in fabricating a typewriter that produced documents indistinguishable from those under dispute. Had the defense called independent experts during the trial instead of relying on the FBI expert who said that the two sets of documents had been typed on the same machine, some doubt might have been established then.

Hiss's appeal to the court of public opinion, like his attorney's appeal for a new trial, casts doubt, too, on the machine that was introduced at the trials. After Hiss was already in jail, his attorney found strong reason to suspect that the Woodstock typewriter rediscovered in April 1949 was not the one that Mrs. Hiss's father had bought in 1929 and had later given to Mrs. Hiss. Chester Lane, the attorney, was able to show that the Hiss typewriter had been used in Fansler's Philadelphia office on July 8, 1929, whereas the serial number on the Woodstock introduced as evidence could not have been dated (in Woodstock, Illinois) before July 3, 1929, and was probably not produced until August. Chambers, moreover, had testified that Priscilla Hiss had typed all of the sixty-five pages, and neither the defense nor the prosecution had offered expert testimony on the idiosyncrasies of the typist or typists. Now Lane had expert testimony that the sixty-five pages had been typed by at least two different people and that Priscilla Hiss (whose letters were available for comparison) had not typed any of them. Lane also had elicited expert judgments that the typeface on Fansler's letters written in 1929 belonged to a model of Woodstock that had not been manufactured after the first few months of that year, and that the typefaces on the Woodstock introduced at the trial had been deliberately altered to produce certain peculiarities (presumably those found in the sixty-five pages and the letters by Mrs. Hiss).

Any of these discoveries alone might raise some question about the justice of Hiss's conviction. As Herbert Packer conceded even while he rejected Hiss's defense, the combination of these and other discoveries seems too strange to be explained by coincidence.[8] The climax of Hiss's long narrative and argument comes in his lucid concluding chapter, "The New Evidence of Fraud and Forgery." There he merges the brilliant arguments, and much of the clear prose, of Chester Lane with some of the strangest inconsistencies and coincidences in the prosecution's behavior during and even after the trials.

Most notorious of the inconsistencies is the conflict between the dates of the State Department documents and the date that Chambers had invariably used throughout a decade of narrating his escape from the Communist underground. During the trials the defense denounced the convenience of his revising the old date (1937) in order to be able to claim that he had still been a spy when the documents had been written and allegedly copied, from January through April 1, 1938. Hiss found evidence during the trial to suggest strongly, though he could not prove, that the Fansler typewriter had been given away before January 1938 and before the end of March—and that therefore Mrs. Hiss could not have typed all the documents, as Chambers swore she had done. (Hiss himself did not know how to type). Only after Hiss was in prison did the defense find a letter and other proof that Chambers had begun translating a book for Oxford University Press before April 1 and that he must have been already hiding from Communist agents by April 4, the first date on which he could possibly have received the last typewritten documents. A vice-president of Oxford University Press then swore that "at the very end of 1937 or the beginning of 1938" Chambers had come to New York to discuss the translation and had "expressed violently anticommunist views and explained to me that he was in fear of his life as he was being hunted by the G.P.U. He gave me the impression of being hysterical and suffering from persecution mania" (399n).

Hiss's attorneys, moreover, had been repeatedly thwarted by questionable FBI and Justice Department behavior during their search for new evidence after the trial. The most sensational coincidences obstructed Lane's effort to establish the date on which the Fansler typewriter and (if there were indeed two machines) Woodstock no. N230099 had been manufactured and sold. Lane and Hiss tell a true detective story. Officials of the Woodstock Company and its successor

give helpful information to the defense but then refuse to sign affidavits. Even the midwestern attorney who has interviewed them refuses
to authenticate in an affidavit of his own the draft affidavit that he has
prepared for those reluctant witnesses to sign—because he says he fears
retribution if he should sign an affidavit related to the Hiss case (377).
Other experts offer opinions but retract them after a visit from FBI
agents. A branch manager of the Woodstock agency in Philadelphia
says that when the FBI interviewed him in 1948 he told them that the
serial number they were looking for would have been manufactured in
1927. Now the same man tells the defense investigators that since the
FBI took away all his records for that period (promising to return them)
he cannot even approximate the date on which no. N230099 would
have been sold. FBI agents now come to see this manager again to ask
what the defense agents were looking for. Lane summarizes his difficulties in two fine paragraphs which Hiss quotes in full. Only if a new
trial were granted, Lane concludes, could the defense acquire the subpoena power necessary to give "the jury in evidentiary form much of
the information which has necessarily been reflected in this affidavit as
hearsay—however reliable" (384).

iv

Twenty-four years after the court refused to grant a new trial or to
compel reluctant witnesses to testify "in the interest of justice," at least
two efforts to open up government files on the Hiss case are going on.
In the summer of 1975 Hiss himself and a writer named William Reuben won permission to look at the "pumpkin" microfilms that were
withheld from the defense during and after the trial. Only a week later
Allen Weinstein, a historian seeking the FBI's Hiss files under the
recent Freedom of Information Act, found himself answered by FBI
representatives who urged the court to deny his request on the ground
that even their sources of 1948, and the families of those sources, deserve the anonymity that the FBI presumably guaranteed to its confidential witnesses twenty-eight years ago. But now a federal court has
ordered the FBI to release more of the documents.

My review of the issues has not covered all the evidence that Hiss
cites. I have skipped past evidence that the jurors who voted for acquittal at his first trial were physically threatened, and evidence that

the prosecuting attorney and the judge at the second trial behaved improperly. Those instances are all part of Hiss's argument and of his experience, and I don't mean to deny their importance to his narrative. Surely the prosecutor's reservation of a surprise witness until rebuttal, when once again the defense had inadequate time to prepare an answer until after the trial had ended, did considerable damage, and Hiss at least has the satisfaction of impeaching that belated testimony in his book. Surely, too, the judge's instructions to the jury on corroborative evidence—instructions much more lenient than those laid down in the first trial—strengthened the prosecution's case. But the central issue on which critics have challenged Hiss's book is the issue of the type-writer and the sixty-five typewritten pages.

The most powerful challenge to the defense claim of forgery by typewriter was written by my former Stanford colleague, the late Herbert L. Packer, in a review of Hiss's book called "A Tale of Two Type-writers." Impressed and troubled by the mysterious conduct of the FBI, by the extraordinary frustrations that defense attorneys suffered in their search for factual evidence concerning the typewriter(s), and by the serial number of no. N230099, Packer argues nonetheless that the claim of forgery raises as many problems for the defense as it solves. Chambers could hardly have performed the forgery alone in 1948, when he was no longer friendly with the Communist underground (presumably the source of the requisite technical skills), and what other help was available? Some people might reply in 1976, "The FBI," but on this question I stand with Hiss and Lane in refusing the obligation to explain the mystery, for it is sufficient to show that someone else could have done the stealing and the typing. The verdict was unquestionably based on the assumption that a typewriter cannot be forged. Whatever the propriety of the judge's refusal to grant a new trial, we no longer have a jury but a group of readers, bound only by what we hope is a commitment to fairness. In the court of historical criticism, where a young historian has as much interest as the aging defendant in calling for the documents, we cannot believe that Hiss's conviction was just if we have serious doubts about the authenticity of the typewriter. Packer himself says that Hiss would have to be acquitted if a jury were not satisfied that he had committed espionage.

But on the larger charge—"Communist involvement" and "Communist activity"—Packer contends that the forged typewriter offers Hiss little help (41). Assuming that for some reason the forger had no access to the original typewriter of Fansler—for why would a forger create a new machine if he had the original?—Packer argues that if Chambers knew Hiss well enough to know where to have the bogus typewriter "planted" so that the defense would find it, then Chambers must have known Hiss more intimately than Hiss ever conceded (30, 38). This is by far the most difficult question about the hypothesis of two typewriters, but here again, although the question is not unanswerable, the presumed victim of a conspiracy is implicitly asked to explain the wiles and motivation of his tormentor. Packer does not mention the few details that we know of the typewriters' discovery in the spring of 1949. Two months before Mike Catlett, son of the Hisses' former servant, came to tell Hiss's brother that he had found the typewriter, the FBI brought Mrs. Catlett herself to the Justice Department to be interviewed by Chambers. Persistent reports, not from the defense but from Richard Nixon, J. Edgar Hoover, and HUAC, say that the FBI found the typewriter late in 1948. If the FBI had been helping Chambers in those weeks before the first trial, when thirty-five agents were reportedly trying to find the typewriter, the most pedestrian investigative skill could have discreetly learned from the Catlett family or neighbors where the typewriter should be planted. Nor, of course, if the original actually was found for the first time through the help of Mike Catlett in April 1949, is it inconceivable that no. N230099 was substituted before the close analysis began. The advantage still rests with the person asking the questions. For me it is harder to imagine why Hiss, if guilty, would have introduced the rediscovered typewriter as evidence than it is to imagine that a forger would have learned only in April 1949 where to plant the counterfeit machine.

But Packer insists that "the other incriminating evidence in the case" will allow doubts about the typewriter—if supported by further investigation—to exonerate Hiss only in "the narrowest and most technical sense" (41). Packer and many others believe that the main issue in the Case is whether Hiss lied about how well he had known Chambers and whether Hiss had been "involved in Communist activity during his years of government service." Packer, like others, complains that "Hiss's book sheds little light on this larger aspect of the problem," and that that is why "his book is so unsatisfactory. Even if one accepts most of the very cogent case he builds against Chambers's veracity, the root question of his own complicity still remains" (42).

Here, as in his study of other ex-Communist witnesses, Packer seeks ways in which further investigation might answer the "larger" question, and he makes some persuasive suggestions for solving some of the remaining mysteries about disputed evidence that I have not discussed: the apparently conflicting testimony of two admitted members of the so-called Ware group, both of whom testified before the Committee after Hiss was already in jail; the origin and date of a rug which Hiss admitted having received from Chambers in the spring of 1936 but which Chambers said was a gift from the Soviet government a year later; the recollection of Timothy Hobson, Hiss's stepson, who was never called to testify; and the testimony of a man who might have settled a conflict between the Hisses and the Chamberses over whether the former had visited the latter during a summer vacation. Yet by treating these questions as perfectly open Packer neglects the premise that I have tried to define as the basis for Hiss's book. Although he declares pointedly that it was the prosecutor who bore the greater responsibility for calling witnesses whom neither side questioned about the disputed rug and the summer vacation, Packer silently dismisses the testimony of the Hisses' maid corroborating Hiss's testimony about both the rug and the allegedly close friendship that Chambers claimed. Packer and others tend to regard the "larger" question as an equal contest in which we the spectators must give equal attention to both sides.

Now Herbert Packer, who died in 1972, was my friend. I am grateful to him for much kindness, and I have learned much from him about the law and about the testimony of Chambers and other ex-Communist witnesses. But I believe that the kind of evenhandedness that he proposes is strongly prejudicial to a defendant in Hiss's position, to a sound reading of Hiss's book, and to civil liberties. If we accept the "very cogent case that Hiss builds against Chambers's veracity," then the entire case against Hiss collapses. If Hiss's book throws grave doubt on Chambers's veracity, then it cannot be unsatisfactory, for then we are forced back to Hiss's public record, against which not one piece of evidence besides the espionage charges was presented to either the Committee or the courts. We must not regard exoneration as a gift that we are free to bestow or deny, a favor for which this man comes pleading after our government has destroyed his reputation and career and imprisoned him for a crime of which he was "technically" not guilty. No, he was technically guilty, so the courts have ruled. But he has shown us in his very cogent and very moving book not only why we ought to reject his conviction, but also why we ought belatedly to accept his record as a public servant. By refusing to give us a confessional book or to show us the "whole human being" that one sympathetic reviewer demanded, Hiss has remained faithful to the dignified principle that I have tried to delineate as the basis for his book. Who are we to demand to know him better? By making his case with such restraint, he challenges us to remember the best qualities in the legal tradition that has done him such terrible damage. If at seventy-one he is a durable confidence man after all, he has at least done us the favor of writing an excellent fiction that shows how a fine character can be assassinated. But I choose to believe him, and I believe that his book deserves much more serious notice than it received when it was reissued in 1972.

II. Perjury, History, and Unreliable Witnesses

The question of motives and allegiance has colored debate on the Hiss-Chambers case ever since Chambers's accusations were first publicized thirty years ago. Chambers, Hiss, and Richard Nixon all considered themselves on the defensive against a resourceful enemy and a misinformed public, and now Allen Weinstein represents himself as a dispassionate historian who refuses to be deceived by the fictions or intimidated by the slanders of Hiss's partisan defenders. Weinstein says that the psychoanalyst Meyer Zeligs (author of a book sympathetic to Hiss called *Friendship and Fratricide*) has been "refuted," but he sees nothing strange in the front-page coverage given by both the *New York*

Section II, a review of Allen Weinstein's *Perjury*, reprinted by permission from the *Virginia Quarterly Review* 54 (1978): 725–32.

Times and the *Washington Post* to the book review in which he himself declared two years ago that Hiss was guilty.[9] The press, he says, is unfamiliar with the historical facts and misguided by Watergate, and so it has rehabilitated Hiss.

Some skeptical inquiry into Weinstein's procedures was therefore probably inevitable. He is not only writing contemporary history about a controversial case. Because of Alger Hiss's durable campaign for vindication, the writer of contemporary history has also become a participant in his own historical narrative. One reason for the extraordinary publicity accorded to Weinstein's judgment in 1976 is that he had sued the FBI for release of documents. When another investigator forced the FBI to concede in 1976 that the deleted offense mentioned in one of the censored documents was homosexuality and that Chambers had confessed to it with great revulsion just before Hiss's first trial began, the reporter to whom the FBI first showed the full text consulted Allen Weinstein. Weinstein was thus able to have his judgment quoted in the very news article that first reported the fact. There, as in *Perjury,* he reasoned that, far from impeaching Chambers's testimony against Hiss, the secret confession tended to support Chambers's veracity, for a married father would not have risked so embarrassing a confession to support a false accusation.

In this case more emphatically than in most factual narratives, then, the historian is a maker of fictions who derives his authority not only from the range and accuracy of his research but also from his appeal to our sense of the way people behave. Why would Chambers accuse Hiss falsely? Why would Hiss, if guilty, give a self-incriminating typewriter to the court? The value of the circumstantial evidence depends chiefly on helping us to ask or (more rarely) to answer such questions. If we reason from Chambers's explicit declaration that he admitted his homosexual behavior because he feared the defense would reveal it to discredit him during the trial, then we may well conclude that this confession does nothing to authenticate Chambers's truthfulness concerning Hiss.

In the history itself, moreover, Weinstein asks us again and again to draw inferences from the motives that he assigns to a large variety of characters as well as to the principals. Consider his treatment of Malcolm Cowley. Neither in narrating Chambers's anti-Communist activities of 1940 nor in reporting Cowley's testimony at the first perjury trial nine years later does Weinstein mention what for me was the most important fact in Cowley's first meeting with Chambers. Instead he quotes at length Cowley's unflattering description of Chambers (including dirty linen), and in order to convict Cowley of bias against Chambers he reports two incidents that did not even occur until two years after the disputed interview. To impeach Cowley's documented testimony about what Chambers actually told him in 1940, Weinstein also cites Chambers's recollection in 1949 that Cowley had had "quite a few" drinks during their luncheon interview nine years earlier (337).

Weinstein does not report that Cowley wrote a sober account of the interview only a few hours after its occurrence, nor does he record Cowley's most important affirmative declaration: Chambers, Cowley wrote in his journal, described himself as a defector from the Communist party's underground who had "learned the technique of the movement and was now going to apply that technique to destroy it." [10]

Besides representing Cowley unjustly, these few pages in *Perjury* do a large favor to the prosecution's view of Chambers's motivation and credibility. Had Weinstein reported here Chambers's alleged intention to use devious tactics against the Left, he would have given the reader a plausible link to other statements Chambers made about using "against the Communist Party exactly the conspiratorial methods which it had taught me to use against others," [11] and (long after Hiss's conviction) about confronting Alger Hiss in a war of annihilation. Other associates of Chambers during the years between his defection and his appearance before the House Committee on Un-American Activities have said that in the late 1930s and early 1940s Chambers made no distinction between Communists and liberal New Dealers in his efforts to cleanse *Time* of the pernicious influence, and Weinstein does report those views. But his total neglect of Cowley's memorandum about Chambers's tactics does more than leave unfair emphasis on Cowley's supposed unreliability. It also screens the reader from one of the most important independent documents—written in 1940 about an interview in which Hiss's name never came up—attributing great ethical latitude to Chambers. Since Weinstein will later deride Hiss's inability to assign Chambers an adequate motive for false accusation, the omission is all the more regrettable.

The Cowley episode is not unique. Having decided that Hiss was guilty and that Chambers's central story was true, Weinstein has written what a reviewer for the History Book Club calls a brief for the prosecution. He uses the defense files, which were opened to him, to highlight every nuance that might show Hiss to have been an evasive or opportunistic character before his alleged conversion to Communism, and (in Klaus Fuchs's words) "a controlled schizophrenic" thereafter (208). In the circular logic of espionage and counterespionage, exculpatory evidence thus becomes potentially incriminating. Weinstein scorns as "defense by reputation" an attorney's plan to show Hiss's actual conduct and opinions that ran counter to Soviet wishes (379), and when he comes to Hiss's apparent support of the Nationalists in the Chinese civil war he remarks that the Soviets, too, opposed Mao's Communists at that point.

The historian's selective skepticism and selective reticence are at work throughout the book. He gives an impressive list of the evidence one must disbelieve in order to believe Hiss's denial of social intimacy with Whittaker and Esther Chambers, but he ignores some of the anomalies one must believe in order to believe Chambers. Nowhere in this very long book can one learn that in 1948 Chambers at first described his six-foot-tall, allegedly intimate friend as about five feet, eight inches tall, but one is told emphatically that Alger and Priscilla Hiss both forgot that Chambers had once worn a moustache. One finds here an elaborate if literal-minded effort to refute alleged similarities between the Hiss case and a novel of betrayal which Chambers had translated, but not one word about the phrase Chambers actually quoted from that novel when he first described Alger Hiss to HUAC. Weinstein never gives a full statement of Chambers's bold fiction that Hiss had transferred his stepson to a less costly private school and had diverted to Communist party dues the money thus saved from the father's tuition payments. Weinstein reports falsely at the very beginning of his narrative that Chambers told HUAC he had broken with the Communist party in 1938, whereas Chambers consistently gave the date as 1937 until he recovered the incriminating documents and found that they were all dated between January and April 1938. (Weinstein has an explanation for the discrepancy, but the reader must persevere through more than three hundred pages before he even learns that the discrepancy existed.) In narrating Chambers's recovery of those documents in November 1948, Weinstein says nothing about Richard Nixon's threateningly urgent demand (reported by Chambers in *Witness*) that Chambers now bring forth whatever additional evidence he might have, in order to save himself and HUAC. Neither in the narrative nor in an appendix that attacks various theories of the Hiss defense does Weinstein mention the discrepancy between the date on which Hiss's incriminating typewriter must have been manufactured and the date of the earliest extant letter typed on it in the office of Mrs. Hiss's father.

Weinstein reports that State Department secretaries swore they never left Hiss's and Francis Sayre's office unattended in the months when the documents were removed and copied, but he ignores Judge Charles Wyzanski's testimony about waiting all alone in Hiss's office for many minutes during a casual visit there. One cannot tell whether he also ignores, or did not elicit from Judge Wyzanski during his interview, a significant anecdote that Judge Wyzanski told me in 1976, the story of asking Hiss whether their former Harvard Law School classmate Lee Pressman should be appointed to a vacancy in the Justice Department that would virtually leave Pressman in charge of all the department's mediation in labor disputes. Wyzanski's recollection that Hiss firmly advised him against choosing Pressman cannot prove Hiss innocent of a plot to get fellow Communists appointed to sensitive positions, but it certainly tends to argue against Hiss's guilt in such a conspiracy, and its absence from *Perjury* leaves the reader almost no basis for doubting Chambers's and Weinstein's sinister interpretation of the relationship between Pressman and Hiss.[12]

Weinstein often uses hearsay, psychological conjecture, and evidence about other people to characterize Alger and Priscilla Hiss. He attributes Mrs. Hiss's reputed hysteria to the strain of upholding a false account of her relationship with the Chambers family, whereas anxiety about the unfavorable publicity and her husband's peril might have been a sufficient cause. In characterizing Chambers, however, Weinstein requires firmly positive evidence on questions that might challenge the accusation of Hiss. Chambers's secretly admitted homosexuality has no bearing on the case, Weinstein concludes—because "no evidence has emerged" to disprove Chambers's declaration that he never mixed his homosexual liaisons and the Communist party's secret work, and because Hiss once told the defense attorneys that he remembered "boastful hints of sexual exploits but no hint of any unnatural sex interests" (146). Weinstein therefore concludes too readily that Hiss's later characterization of Chambers as a "spurned homosexual" (146) must be false. Chambers's complex attitude toward his homosexual past might very well have affected his treatment of men whom he came to portray as his former coconspirators or intimate friends.

In this continuing debate over plausible characterization, the advantage lies with the debater who is asking the questions. Weinstein does not ask in this book why Chambers, whose prodigious memory allowed him to testify at length about an old Ford that he helped Hiss to dispose of, would have forgotten all about a $400 loan from the Hisses a year or two after that transaction—a loan with which Chambers bought his own car. Not even in the growing danger of the slander suit, when urged to find every proof of intimacy with the Hisses, did Chambers remember that alleged loan—not until several days after the FBI found in the Hisses' bank records for 1937 a $400 withdrawal. Weinstein concentrates on challenging Hiss's explanation of the withdrawal, and on displaying the FBI records to show that no evidence about the Hisses' withdrawal of the money was sent from the Washington office to New York before Chambers's memory of the alleged loan revived. I find it easier to believe that the FBI's discovery came in some unrecorded way to Chambers than that Chambers remembered Hiss's old Ford but not Hiss's relation to his own car. On numerous occasions in *Perjury,* Weinstein uses similar yet weaker coincidences of amnesia and memory to incriminate Hiss.

The most damaging of these, and the central document in Weinstein's argument for Hiss's evasiveness, is a memorandum that he found in the defense files, a report that in the general search for the typewriter owned by the Hisses in 1938 one of the defense investigators in Washington had been told by Hiss to look up the Catletts, the servant's family to whom (as it later turned out) the Hisses had actually given the machine. Weinstein believes this memo proves that Hiss remembered even before his interrogation by the grand jury exactly how the incriminating typewriter had been disposed of ten years earlier, and he builds a strong argument to show that Hiss denied this knowledge not only to the grand jury but also to his own attorneys. Here as earlier, however, Weinstein fails even to ask questions that occur promptly to a reader less sure of Hiss's guilt. If Hiss knew all along that the typewriter would help to convict him, why did he voluntarily tell the FBI that it had been given to his wife by her father, a Philadelphia insurance agent, and why did he volunteer the name of the insurance firm—evidence that would surely lead to the typewriter's serial number? And why did Hiss ever tell one of the defense investigators about the Catlett family, among whom he didn't want even the defense to inquire?[13] Why, if guilty and only recently reminded of the dates on the papers Chambers had copied, did the Hisses volunteer that they had kept the typewriter until after 1938?

I don't mean to say that none of these questions can be answered. It is possible that Hiss behaved, in Chambers's words, "like a complete swine," but "not a very bright swine" (539). My objection is that Weinstein doesn't ask the questions. He is too intent on showing that Hiss deceived the defense attorneys, and he therefore neglects to consider other possible explanations of the memo. He compounds the difficulty by representing Hiss throughout this hectic period as a man perfectly in control, so that the blunders (if blunders they were) are the more difficult to believe. And when he comes to the critical decision of Hiss's attorneys to introduce the typewriter in court, he offers baffling if not misleading documentation for his reasoning. "Stryker and the other lawyers," he says, "planned a strategy of candor. They would introduce the Hiss Woodstock as if the defense had nothing to hide in connection with it" (397). For this damaging inference about Hiss's attorneys, the only source that Weinstein cites is a letter not from one of the attorneys but from a documentary expert to Hiss's trial lawyer (397, 633).

Nothing that I have said here settles the tangled question of Chambers's credibility or Hiss's guilt. I have deliberately concentrated on flaws in the method and the argument, because the favorable reviewers in the national press—largely survivors who long ago declared their belief that Hiss was guilty—have praised Weinstein's impeccable objectivity, and because several of them have announced that his book closes the case. The tone of the book is generally dispassionate, and the evidence voluminous, the narrative organization extraordinarily complex. Few disinterested readers are likely to work their way through the entire narrative while paying close attention to the notes at the back of the book, and those few readers may be fatigued and submissive by the time they reach Weinstein's treatment of some of the most debatable evidence. A skeptical reading like my own, motivated by previous commitment to doubts of Hiss's guilt, may help to alert the weary to the historian's role in assembling and shaping the evidence—whether he is using evidence about Noel Field and Klaus Fuchs to characterize Alger Hiss, or inexplicably reporting as fact in 1978 a statement he publicly called an error in 1976.[14]

Yet the defense and anyone else interested in the mystery of this case ought not merely to dismiss this massive book. I continue to believe that if Hiss was innocent he cannot be expected to solve the mystery of all the evidence marshaled against him, but of course many people cannot be persuaded to exonerate him unless he does explain that evidence. On several questions—especially the content and routing of the documents, and the defense's treatment of the typewriter—Weinstein's substantive arguments deserve to be answered on the merits. His unfairness, though a legitimate issue, is not the only issue worthy of careful response.

III. *Coram Nobis*

On the rare occasions when a legal brief is printed for sale by a trade publisher, one might expect it to be reviewed by an attorney. In this historic case, however, a professor at the Yale Law School introduces Alger Hiss's long-awaited petition explicitly for the general public, and it seems reasonable for an informed layman to consider questions that will trouble conscientious citizens even though the legal case may be decided on other grounds.

Whether or not it persuades the federal court to issue a writ of

Section III, a review of *In re Alger Hiss*, edited by Edith Tiger, with an Introduction by Thomas I. Emerson, reprinted by permission from *The Nation* magazine / The Nation Co., Inc., © 1979, 229 (1979): 506–7.

error *coram nobis,* Hiss's petition ought to persuade any fair-minded reader that the Federal Bureau of Investigation and the prosecution misbehaved outrageously thirty years ago in their effort to convict Hiss of perjury. So lucid is the text of Victor Rabinowitz's brief that lay readers may follow the argument easily. The mass of supporting documents will require more patient study, but these, too, are arranged in an order that is admirably clear. The pattern of official misconduct is more troubling than the question of Hiss's guilt. Even those who believe Hiss was guilty ought to deplore that pattern.

As articles published in the *Nation* reported several years ago, the prosecution and the FBI concealed or misrepresented evidence undermining the validity of the notorious Woodstock typewriter, and months before the first trial began the FBI had an informer among the private investigators working for Hiss's attorneys.

The details of those misdeeds gain new power in the context of deception that was even worse. The most reprehensible acts of the prosecution and the FBI in this perjury trial were lying to the court and allowing witnesses for the prosecution to perjure themselves. In disclosure proceedings, though ordered to show the judge all written statements made to the FBI at different times by Whittaker Chambers, the prosecution deliberately concealed the existence of a 184-page narrative, which the government had asked Chambers to write but not to sign. Not only was the defense thus denied access to the most extensive account that would have revealed inconsistencies with Chambers's other statements, but the very existence of this account was deliberately withheld from the judge, in evasion of his explicit order. One is reminded of the Ellsberg trial.

Besides Chambers's denial that any such narrative had been written, the most egregious perjury disclosed in the Hiss brief is in the testimony of Edith Murray. She was called in rebuttal by the prosecution to surprise the defense at the end of the second trial by corroborating Chambers's testimony that Alger and Priscilla Hiss had indeed visited Chambers in his Baltimore apartment. Murray falsely denied that the FBI agents had told her the names of Alger and Priscilla Hiss when the agents had first shown her a photograph of the Hisses.

The false testimony of Edith Murray and of another rebuttal witness is exposed in Hiss's brief through documents recovered under the

Freedom of Information Act. Almost all those documents are concerned with the government's behavior. But of all the papers that Hiss's brief reproduces from the files of the FBI and the prosecution, none was more interesting to me than a memorandum by Edward McLean, the chief attorney for Hiss's defense in December 1948.

Hiss's brief properly introduces McLean's memorandum to help demonstrate that the prosecution was spying on the defense. In the continuing debate over Hiss's guilt, the memorandum has a greater significance, for it undermines one of the most damaging arguments in Allen Weinstein's *Perjury*. Using a letter written by a private investigator in Washington on December 28, 1948, Weinstein argues that Hiss had inadvertently disclosed the identity of the Catletts, to whom he had given his incriminating typewriter, but that then Hiss had continued to obfuscate and conceal from the government and even his own counsel information concerning both the typewriter and the Catlett family. In *Perjury*, moreover, Weinstein declares that Hiss's chief attorney—though he knew who had the actual typewriter—"held off" looking for the Catletts until the FBI "forced his hand" at the end of January 1949 by finding them. Until January 21, Weinstein contends, the only mention of the Catlett family in McLean's files occurs "at the bottom of a list of things" for a defense investigator to do (386). Perhaps Weinstein may be excused for having overlooked McLean's memorandum in the prosecution's files.[15]

This memorandum proves that McLean knew about the Catletts and had an address for them even before he received the letter from his investigator in Washington. It also shows that McLean had ordered a thorough inquiry about the typewriter among all the Hisses' former maids, including the Catlett family. The order for this investigation stands second among fifteen headings on McLean's agenda, nowhere near the bottom of the list. Far from holding off until the FBI forced his hand, McLean was searching right along.

Several favorable reviewers of *Perjury* made a major point of Weinstein's argument that, except for one unexplained lapse, Hiss was trying to conceal the whereabouts of the typewriter from his own attorneys. McLean's newly published memorandum forces one to ask how, if that was so, McLean learned the names and address of Claudia Catlett and her sons. The reasonable inference is that he learned them from Alger or Priscilla Hiss, along with the misinformation that Claudia Catlett had died. Since it was her sons who got the typewriter, the false report of their mother's death loses the incriminating significance that Weinstein attributes to it.

Besides revealing the government's misconduct, Hiss's new brief reminds us that on this matter and others the documentation in *Perjury* should be checked with great care.

Notes

1. Whittaker Chambers, *Witness* (New York: Random House, 1952).

2. Alger Hiss, *In the Court of Public Opinion* (New York: Alfred A. Knopf, 1957; rept. New York: Harper and Row, 1972); Richard M. Nixon, *Six Crises* (Garden City, N.Y.: Doubleday, 1962).

3. See Leslie Fiedler, *An End to Innocence* (Boston: Beacon Press, 1955), p. 8; Irving Younger, "Was Alger Hiss Guilty?," *Commentary* 60 (1975): 23–37, and letters in response, ibid., pp. 4–18.

4. Mark De Wolfe Howe, "The Misfortune of a Nation," *Nation* 184 (1957): 442–43.

5. Preface addressed to "Christian Reader," by fourteen ministers, for Increase Mather, *Cases of Conscience,* in David Levin, ed., *What Happened in Salem?,* 2d ed. (New York: Harcourt Brace Jovanovich, 1960), p. 118.

6. Richard Challener, "New Light on a Turning Point in U.S. History" *University: A Princeton Quarterly,* no. 56 (1973): 3,28.

7. Lionel Trilling, *The Middle of the Journey,* with a new introduction by the author (New York: Avon Books, 1976), p. xiii.

8. Herbert L. Packer, *Ex-Communist Witnesses: Four Studies in Fact Finding* (Stanford: Stanford Univ. Press, 1962), pp. 21–51.

9. See Allen Weinstein, "Was Alger Hiss Framed?" *New York Review of Books,* April 1, 1976, and *Perjury* (New York: Alfred A. Knopf, 1978). See, for example, the *Washington Post,* Sept. 10, 1976.

10. Malcolm Cowley showed me his original journal entry, dated Dec. 13, 1940, when I interviewed him at his home in Sherman, Conn., in June 1978.

11. Chambers, *Witness,* p. 445. Compare similar statements made by Chambers and attributed to him by others in Meyer A. Zeligs, *Friendship and Fratricide: An Analysis of Whittaker Chambers and Alger Hiss* (New York: Viking Press, 1967), pp. 233, 304, 306.

12. Interview with Charles Wyzanski, Oct. 15, 1976.

13. In a note on p. 289, Weinstein does concede that nobody has ever explained Hiss's alleged decision to give the information to a defense investigator while concealing it from the chief defense attorney; but see below, section III.

14. See the *New York Review of Books,* May 27, 1976, p. 46. There Weinstein responds to doubts that a secret Communist trying to transfer his car to a fellow conspirator would have notarized the transfer at the largest Ford agency in Washington: "In 1936," Weinstein declares, "the Cherner Motor Company was not the largest Ford agency in Washington." But in *Perjury,* without explanation, Weinstein describes the same company as "Washington's largest auto dealership," p. 41.

15. See *In Re Alger Hiss: Petition for a Writ of Error* Coram Nobis, ed. Edith Tiger (New York: Hill and Wang, 1979), pp. 153–54.

Part Two

Biography, Autobiography, and Memoir

8.

___

Trying to Make a Monster Human
Judgment in the Biography of Cotton Mather

I

At a book-author luncheon in Charlottesville in 1978, I had the good fortune to follow a speaker who had written a biography of Douglas Fairbanks and Mary Pickford. With an emphasis that a biographer of Cotton Mather could only consider providential, my predecessor declared that Fairbanks and Pickford had once been the most popular names in the world. It was all too easy then for me to begin by asking how many in the audience had known Cotton Mather's name before this fund-raising event for our art museum had advertised it throughout Albemarle County, Virginia. Every one of those two hundred auditors claimed to have known Cotton Mather's unique name, and I did not need to tell them that, well known though it surely is, it is not among the most beloved in our history. Everybody seems to know the name, and that it signifies something puritanical, perhaps both bookish and superstitious, but few know much more about it. After my remarks in Charlottesville, one brave woman came forward to protest that Mather had been cruel to children. When I asked what kind of behavior she referred to, she said he had told children they were like a spider hanging over a flaming pit. I suspect that her opinion did not change when I credited that image to Jonathan Edwards.

Whether the Puritan ogre is Jonathan Edwards or Cotton Mather matters even less as a challenge to the biographer than whether the representation of hell asks the sinner to imagine himself as a dangling

Reprinted by permission of the editors from *The Yale Review* 73 (1984): 210–29, copyright Yale University.

spider (Edwards) or a glowing coal (Mather). A biographer finds Cotton Mather's high name-recognition factor peculiarly embarrassing because the false or distorted image not only appears in surprisingly lowbrow media but also glowers or simpers at us in the work of both the middle and the highest brows. Let me display just a few examples that will establish a context for my discussion of some biographical challenges.

I won't bother to quote from the comic book, lent to me several years ago by a student, in which science fiction brings us a witch-hunt led by a drooling priest named Cotton Mather, but I do want to record the actual language of several other recent examples from my extensive collection.

A physician in Richmond, Virginia, wrote the following letter to the *Boston Globe* in 1979:

> With regard to Laetrile and the Chad Green family [who had been forbidden to give their child Laetrile and had taken him to Mexico for treatment], I was surprised to learn that Massachusetts is still burning witches.
>
> Fortunately, the Green family had the intelligence and resources to flee the inquisition.
>
> Has anybody checked Cotton Mather's grave?[1]

I suspect that the physician would not have changed his mind if I had told him that no witch was ever burned in Massachusetts, or even if I had reminded him that Cotton Mather's pioneering defense of inoculation during one of Boston's worst smallpox epidemics had provoked fierce opposition, including an effort to bomb his house.

My second exhibit comes from the lead article in the sports section of the *Washington Post* on a Sunday near the climax of the American League pennant race in September 1978. The New York Yankees had just won five games in a row from the first-place Boston Red Sox, and this article by Thomas Boswell focused on the vindictiveness of baseball fans in Boston. "If Cotton Mather were alive today," said the lead sentence, "he would be a Boston Red Sox fan. And he would be mad." Several hundred words later, the name that Cotton Mather repeatedly begged the Lord to save from obloquy and from bringing shame on the true religion figures again in Boswell's conclusion. In the stands above the Boston locker room, the fans, Boswell says, "continue to boo. Cotton Mathers do not console a sinner. They give him a free courtesy road map to the eternal five."[2] (I took the last word to be a misprint for *fire* although "the eternal five" might be an allusion to the immortal Boston Celtics. Even so, the editors of the *Post* chose not to print my brief letter pointing out that Cotton Mather had indeed consoled condemned murderers and even condemned witches. Perhaps they were indifferent to my pedantic insistence that if Cotton Mather were alive on any Lord's day in September he would not be in Fenway Park but in church.)

Nor was the editorial page of the *New York Times* better able than the sports page of the *Washington Post* to resist the ubiquitous image. In a sentence that obscurely hinted at reactionary or troglodytic economic policies, an editorial chiding the secretary of the treasury under president Ford called William Simon "the Cotton Mather of fiscal orthodoxy."[3] My unpublished letter in response to that slander of the dead conceded that without further explication I could not say whether William Simon was the Cotton Mather of fiscal orthodoxy in our time; I could only insist that Cotton Mather—author of a pamphlet on the value of paper money and deficit financing—had not been the William Simon of seventeenth-century fiscal policy.

Dragged forth in the company of a villain even more despised than William Simon, the image of Cotton Mather has also been haled before the voluble court that sits in the Letters column of the *New York Review of Books*. In a *NYRB* article Renata Adler had referred to a former Virginia congressman as "an obscure fanatic." When a Virginian protested that the man in question had won a congressional Medal of Honor as well as his election to the House of Representatives, and that it was therefore inaccurate to call him obscure, Adler replied with an economy that in those pages deserves to be called laconic: in comparison to notorious fanatics, she explained, a Medal of Honor winner might justly be called obscure. Her examples were Carrie Nation and Cotton Mather.[4]

I wrote no letter about that pairing.

For different reasons I also refrained from writing to correct the most powerful of these exhibits, which appeared in the *New York Times Book Review* within a few weeks after Robert Lowell's death in 1977, but I was persuaded by my publisher's editor to consider a different kind of reply, which will bring me soon to the biography itself. Under the title "The New England Spirit" the *Times* printed an excerpt from an unpublished essay by Robert Lowell on New England writers. I was more troubled to see that Meyer Schapiro had read this passage to the distinguished audience at the New York memorial for Lowell than to know that it would be read by the general public. (Later I learned that somebody in Lowell's family had chosen the passage for Schapiro to read.)

Here our problem as readers is slightly more difficult than in the other exhibits, for Lowell is perfectly aware of reviewing images— "Cardboard men" he calls our image of the first-generation Pilgrims, "silhouetted in the famous steepletop hats"—and he introduces the later version of the "pilgrim" as a different kind of image: "not a cut-out for children," he says, "but an effigy to be trampled on by a dubious Enlightenment." Then, without a pause but in a new paragraph, he comes to our unloved hero: "The pilgrim," Lowell says,

> has learned to grow twisted with subtlety, like the dark, learned, well-connected Cotton Mather. The supreme bookman: Mather wrote 450 books [a slight exaggeration], all printed [a larger exaggeration]. It seems a slander that he could have done so much harm when all his nights and days were spent writing and looking up brilliant quotations.
>
> Mather, the Salem witch-hanger, was a professional man of letters employed to moralize and subdue. His truer self was a power-crazed mind bent on destroying darkness with darkness, applying his cruel, high-minded obsessed intellect to the extermination of witch and neurotic. His soft bookish hands were indelibly stained with blood—a black image to set against our white busts of Washington and Lincoln. Perhaps in his cross-examinations of the harmless and foolish, Cotton Mather oddly exposed a deep, symbolic, incongruous intelligence that nearly made him immortal.[5]

There the passage ends. Despite the allusion to black and white images near the end, it seems clear that the statements of supposed fact and the evaluation, as well as the identification of Mather's true self as a power-crazed mind bent on exterminating witch and neurotic, represent Lowell's own judgment.

The effigy that Lowell re-creates so powerfully has a long life in our national literature—a life and utility of its own. Long before

Washington Irving's Headless Horseman drives Ichabod Crane from the state of New York in "The Legend of Sleepy Hollow," the narrator has associated the credulous pedant with Cotton Mather's writings on witchcraft, and the tin can that a seventeenth-century antagonist tied to Mather's effigy in 1700 has rattled through the works of James Fenimore Cooper, Nathaniel Hawthorne, William Carlos Williams, and Katherine Anne Porter. Even the historian Samuel Eliot Morison, who invented the metaphor of Robert Calef's rattling tin can, once wrote that undergraduate life at Harvard in the 1670s must have recovered its vigor if "that insufferable prig Cotton Mather [then only eleven years old] was being kicked about, as he so richly deserved."[6]

The problem for the modern biographer is not how to defend Mather. Answering such distortions tends to perpetuate the effigy both by repeating the memorable rhetoric and by casting the discussion or the characterization in the rigid mold of prosecution or defense. Even if one avoids the temptation to whitewash the black image, answering the charges limits one's freedom to portray the character according to one's best judgment of the historical record. I would feel ridiculous if I were to demonstrate that Cotton Mather did not spend all his nights and days looking up brilliant quotations, and only slightly less hampered by anachronistic distortions if, in order to prove that he was not bent on destroying witches and neurotics, I should set out to describe Mather's therapeutic treatment of his parishioners' anxiety.

When I say that the effigy has a life of its own, I don't deny that it has genuine contemporaneous value; I only recognize that sound history or biography can do little to modify the caricature. Historical correction of Robert Lowell's effigy or Katherine Anne Porter's brilliantly inaccurate satirical portrait would be as useless as similar modifications of Shakespeare's Lear or Richard III. Although both Lowell and Porter claim the authority of history in a way that I believe is quite different from Shakespeare's, they are much more interested in what Mather has come to represent—in Lowell's words, the professional man of letters employed to moralize and subdue—than in justice to poor old Cotton Mather.

Against the advice of my editor, therefore, I decided that the best way for my biography to deal with the effigy was virtually to ignore it. The manuscript was being copyedited when Robert Lowell's comments appeared in the *New York Times Book Review*, and my editor urged me to get some of Lowell's language into the preface. I did write two paragraphs explaining why my biography would not deal with the legendary figure, but Lowell's rhetoric made the effigy so formidable that arguing its irrelevance to serious history and biography was self-defeating. The mere mention of those soft bookish hands made the effigy and the bloodstains more memorable than any materials with which I might try to fabricate a human characterization. I decided not to use the new paragraphs. Although I would not try to absolve Mather of all culpability for his part in the Salem witchcraft trials, I was determined not to be bound by the narrow language of approval or condemnation. Hardly a page in my biography lacks strong judgments of character and conduct, but most of those judgments are too complex to be expressed as approval or disapproval, guilty or not guilty.

My resolution to ignore the effigy was strengthened by my awareness that all Mather's biographers (except Katherine Anne Porter in the few chapters she published) had portrayed him sympathetically. Beginning with George Lyman Kittredge, moreover, a distinguished succession of modern scholars—from Samuel Eliot Morison, Kenneth Murdock, and Perry Miller to Sacvan Bercovitch and Robert Middlekauff—all these scholars, each working independently and from a different perspective, had written hundreds of pages recognizing Mather's intellectual and literary achievement; his enlightened views on smallpox inoculation and a number of other scientific, political, and religious issues; his energetic determination to advance learning while preserving what he considered the best traditions of New England Congregationalism. Several other scholars—most recently Chadwick Hansen in a 1969 history of the Salem witchcraft trials—had published fresh narratives of Mather's efforts to restrain the court and protect the defendants' rights in 1692.

This voluminous record helped me to perceive two paradoxical if not contradictory truths that confirmed my decision about the effigy—first, that it was unnecessary to rescue Cotton Mather's name from the bloody pool in which his hands had been drenched, because other scholars had already fished him out; but second, that not even mouth-to-mouth resuscitation could make any historically human characterization vigorous enough to compete with the effigy for public attention.

More than fifty years ago, in the very first issue of the journal *American Literature,* a reviewer praised Kenneth Murdock for having represented Puritanism not as a reproach but as a subject crying for further study. For half a century scholars, while conducting that intensive study, have been introducing their reviews or essays on Puritanism or on Cotton Mather with allusions to H. L. Mencken's definition of a Puritan as a man who fears that someone somewhere may be enjoying himself. And they have regularly warned us to forbear caricature, to study Puritanism for what it actually was. I was not surprised, therefore, when a Pulitzer Prize–winning historian set his very generous review of my biography first in the framework of Mencken's satirical definition and then in the clockwork of a pendulum swinging from disapproval of Mather toward approval.[7] My resignation became complete when the *Charlottesville Daily Progress* drew attention to an article about my book with the banner headline: "COTTON MATHER NOT A MON-STER," and when the *Palo Alto Times* review bore the headline: "COT-TON MATHER MORE THAN A SOUR PURITAN."[8] I even decided prudently that since I couldn't beat the headlines that invoke the effigy, I might as well join them by incorporating the monster in the title of this essay. Our judgment is inevitably complicated by the effigy and by our disposition to judge Puritans—especially if we sus-pect in any of them a motive slightly lower than angelic—our dispo-sition to judge Puritans with a decisiveness that may seem poetically just for a tribe who called themselves the Lord's People and who tried to divide mankind into the elect and the reprobate.

Nowhere is that disposition more evident than in Edmund Mor-gan's review of my book in the *New York Review of Books.* Morgan has earned much of his preeminence among American historians by writing with sympathetic understanding about the Puritan family, John Win-throp, and the government of Puritan congregations. Yet his essay on Cotton Mather is called "The Puritan You Love to Hate." And the page is dominated by a superb caricature drawn by my near namesake, Da-vid Levine. When I saw that headline, Levine's caricature, and then the review itself, I was struck by what Cotton Mather himself would surely have called a Providential sign. I felt almost as if I were reliving the experience in which Mather had set aside his prepared sermon dur-ing a thunderstorm one Sunday in 1694 and had preached extemporaneously on God's voice in the thunder, only to be interrupted by a messenger with the news that Mather's own house had just been struck by lightning. In the Levine caricature the head is narrow and the soft bookish hands are enormous as they virtually surround a large book, along the board of which one hand lies not quite reverently. And Morgan introduces his essay-review with a three-column introduction that asks, and then tries to answer, a question I, too, had posed in an essay published in 1963, the question that we have been implicitly considering here: Why, Morgan asks in his very first paragraph, is it almost impossible to speak of Cotton Mather without taking sides?[9]

I am sorry to say that Edmund Morgan strengthens the point of our concurring introductions by taking the negative side. He admits forthrightly that the proximity afforded by my characterization of Mather only reinforces his contempt for the man—he says "our contempt," but he means the reader's and his own, not mine—he declares that Mather's part in the witchcraft episode now seems "all the more odious," and he concludes that Mather was not only an egomaniac but a nauseating egomaniac. He generously suggests that it is Mather, and not I, who must be blamed for these reactions, but since I had hoped to elicit more understanding than disgust, I can take small comfort from my conviction that words like *odious, contempt,* and *nauseating* usually do not issue from objective correlatives. I am moved by Mather's early life not to nausea but to a mixture of compassion, disapproval, wonder, respect, admiration, and comic irony. I find the act of trying to understand him in historical (including psychological) circumstances so demanding that no judgment of condemnation or exoneration can adequately represent it. Grateful though I am for the approval of historians who reviewed my book, I cannot agree with one of them that I set out to "defend" Mather.[10] I don't believe that to understand all is to forgive all, nor do I believe that my willingness to consider Mather sympathetically is entirely attributable to my strong stomach.

That sympathy is enlisted in an effort to approach a just understanding of Mather's life and to speak to our own historical consciousness. I agree passionately with the late historian Garrett Mattingly that although it cannot now make much difference to the dead whether we treat them fairly, the effort to achieve a just understanding ought to make a great difference to us, helping to define our own humanity by affecting our approach to contemporary affairs and our modification of the record for our successors.

II

My biography, then, tries to narrate the experience of an extraordinary man in a way that makes it comprehensible in the historical circumstances. Taking off from Nathaniel Hawthorne's call for a biographer who might base a life of Mather on love, I concede in the opening lines of the preface that I have not learned to love Cotton Mather, but claim that I have learned to see why others loved him. One major challenge in the historical circumstances is that Mather was obviously a popular figure until the Salem witchcraft trials and their aftermath damaged his reputation—and well liked by many New Englanders even after he had become the controversial figure we recognize in the caricatures. Cursed as well as blessed from birth with the name of his maternal grandfather, John Cotton, he was a transitional figure almost from the beginning. His father had not only named him in honor of John Cotton but "designed" him, the father said, for the ministry.[11] Our conventional wisdom has found it easy to explain in general terms the anxieties caused by such a genealogy, and therefore to explain Cotton Mather's hypertonic efforts to assuage them: the prodigious piety and learning, the self-exaltation and self-accusation, the boyhood stammer and the prolific writing. (As I read laboriously through Mather's four hundred published books, I often wished that some of them had not survived, and my private image of him merged with that of Danny Kaye in a film called *Wonder Boy,* sitting in a public library and reading two books at once, taking notes on one book with his left hand and on the other with his right.) What I thought had not been adequately represented were the sources of strength in the boy's family, community, and character. How did he come to accomplish all that he did? Why did his congregation insist on calling him to be pastor despite the apparent opposition of his own father, the incumbent teacher in the same church? Why did a condemned murderer, who had killed a friend in a drunken rage, invite young Cotton Mather rather than some other minister to preach a sermon before the execution and to counsel and pray for him on the way to the gallows? How did Cotton Mather come at the age of only twenty-six to be chosen to write the declaration of English liberties and colonial grievances in the revolution against the royal governor? I believe that emphasis on Mather's transitional role in the movement from seventeenth-century piety to eighteenth-century moralism, or from Puritan orthodoxy to the glories of the Enlightenment, has distorted his actual experience in a way that has made it all the more difficult to understand and represent the life he actually lived. My biography does not claim to answer all the questions that I have just posed, but it does try to represent his attractive and repellent qualities as believable components of the same character. If we are nauseated by his vanity, we may recoil from it or condemn it rather than see its nature and significance.

Here I can only sketch the general argument of the narrative and then give a few examples that illustrate different kinds of judgment. I try to show in Mather's childhood the sources of both his strength and his anxieties: the strong family approval and encouragement as well as the frighteningly high expectation and example; the mother's and father's tenderness and wisdom, as well as the father's terrifying breakdown after the paternal grandfather's death, when Cotton was six years old. These domestic relationships and events occur in a political and theological context that ties the family's life to national and even cosmic issues. The father has been driven from England after the Restoration of Charles II to the throne in 1660, and royal agents threaten the autonomy of Puritan Massachusetts throughout young Cotton's childhood and youth. Soon after this drama culminates in the cancellation of the Massachusetts charter, Increase Mather (escaping royal agents who want to arrest him in Boston) goes to London to plead the colony's case before King James II. Cotton Mather, in his twenty-sixth year, must therefore minister alone to the largest congregation in the English colonies, must confront the Devil in an astonishing witchcraft case in his own congregation, and must act as a leader in the revolution against the royal governor.

Here the biographer, while keeping his own judgment separate from that of his characters, must avoid condescending to their experience and must show how their interpretation of that experience was supported not only by their strange perspective but also by historical events. Cotton Mather's calculation that the Millennium—the end of Antichrist's reign and the beginning of Jesus Christ's thousand-year rule on earth—would begin in 1697 was strengthened by evidence in his father's first book, *The Mystery of Israel's Salvation,* published when the boy was only six years old. Twenty years later the father's mission in the royal court (1688–91) during the time of the Glorious Revolution against the Catholic king in England seems to be Providentially timed, and so too does Cotton Mather's own participation in the subsequent revolution in Massachusetts. At the same time devils and witches attack a Christian family in Boston, and three years later they attack Salem, almost at the moment when the new Protestant king of England has allowed Increase Mather to name as royal governor under the new Massachusetts charter a member of the Mathers' own congregation, whom Cotton Mather himself had baptized. All these historical events support whatever pathological and theological peculiarities have led Cotton Mather to a grandiose view of his historical destiny. His own vision of an angel, whose flattering predictions several years before these events now seem to have been proven accurate, encourages both his apocalyptic reading of contemporary events and his craving for more experiences of the supernatural world.

But the coincidence of the witchcraft trials and the new charter, which broke the monopoly of Congregationalist power in Massachusetts, makes it virtually impossible for Mather to maintain this exhilarating unity of his personal and spiritual life with the colony's progress toward the Millennium. Throughout the last decade of the century he manages to keep the effort going as he writes his grand history of New England, fights political enemies in Boston, and prays for the divinely promised overthrow of Louis XIV and for the second Reformation of Europe and England. At last, near the end of his fortieth year, the failure of two specific promises that have been repeatedly given to him in meditative visions shakes his faith in all such connections between the spiritual world and historical events, and completes the separation of his personal, psychic, and spiritual life from the political history of Massachusetts. The book ends soon after the death of Mather's first wife contradicts repeated promises, which he received in overwhelming visions, that she would be granted a miraculous recovery from consumption.

Now I would like to discuss a few of my efforts to solve specific problems of judgment.

Consider first the narrative of Cotton Mather's stammer, its onset, and its apparent cure. Increase Mather's first surviving allusion to any difficulty in his son's speech occurs in his diary in October 1674, some months after the boy, an eleven-year-old freshman at Harvard College, has been withdrawn from the college during a fierce but obscure controversy over hazing and student discipline. This conflict eventually closed the college for a time and forced the removal of the president, whom Increase Mather, a member of the Board of Overseers, had strongly supported. What I wish to show here is both the coincidence of emotional pressures and historical events in the child's life and the very strong support given him by his father and other exemplary males.

Judgment here consists in recognizing in the father and son, in an old schoolmaster named Elijah Corlet, and in the community's values qualities that might help to account for the complex result. Beginning with the anxiety that we so easily and justly perceive in Puritan nurture, I conclude with its strength. Two scenes that I found in the Mathers' own writing enabled me to represent the combination dramatically. In the first, Increase Mather summons his wife and their eleven-year-old son to pray with him in his study, at the end of a day that he has spent there in fasting and solitary prayer. The parents kneel and the father weeps as they bewail their sinfulness, plead for relief of the child's stammer, "solemnly" give him to God, and "beg the Lord to accept him" (32). All Boston and Cambridge know that this boy is meant to be the hope of his generation, and his own awareness of that burden increases the tension that his painful experience and the crisis at Harvard have already aggravated. Providence seems to be punishing the family, or at last warning them not to carry out the father's plan to educate his first son for the ministry. How could a stammering minister preach two sermons every Sunday and a third on every fourth Thursday? Surely, I argue, "the very ardor of parental support, the parental hope, the parental entreaty (like the boy's own eagerness to shine) . . . had a choking effect as Cotton strove to break free into speech" (32–33). Even his father remembered, several decades later, having been "much (more than I should have been) exercised in my spirit . . . lest" the stammer should block Cotton's entry into "the ministry, whereunto I had designed him" (33).

The second of these documented scenes occurs after Cotton's return to Harvard College, when he is struggling to control the stammer. He fears that it is God's way of "continually *binding*" him, and he lives in constant anxiety because "every business and every company" make him wonder "in pain, how to get through the speaking part" of the occasion (35). He begins to study a book by Hezekiah Woodward, an English preacher who had been a stammerer and had written a guide for the young. It is from this book and from other Puritan elders that Cotton Mather receives his Providential answer to the affliction: he must pray harder, study harder, and "mightily labor" for "a *prudent conduct*." "The key to his developing character," I insist, "is not only . . . the anxiety but the labor to make the most of it." He resolves to "'make the experiment' of seeing how far prayer might bring him . . . toward divine favor" (37). But he also resolves to use all the practical means available to him, and it is the visit of Elijah Corlet to Mather's room at Harvard that enables me to dramatize my judgment.

Corlet speaks abruptly. His only reason for the visit is to offer advice about the boy's infirmity, "because I suppose it is a thing that greatly troubles you." He tells the boy bluntly that he will always have to speak slowly, and warns him that if he tries to "snatch at words . . . you'll be stopped a thousand times in a day." Mather must develop "a very *deliberate* way of speaking; a *drawling*," Corlet says, "that shall be little short of *singing*." This habit of deliberation might give a stammerer time to find a pronounceable word whenever "you find a word likely to be too hard for you." The habit can gradually allow for an improvement in pace, but the Puritan schoolmaster will not give out false hope: "You must beware of speaking too fast as long as you live" (38).

My judgment gives great weight to this scene, which Mather described thirty-five years later, because it exemplifies both the kind of support that helped "young people to master the anxieties induced by their creed" and the habits of thought that Puritan nurture, at its best, encouraged. "The great emotional burden of young Mather's inheritance," I argue, "was alleviated if not balanced by the solicitous and resourceful example of several paternal figures." His father and several other ministers and teachers gave him "memorable experience of practical thought, shrewd psychology, arguments from experience, careful study of evidence, and strong encouragement to live with, while trying always to overcome, [his] limitations" (38–39). Notice that in the latter scene as Mather preserved it, and as I have re-created it, Elijah Corlet does more than propose a way of curing the stammer. He directs a reassuring question to the boy's own experience: "Did you ever know anyone stammer in singing of the Psalms?" He exemplifies his method by intoning some lines from Homer. He offers several shrewd arguments for the value of his method. And he supplements his practical advice with two prudent admonitions: "Make what you speak be worth waiting for, and remember that for the rest of your life you will have to beware of speaking too fast" (39).

In my version of it, then, this episode does not defend Mather against secular moralizing that had portrayed him in our century as an Infant Prodigy and a tattletale, a figure I once referred to as the Sid Sawyer or the Master Blifil of colonial New England. Instead my judgment removes the subject entirely from the jurisdiction of praise or blame.

It is in his so-called diary as well as in the rattling of Robert Calef's tin can that Cotton Mather's historical image was most severely damaged, and the tin can that Mather tied to himself in those pages is labeled PRIDE. The vanity of the man is the most difficult quality for our age to accept and to portray. It is "the ravings of an egomaniac" that Edmund Morgan finds nauseating. The second passage that I shall consider is one of several that characterize Mather's pride. Here, having set his protracted self-examination in a long Puritan tradition of meditation, I try to portray his awareness of his own subjectivity as a major part of his experience, even as I maintain the perspective of a modern observer privileged to see other kinds of explanation. Then I must assess his pride or vanity even as he compounds it in his very effort to subdue it. Here again it is his perplexity that moves me even as it amuses me. The epigraph to this chapter, which describes his conversion in his middle teens, is a line from his diary: "Proud thoughts flyblow my best performances" (57).

Whether or not we call him neurotic, we cannot measure the

intensity of Mather's private religious experience any better than his
contemporaries could measure it. We have no reason, besides the dubious generalization that piety was declining in his generation, to discount "the mixed feelings of anticipation and dread" with which he
says he came to his days of prayer and fasting (61). It seems likely that
the conventional nature of his very strong language—"glorious conflicts, horrors of mind, horrible amazements, agonies" (61)—gave him
some comfort in the implicit knowledge that others had shared such
experience. But I believe that the key to the genuineness of these experiences is in his self-awareness, his recognition of the repetitive pattern, his perception that the agonies "came over me without my calling
for them" and that a repetition which began with "inexpressible bitterness," a dread of suffering through the process once again, almost invariably ended in "a sweet satisfaction of mind." Even if we read
Mather's struggle as a repetitive quest for his father's approval, forgiveness, and reassurance, we must notice that Cotton Mather himself
eventually recognized what we might call the compulsive pattern:
"Thus I was (while an ignorant youth) strangely led on by the Spirit of
the most High, to go the whole work of conversion often over and over
again. And though at the beginning of a day set apart for such devotions, I should even tremble at the thoughts of the travail that I foresaw I should pass through, yet I comforted myself that my frequent
renewing of this action would be my assuring of it" (61).

But the genuineness of Mather's spiritual concern and his recognition of subjective patterns do not negate real biographical distinctions, not even in what I call the spiritual region of Mather's world.
Every saint might bewail his pride, but some saints, I contend, "had
more cause than others to find pride among the incurable corruptions
of their hearts" (61). Cotton Mather had always had "extraordinary
reason to feel that he must not bring shame upon either of his distinguished names, and he displayed throughout his life an extraordinary
sensitivity to public attacks upon them. The very vanity that Benjamin
Franklin later placed among the comforts of life was pushing Cotton
Mather to achieve prodigies which inflated his pride and cried out for
mortification" (62). He was the only Harvard graduate to preach his
first sermon at the age of sixteen, to preach with great success at
Grandfather John Cotton's First Church in Boston at eighteen, and to

be called as pastor of the New Haven church in the same year. His journal's repeated warnings against pride culminate in recognition of his perplexity and (once again) in his acknowledgement that the glory of divine mercy is worth the perpetual striving. He vows that he "will never give [the Lord] or my own soul rest, until my dearest lust become as bitter as death, as hateful as Hell to me" (62). Proud thoughts did flyblow some of his best performances. Nor did pride in his language, his learning, and his name ever become hateful to him. The best he could do, my judgment declares, was "to drive that pride in an unflagging parade of talent expended in the Lord's work" (62).

By the end of the book Mather's vanity has been so closely joined with grand events and aspirations that vanity (as well as egomania) becomes an inadequate word for what he strains to express. Pride and vanity are swallowed up in a merging of self with divine intentions to use the author's pride, vanity, and learning to extend divine glory. Mather seems at times to be standing aside and watching the instrument of his mind in operation. Whether or not such an attitude repels us, we cannot judge it fairly by merely damning it with a name drawn from anachronistic pathology.

III

The persistence of Mather's perplexity and blindness in the midst of fine acuity and grand assurances gives his life at times a note of hilarity, as when he literally wrestles with the Devil while trying to cure a possessed girl, but that combination also becomes awesome when an angel, who Mather plainly knows might be a diabolical delusion, appears in his study, and the mixture becomes downright pathetic when Mather conducts nightly vigils and brings on more and more explicit promises during his wife's mortal illness. I want to conclude with two brief episodes to illustrate varieties of tone and judgment in the narrative of those differing encounters with the supernatural. In both episodes literary explication becomes essential, for both depend on Mather's own writings as their chief authority. Both help to demonstrate why I find it appropriate to place the composition of Mather's *Magnalia Christi Americana,* his history of New England, in a climactic position in the narrative, and why I find one of that history's central themes, the representation of the saints' perplexity, a moving statement of his own situation.

Toward the end of his twenty-second year Mather has an ambiguous, overpowering vision which I decided to present from his own point of view, letting the angel appear in his study. Mather looks up from his prone position on the floor and sees a robed, winged angel with a clean-shaven, human face that shines brilliantly under a magnificent tiara. This splendid emissary tells the fasting youth of glorious prospects—books to be published in Europe as well as New England, leadership in the imminent revolutions that may overthrow tyrants— but he prefaces the entire prophecy with a quotation of Ezekiel (31: 3–9):

> Behold he was a cedar in Lebanon with fair branches, and with a shadowing shroud, and of a high stature, and his top was among the thick boughs. . . . His height was exalted above all the trees in the field. . . . Nor was any tree in the garden of God like unto him in his beauty. [107]

Mather, of course, was dazzled by this apparent promise that his most ambitious hopes would be fulfilled, but he ended his secret account of the vision with a prayer begging Jesus to defend him from the Devil's tricks. He knew that Satan could impersonate an angel of light, and his concluding prayer led me to study the context of Ezekiel's splendid image. There I found what Mather surely knew all along, that the angel had borrowed Ezekiel's description of Asshur, king of the Assyrians, an admonition that Ezekiel shows to Pharaoh to demonstrate the Lord's power (31:10–15):

> Therefore thus saith the Lord God, Because he is lift up on high, and hath shot up his top among the thick boughs, and his heart is lift up in his height, I have therefore delivered him into the hands of the mightiest among the heathen. [108]

It is only fair to conclude with witchcraft. Cotton Mather's role in the notorious Salem trials is too complex to be adequately represented here, but I can say that I find a similar perplexity, a similar mixture of qualities, even in Mather's behavior in the frenetic summer of 1692. Here I choose instead an episode three years earlier, a case of bewitchment in Boston. Once again the judgment requires us to imagine the reality of the supernatural world. In this Goodwin-Glover case, just before and then overlapping with the revolution to which I have so often referred, Mather advises that the four bewitched children be separated from one another, and he takes the eldest, a thirteen-year-old girl, into his house and eventually, after several months, cures her.

My comical judgment of this episode portrays Mather as a medical and spiritual healer trying to cure the afflicted child, even as he tries to study her symptoms, and the Devil's power, with the precision of an empirical scientist, and even as he fights in the Lord's war against the Devil. Mather asks skeptical questions about the afflicted children's behavior; he even takes pains to prevent collusion among them, and he perceives once or twice that his own vanity has been teased. But he becomes so deeply entangled in the conflict, and so passionately curious about the phenomena he is studying, that I feel compelled to stress what he saw and what he failed to see. When the devils afflict her, Martha "coughs up a ball as big as a small egg" and chokes on it until stroking and drinking bring it down again (153). She rushes toward the fireplace, and when Mather tells her to cry to the Lord for help her face is paralyzed, her jaws locked. When he tells her that she can at least look up to Heaven, her eyes are "pulled into her head, so far that one might have feared that she would never use them more" (153). More than once she seems to contrive to bring Mather into physical contact with her, most dramatically when the demons carry her about his house on an invisible horse which climbs the stairs but shies away from the door to Mather's study because (she tells him later) the demons cannot enter the room of a man of God. When Mather invites her into his study as a sanctuary, then, his very invitation provokes terrible fits: "it gave me much trouble to get her into my arms, and much more to drag her up the stairs. She was pulled out of my hands, and when I recovered my hold, she was thrust so hard upon me, that I had almost fallen backwards, by their compressions to detain her. . . . With incredible forcing (though she kept screaming, 'They say I must not go in!') at length we pulled her in; where she was no sooner come, but she could stand on her feet, and with an altered tone, could thank me, saying 'Now I am well'" (155–56).

Eventually Mather succeeds in curing Martha by prayer and

faith—and by kindness and forbearance, even when she throws things at him, hides his manuscripts, and warns him that the book he is writing about her will "quickly bring him to disgrace" (156). It is the uncanny blending of pathology, demonology, wish fulfillment, and therapy that gives the episode its human richness. Mather has the sense to give Martha an empty sheath when she demands a knife so that she can decapitate the invisible horse as she rides past Mather and the guests he has invited in to witness the spectacle. When Martha slashes at her own throat and protests that his "knife" doesn't cut (156), I still stand amazed at the mixture of shrewd prudence and credulity. When I notice that Mather asks her about the invisible human beings who "ride" with her and torment her, I must also report that he never revealed the names of the three people she identified.

I remain convinced that we cannot reach a fair judgment of Mather's role in the witchcraft cases until we recognize his personal experience of the supernatural, his historical convictions about the imminence of the Millennium in Massachusetts, and both his humane pleas for defendants' rights and his fierce detestation of witchcraft. But I have learned a degree of resignation in the face of the effigy. In a letter dated March 11, 1983, and signed by Senator Bob Packwood, I received an excerpt from the *Congressional Record* in which the brave senator tries to make Margaret Heckler, President Reagan's nominee as secretary for health and human services, confess that she would support a proposed statute limiting the Supreme Court's power to rule on cases involving abortion. After several pages of dogged but futile pursuit of his evasive witness, the senator blames the campaign to limit the Supreme Court's powers on "a fury of contemporary Cotton Mathers who want to reverse a decision they do not like." [12] Now I know that Mather scrupulously abstained from commenting on the powers of the Supreme Court and Congress; and I don't believe that he ever committed himself on what Senator Packwood calls pro-choice. But I will probably not write a letter to set the *Congressional Record* straight. I will just have to hope that serious students of history and biography attend to another kind of record. I have deliberately avoided here the passages and incidents that show Mather's most enlightened conduct, so that I could show how I have expressed my judgment of some of his less winning traits. In the man as I have sketched him here we have reason to celebrate the extraordinary combination of weaknesses and strengths and at least some of the ways in which history, politics, religion, and psychology merge to make his experience thoroughly human.

Notes

1. *Boston Globe,* Feb. 3, 1979, p. 18.

2. *Washington Post,* Sept. 10, 1978, pp. D1, D5.

3. Editorial, *New York Times,* Oct. 12, 1975, p. 4:12.

4. Renata Adler, response to a letter in *New York Review of Books,* Feb. 23, 1978, p. 45.

5. Robert Lowell, "The New England Spirit," *New York Times Book Review,* Oct. 16, 1977, p. 7:34.

6. Samuel Eliot Morison, *Harvard College in the Seventeenth Century,* 2 vols. (Cambridge: Harvard Univ. Press, 1936), 1:82–83.

7. Michael Kammen, *New Republic,* Nov. 4, 1978, p. 50.

8. *Charlottesville Daily Progress,* Oct. 8, 1978; *Palo Alto Times,* Nov. 4, 1978.

9. Edmund S. Morgan, "The Puritan You Love to Hate," *New York Review of Books,* Jan. 25, 1979, p. 32.

10. David D. Hall, review of *Cotton Mather,* in *William and Mary Quarterly,* 3d ser., 38 (1980):154–55.

11. David Levin, *Cotton Mather: The Young Life of the Lord's Remembrancer, 1663–1703* (Cambridge: Harvard Univ. Press, 1978), p. 14.

12. *Senator Bob Packwood's Pro-Choice Report,* March 11, 1983, [p. 4], transcribed from *Congressional Record* 129 (March 3, 1983).

9.

Cotton Mather's Misnamed Diary
Reserved Memorials of a Representative Christian

Among autobiographical works by seventeenth- and eighteenth-century Puritans, two overlapping manuscripts by Cotton Mather which were not published until the twentieth century hold a central place. *Paterna,* copied largely from Mather's "Reserved Memorials," puts a very thin narrative frame on an anonymous father's record of personal religious experience for his son. And the much more widely read "Reserved Memorials," usually referred to as Mather's diary, express the pious hopes, exercises, and literary and pastoral activities of a Christian who tries for more than forty years to bring his behavior into conformity with the will of God as events in his own life reveal that divine will to him. Close attention to some representative passages from different sections of the "Reserved Memorials," ranging from the 1680s to the 1720s, should demonstrate both the cost of misreading the work as a mere diary and the value of noticing the narrator's retrospective emphasis.

I

Although most allusions treat the work as if it were a daily record like *The Diary of Samuel Sewall,* the two fat volumes published in 1911–12 as *The Diary of Cotton Mather* have long been known to be not strictly a diary at all.[1] In the first few years, Mather refers more than once to having "at this Time . . . kept a *Diary* of my daily *Actions,*" and he

Reprinted by permission from *American Literary History* 2 (1990): 183–202, © 1989 Oxford University Press, Inc.

says that "I will here transcribe only the Actions of one Day, namely the first occurring in that part of the Diaries then written by me." Here, in terse Latin, he quotes the diary for August 28, 1683, in order to "exemplify the Watch which the Lord in those Dayes helped me to keep over my *Walk*."[2] Having quoted that example from his diary, he concludes the entry in "Reserved Memorials" by announcing that he has burned the diaries (1:72). Some time "afterward," he says, he stopped recording such tedious details—or perhaps he stopped recording his efforts to dedicate each of these actions explicitly to God. In the margin of the surviving memorial, he concedes that he doesn't want it "thought that I have *every Day* been so watchful; however the *Free-grace* of God helped me not a Few" (1:72–73). Twenty-six years later, in April 1709, he refers casually again to a daily record; under the date of April 1 he says that "little remarkable" occurred as this month "has rolled away," and he seems to refer prospective readers to "my Book of daily Memorials" to find hints of his "Special Services, attempted or purposed" (2:5).

Even the few lines that I have quoted indicate, moreover, that under a specific date in Mather's "Reserved Memorials" the retrospective range includes much more than twenty-four hours. Such phrases as "at this time" and "in those days" abound, especially in the first volume of the published work (1:41, 51, 56, 114, 118, 128, 134, 136). One entry, postdated October 30, 1681, says that "In the Month of November," the church at New Haven, Connecticut, invited Mather to serve as pastor. After reporting that he declined the call, Mather expresses the pride that he felt on receiving such an offer at the age of eighteen, and he transcribes the thoughts that "I yet wrote" to quell that pride (1:42–43).

Beginning in 1710, Mather follows a new practice that seems to make the entries much more like a traditional diary. He lists a "Good Devised" (G.D.) for each day of the week, and he often restricts the entry to statements of the proposed benevolent action. Especially in 1717, for example, some of these entries (2:484–90) read as if one item had been entered each day. Yet many other Goods Devised were written at intervals of at least a week. Mather still records extensive observations concerning Saturday fasts and days of thanksgiving, and internal evidence (as on 2:445–46, in March 1717; and on November 12, 1712)[3] makes the postdating unmistakable. In 1719, moreover, Mather writes that he has been obliged to hide some of the memorials because his wife has destroyed some others. Here again his account ranges back over a year as he tries to contrive a way of protecting his children from what he calls "a furious and froward Stepmother" (2:583–86, 590–91). And when he returns to listing the next Good Devised, he clearly implies a concern for prospective readers, with this brief paragraph (586): "I will now go on."

Large sections of these "Memorials" thus consist of selected revisions or transcripts of diaries that no longer exist. And specifically dated entries often range over weeks and months, rather than report on the events of a single day. In the middle of one of the most intense crises of Mather's life, when his first wife seems obviously to be dying of consumption but he keeps receiving divine assurances of her recovery, an extraordinarily passionate entry dated August 30, 1702, is short-circuited by an abrupt reminder that the narrator is writing weeks or months after the event: "Little recordeable occurr'd unto me, in the next Month; only in several *Vigils* from Time to Time, I enjoy'd some intimate Communions with Heaven" (1:441). The retrospective range rarely exceeds a year, for Mather consistently begins a new year on February 12, the anniversary of his birth.

Perhaps the most interesting of these anachronistic entries for modern readers is dated Saturday evening, May 14, 1692. Mather records the long-awaited arrival from London of his father and Sir William Phips, the new royal governor, in the midst of the Salem witchcraft crisis and then proceeds to comment on events not only of the next day but of the entire year 1692. When he writes (still under May 14—1:150) that "The Rest of the Summer was a very doleful Time, unto the whole Country," he obviously comments from a perspective that is almost surely as late as December, several months after the last execution (1:148–54).

Although he is not anonymous here, as he claims to be in *Paterna*, the autobiographical work that he culled from these "Memorials" in the eighteenth century for his sons, Mather creates in these early years a persona, a representative figure who offers selective meditations, prayers, and pious devices to instruct "my little Folks, for whom these Papers are intended" (1:41). The eighteen-year-old's little folks, five years before his marriage, are his younger brothers and sisters.

What difference should these distinctions make to a reading of *The Diary of Cotton Mather?* For the early years, at least, they confirm and intensify our awareness of this man's inexhaustible, repetitive scribbling. Mixing his own ink, fashioning his own pens, he reviewed his original records, copied out large sections in his "Reserved Memorials," and then, when he began to write *Paterna* in early middle age for his son, copied almost all of that exemplary and anonymous autobiography from the "Reserved Memorials," editing and condensing the prose as he went along.[4] Whether afflicted with egomania or merely determined (as he said every minister should be) to spin moral instruction out of the bowels of his own experience, this man of the word reedits versions of his life at different stages. Year by year, especially on his birthday, and in many of the individual retrospective entries, he writes as if acutely aware that this incident or observation is part of a larger narrative.

Both internal evidence and textual comparisons show that Mather selected and shaped these passages for his new purposes. Of course, the surviving texts do tell us much about the attitudes and preoccupations of Cotton Mather, but because his personal peculiarities make such a strong impression we need to recognize explicitly that the so-called diary does not record the whole range of his daily activities or thoughts. In the early and middle years, weeks regularly intervene between one entry and the next, and one can even see a pattern: a series of entries on Saturdays, set aside for prayer and fasting or thanksgiving, varied by entries recording church services and private spiritual activities on Sundays or Lord's Days (1:6–18, 87–91, 196–203, 409, 434; compare 2:2–5 [1709], 266, 275 [1713]). For many of the private fast days, sometimes at intervals of several weeks, Mather describes his actions and transcribes his favorite meditations and prayers. If we think of these entries as though they constituted his original diary, we may overlook the pattern; we may neglect to infer that much more varied days and nights intervened.

By noticing the selectivity of Mather's "Reserved Memorials," we also lessen the risk of misunderstanding and misjudging his self-consciousness. Abundant evidence does reveal discrepancies between motives professed by this persona and motives that seem unmistakable to us—most obviously when Mather seems caught between his pride in some achievement or blessing and his obligation to protest its bestowal on "poor, vile sinful *me*" (1:234). But the mind that chooses such conventional language acknowledges its paradoxical duty to be both proud and humble, both submissive and assertive:

> And while I was, with much Amazement of Soul, considering the incureable Corruptions of my Heart, that as it were, defy'd all the Means of Mortification, yea, and even my best Endeavours to put my Heart into the Hands of the Lord Jesus Christ for cure, I yet wrote the following Thoughts.
>
> "I think, *first,* the Lord will not utterly destroy me. He has wrought those Works in me, that, I hope, He will never disown or forsake. If He *do,* I shall be the direfullest example of a deluded and an exalted Hypocrite, that ever was! *Lord, let my Soul tremble!*
>
> "But, *Secondly,* the Lord will bring my Soul down into the Dust, and under all Enlargements and Attainments, cause me to abhor myself. If ever I am lift up with Pride, I shall be, (*Lord, I here own it under my Hand!*) a most *unreasonable Wretch.* I must walk softly and sorrowfully as long as I breathe on Earth. Shame is to be my Garment, *Grief* my meat, *Tears* my Drink, and Sighs my Language, as long as I am related unto this *vile Body!*
>
> "And, *thirdly, Strength against Sin,* is a Mercy so glorious, that the Lord will have me stir up myself and *wrestle* and *struggle* to purpose, before I shall attain it. Wherefore, *Lord,* I here make my *Vow,* that *I will never give Thee, or my own Soul rest, until my dearest Lust, become as bitter as Death, as hateful as Hell unto me.*" [1:42–43; cf. 80–81]

By placing the narrator or memorialist at a distance, Mather also makes his persona self-aware in a way that may help prospective readers dare to risk the intense self-examination of fast days. In the "Reserved Memorials" he clearly implies the same double consciousness that he would describe explicitly when he transcribed some of these passages once again for *Paterna.* There he would need no modern interpreter to find the pattern of self-accusation, self-abasement, and exhilarating pardon in his private rituals. He himself would notice in retrospect that in his days of humiliation "I was (while an ignorant youth) strangely led on by the *Spirit* of the most High, to go the whole *work of conversion* often over and over again. And though at the beginning of a day set apart for such devotions, I should even tremble in the thoughts of the *travail* that I foresaw, I should pass through, yet I comforted myself, that my frequent *renewing* of this action, would be my assuring of it."⁵

As those paragraphs represent Mather's spiritual persona at its best, so one other brief anecdote may help us to reconsider the presentation of self near the supposed diarist's rhetorical worst. If we remember that Mather deliberately placed some distance between the daily record and the representative or exemplary persona, we may resist what might otherwise seem an irresistible provocation to judge him severely. Consider this anecdote taken from the first entry, on his forty-sixth birthday, in 1709:

> About this Time, a small Accident befel me which look'd like a very particular Answer of Prayer.
>
> Tho' I am furnished with a very great Library yet seeing a Library of a late Minister in the Town to be sold, and a certain Collection of Books there, which had it may be above six hundred single Sermons in them; I could not forbear wishing myself made able to compass such a Treasure. I could not forbear mentioning my Wishes in my Prayers before the Lord; that in case it might be a Service to His Interests, or to me in serving His Interests, He would enable me in His good Providence, to purchase the Treasure now before me. But I left the Matter before Him, with the profoundest Resignation willing to be without every Thing that He should not order for me. Behold, a Gentleman, who a year ago treated me very ill; but I cheerfully forgave him! carried me home to dine with him; and upon an accidental Mention of the Library aforesaid, he, to my Surprize, compelled me to accept of him a Summ of Money, which enabled me to come at what I had been desirous of. [2:2]

If we treat this conventionally exemplary anecdote as simply a page from Mather's diary, the little nudges that immediately strike us as self-serving—the careful wording of the prayer to conform with submission to God's will, the "profoundest" resignation, the "cheerful" forgiveness of the gentleman's ill treatment, the "accidental" mention of the library—will surely seem much more offensive than if we separate the anecdote from Mather's daily self and recognize the "small Accident" and the narrator's deliberate projection of an idealized self who unconsciously becomes worthy of the Providential gift. The readers for whom Mather wrote may well have been prepared to accept that projection with a readiness that modern skeptics, ironically provoked to judge the sincerity of a seventeenth-century believer's faith and repentance, cannot recover without a strenuous exercise of historical imagination.

The same kind of variation in judgment will be even more emphatically necessary if we reconsider the longer entry dated March 4, 1709. Here the retrospective narrator complains that "About this Time" he was so poor that "I had not Cloathes fit to be worn; I was *cloathed with Rags.*" His elaborate meditation brings him to acknowledge his true wealth and then brings him "not only to Submission but even to Cheerfulness, under my Humiliations" (2:4). With help from the discipline of meditation and from the distance of retrospective calm, Mather's little narrative can take his persona beyond resignation to the very condition he remembered that his father had exemplified long ago. As a child, Cotton Mather confessed, he had been perplexed by his father's expression of joy and pride when Cotton had been beaten by some "play-mates" whom he had "Rebuked . . . for their Wicked *words* and *wayes.*"[6] By the time he wrote the entry about his financial "Wants and Straits," he had long since attained a better understanding of his father's "Heavenly principle." Just as we know that Increase Mather was actually furious when young Cotton was hazed at Harvard, so we may doubt Cotton Mather's cheerfulness when he actually had to face once again the "Negligence" of the church members who (according to his hyperbole) kept his family in rags. But the triumph achieved in his meditation, and its function in his "Reserved Memorials," may be more understandable—we may resist the temptation to hunt for our own triumph in the exposure of his insincerity—if we consider the passage as a conventional meditation written some time after March 4, 1709, as part of a larger set of memoirs that could allow selected entries dated February 12 and March 1 to include narratives beginning "About this time."

II

Somewhere between diary and autobiography, Mather's "Reserved Memorials" may properly be said to form a narrative of key incidents at different stages in a unique but representative Christian's spiritual life, with special emphasis on his prayers and his writing. The narrator's chronological distance from the dated entries varies from less than one day to the better part of a year and perhaps even longer—if the retrospective memorial dated 1692, for example, was written a year or two later, as the account dated 1693 probably was.[7] Looking back over the year just ended, he usually exercises his most extensive autobiographical control on the entries dated February 12. But in entries describing particular incidents, too, he strives early and late to cast his narrative in spiritual terms. It is this very effort that creates not only the rhetorical and moral discrepancies to which I have already referred, but also a dramatic tension powerful enough at times to send surges of immediate feeling pulsating through the retrospective, abstract exempla.

Mather the Christian and his persona in the "Reserved Memorials" aspire to perfect obedience to God's will, total dedication to God's purposes, perfect love of Christ, resolute imitation of Christ (1:344–45), and exemplary resignation. As late as 1714, when he is fifty-one years old, he lists as one of the few specific sins to which he is drawn his "horrible Temptations to the *Paulician* Heresy"—by which he presumably means an excessive effort to model his own life on that of Jesus or to think of Jesus as inspiring him directly (2:282).

Other people as well as Mather himself therefore appear here as abstractions. The "gentleman" who mistreated him and yet bought him the coveted sermons; "a very religious young Minister" (1:427); "a Kinsman, the Son of my Sister, at *Roxbury*" (2:268); "a poor Woman" in Mather's congregation who is afflicted with cancer (2:274); "a new Brother-in-Law" acquired through the "Marriage of a Sister" (2:274)—these are only a few of the people who appear anonymously. Not only father and mother but wife ("my dear Consort" [1:430]), sisters, brothers, and children ("my only and lovely Son," [1:336]) often appear without names.

As Daniel Shea noted long ago, Puritan autobiographies tend to become allegorical, and much of their dramatic quality derives from the tension between unique historical incidents and their allegorical or spiritual significance (90ff.). In Mather's memorials of an imitative life, that tension sometimes increases because of the conflict between his retrospective position and the immediate feelings and facts. Sometimes his passionate feeling about an incident or issue gives an abstract or representative character a unique particular significance in the narrative. Sometimes the retrospective entry arouses in the narrator a passion much more earthbound than the longings and remorse of the pious, representative persona. Sometimes the retrospective narrative contains the tension between the representative Christian's own will and his quest for resignation. And the accumulation of historical phenomena over the years creates a larger narrative that celebrates variety within uniformity.

To illustrate the value of reading Mather's "Reserved Memorials" in this way, I would like to consider four examples of passages we can understand better for having considered them as deliberate, retrospective parts of a longer narrative, the life of a representative Christian writer who is always alert for remarkable anecdotes of God's Providence.

In the spring of 1702, several weeks before his wife's terminal illness begins, the narrator records two exemplary incidents that fill him with delight. On April 16 he receives "a short Letter from an holy Servant of Christ," thanking Mather for *Maschil, or the Faithful Instructor,* a catechism Mather published in 1701. Both the letter and Mather's comment emphasize exemplary piety that deflects attention from the self to "the Lord JESUS CHRIST"; the letter writer feels a new sense of Christ's "Excellency" for having "by His Holy Spirit so fill[ed] one of His Admirers, that he [Mather] is Enabled to fill a Book with such excellent Things!" Mather's delight responds to the exemplary language: "That holy ones, whose Hearts are set upon glorifying of the Lord Jesus Christ, should by any Thing of *Him* in me, be led unto the Contemplation of His Glories! This, this is the highest Pitch of my Felicity; I aspire to nothing higher than this, throughout eternal Ages. Now my good God has begun to grant me this Felicity; I despise the Diadems of Emperours, in Comparison of it. I am happy, I am happy. *Lord,* I am swallowed up with the Extasies of thy Love!" We need not question the genuineness of Mather's emphasis on God's generosity in granting him this felicity when we notice that here one of the narrator's most enraptured moments in all the "Reserved Memorials" expresses his reaction to a note in praise of his writing (1:426).

Even as we notice the intensity of this moment and the expression of Mather's personality here, we err if we assume that the passage was written on April 16. Presumably the narrator is not still swallowed up in ecstasies when he writes the next line: "About this Time, I considered, that there are in the Skirts of our Colonies, divers Plantations, that live destitute of any evangelical Ministry. Wherefore I drew up as Pungent an Address as I could." The entire entry, then, moves from the testimonial by "an holy Servant of Christ" who has already learned from Mather, to Mather's own composition of a letter for "ungospelized, and paganizing Plantations" (1:426). The passion and the personality do come through; the spiritualized narration has captured the ecstasy that Cotton Mather feels when his writing elicits praise. The narration is nonetheless intricate, retrospective, and controlled. If our approach is primarily psychological, we may say that the narrator gets control of his ecstasy by shifting attention to his care for the ungospelized. Even so, the chronology of composition obliges us to notice that the shape of the entire passage implies Mather's intention to use both letters from the moment he wrote the first line. Like the quoted passage from the first letter, the date of its arrival is specific: "16 d[ay]. 2 m[onth]. This Day, I received a short Letter"; like the generalized comments about Mather's own letter to the ungospelized, the timing of that second, balancing letter is generalized, and its vague date ("About this Time") follows immediately after the exclamation of delight in ecstasies.

Dozens of brief, exemplary anecdotes of this elegant sort are sprinkled through the "Reserved Memorials." On first reading them, of course, we are likely to notice their sameness, Mather's narrative economy in moving toward the exemplary meaning. Within that narrow compass, however, we can see a celebration of variety.

Only one entry separates my first example from my second, which describes an exemplary incident that Mather says occurred three weeks later, presumably in the evening, after one of his Saturday fasts. This time the central figure is "a very young Minister (and one doubtless of much more Grace than myself)" who says he is "fully convinced" that he is *to this Day an unconverted and unregenerate Creature.*" Mather casts this narrative as a dialogue, and he introduces it with a conventional declaration: "if one so much better than I hath such Thoughts of *his*" spiritual condition, Mather had better study his own. But he finds that "setting myself to comfort" the distressed colleague brings "a wonderful Comfort . . . unto my own Soul."

Mather does not note here, if he indeed remembers, that the dialogue reenacts an argument his father had offered him two decades earlier, in response to similar doubts.[8] Here he simply casts himself as the resourceful, Socratic counselor. He asks the minister to identify an object on the shelf of Mather's study (Answer: *"A Repeating Clock, and a very Curious One."*) and then asks, "What use do you think I will put it to?" When he has elicited the desired reply, he asks how the minister knows Mather will not use the clock as a stool or as a backlog for the fire. Again the desired answer—"workmanship"—advances the argument, and Mather delivers an intricate little homily that plays on workmanship, work, use, and fire:

> Well then: Have not you upon your Soul a divine Workmanship, far more excellent than the most curious *Clock-Work* in the World? A Work of *Grace,* is a Work of *God;* even of Him, who *does nothing in Vain.* You find in yourself a Disposition, a strong Disposition and Inclination to glorify God, and serve the Interests of the Lord Jesus Christ, and slay all Sin as being most contrary unto Him. This is a Work of *Grace.* You know no delight comparable to that of Serving the Lord Jesus Christ. God has *wrought* this in you; and herein He has *wrought you, for that selfsame Thing,* of being to the *Praise of His Glory* forever. What use can you think He will now put you to, but that [of] serving the Lord Jesus Christ, in His heavenly World? Such a peece of *Workmanship (created unto good Works)* as what is wrought in you, was never intended to be thrown into the *Fire of Hell.* No, there is no use of it there. God intends you for an heavenly Use, undoubtedly.

From Mather the vain diarist of our scholarly folklore, one might expect a self-comforting report that his dialogue brought new assurance to the young minister. In this entry, however, Mather the retrospective narrator completes the frame by returning to the dialogue's spiritual effect on himself. Here, for once, he will not celebrate the conquest or service that Providence has allowed him to do for someone else. The anecdote stands in virtual apposition to my first example, for Mather concludes the entry for May 9 with a one-sentence paragraph that gains resonance when we remember that this Saturday's fast, though "not without some Irradiations from Heaven," had been "poorly attended" by divine responses. Mather concludes that his dialogue with the troubled minister "gave to *me,* an inexpressible Consolation, whatever it gave to him to whom I directed it" (1:427–29).

Among all the passages that concentrate on himself, as well as in the contrast to his anecdote about the gentleman who has praised Mather's *Maschil,* this story of the young minister reverberates as singular. Of course the baroque intonations of *work* and his mastery of the situation do celebrate himself. But in the abrupt turn that shows how Providence, having withheld the coveted irradiations that Mather expects from Heaven on his days of fasting, brought him wonderful comfort after all, I see a fine example of the narrator's skillful effort to show the richness of Providential variety within a narrow range.

The issues in Mather's battle with Samuel May, in 1699 and 1700, combine with historical circumstances to make my third example stand for a number of political or professional crises in which the narrator's personal reaction threatens to overpower, but remains subsumed by, his representative or exemplary piety. By 1699 the "grievous decade" described in Mather's ecclesiastical history of New England had ended, but the Millennium, which Mather had confidently expected to begin in 1697, had obviously not begun. As the century ends in his "Reserved Memorials," a crisis threatens the narrative of Mather's development as a Christian writer seizing and recording every opportunity to glorify God with his talent. The persona who has repeatedly marveled at Providential uses of his literary skill must now report objections against his meddlesome efforts to do good, and even (in 1700) that "people were now prejudiced against mee for printing so many Books"! At least one Christian even advises him to publish no more (1:340).

In these two years, then, the alternation between joy and gloom—one of the chief patterns in Mather's and other Puritans' spiritual records—becomes most intense. Before he encounters Samuel May, Mather has begun to experience Particular Faiths, explicit divine promises that certain blessings will be granted him: a very sick daughter will survive convulsions; the infant named Increase in honor of Cotton Mather's father will survive to glorify and serve Jesus forever (1:305, 307); in separate Particular Faiths both the father and the grandfather receive assurances that Grandfather Increase will be sent to London on an important mission for Harvard College (353). Cotton Mather receives heavenly assurances "that *France* will quickly undergo a wonderful Revolution" (301), and he publishes works that promise to have some effect (with millennial significance) across the world—a catechism designed to convert Jews, a "compleat system of the Christian religion" in Spanish, a letter of advice to English dissenters proving that they represent the true Church of England (312). Yet political, religious, and personal disappointments that have been accumulating and brewing ever since the Salem witchcraft trials and the new charter of 1692 boil onto these pages with extraordinary force.

Mather manages to adhere to his usual anonymity in describing the misguided antagonists who (in his version) break their word and violate first principles by calling to the pulpit of their new congregation (the Brattle Street Church) a man who has already been ordained in England and whom they therefore see no need to ordain in the usual Congregational way (326). Another antagonist, too, a young minister, remains anonymous when our narrator expresses ingenuous astonishment; Mather cannot understand why the young man should vehemently resist Mather's benevolent efforts to reverse the decline of Boston's very first church by recruiting an older minister to become the young man's senior colleague (316–17)! The name of Samuel May, however, a Baptist interloper, Mather cannot omit from the record.

Here again Mather represents himself as having striven to save a neighboring church—this time a congregation of Baptists—from the worst consequences of its own imprudence. His role as the exemplary Christian citizen gains dramatic force from his plaintive reminder that he has treated the Baptists with more tenderness and civility "than all the Ministers in New England" have shown them (318). At first, under the date of August 19, 1699, but writing several weeks or months later, Mather represents "that pernicious Incendiary S. May" as "a wondrous Lump of Ignorance and Arrogance" who has come to Boston from England "and sett up for a public Preacher" (313)—one of "several Wretches" who have "arrived among us" claiming extraordinary zeal.

"But the flaming Eyes of the Lord Jesus Christ" quickly expose "those hypocritical Intruders . . . by Detecting some scandalous *Plagiarism* in their Sermons." Our exemplary narrator attends one of May's sermons at a private meeting, prays secretly for the exposure of May's "Cheats," and finds his prayer quickly answered by a remarkable providence: On hearing Cotton Mather's summary of May's sermon, Increase Mather finds the original in a book of sermons (by Samuel Bolton) that he has "newly" bought (315). Although the people in Mather's neighborhood "admire the Providence" that has exposed May's fraud so promptly, "the hardened Wretch" denies that he has ever seen Bolton's book and insists that the sermon is entirely his own work (315–16).

May's role in the intricate narrative gives the exemplary narrator his best chance to win a specific victory in a season of perplexing defeats. Interspersed with typical days of fasting or thanksgiving, and with more generalized accounts of the controversies in the summers of 1699 and 1700, Mather's entries about this impostor portray himself as a forthright, indefatigable prophet. Mather's tenderness and civility toward the Baptists do not require him to withdraw from the controversy once he has informed them of May's plagiarism. He asks them for a private meeting so that he might "convict the New-*Holder-forth*" of "repeated *Lying* against his Conscience," but they astonish Mather by declaring that they intend to take no notice of his charges. One Baptist tells Mather that "the *Church of England* Men" are hatching a private plot against him, whereupon our narrator can represent himself in the language of Jeremiah (l. 18)—and with the defiant gusto of the biblical Sampson—against both Baptists and Anglicans: "*Go to the Church of England Men,*" Mather replies, "*tell them from mee, that as for them, God has made mee a defenced City, an iron Pillar, and a brasen wall; and lett 'em fight never so cunningly against mee, they shall never prevail to do mee any Harm. Go tell 'em also, that tho' I am every way little, yett I hope, thro' the Help of Christ, I may live, to do for them the same Kindness, that* Sampson *did for their* Philistian *Brethren, and pull down their Temples about their Ears*" (318).

By December 7, more than two months after his report of his defiant response to the Baptists, Mather can report further mistreatment by them, and further vindication as well. The exemplary narrator has continued to speak truth to the face of falsehood, telling May himself that *"the glorious Lord Jesus Christ will certainly and speedily detect you,"* but (with God's help in resisting the temptation to respond vengefully to the Baptists who "ly and rail, and rage against mee, on all Occasions") has remained patient and cheerful. His prayers are answered once again when Samuel May, "having chous'd the foolish People of a great Summ of Money," goes off to England "with a Stink!" (324)

Even after May's malodorous departure, Mather's narrative adds new Providential disclosures and seals the exemplary meaning of the story of "this detected Wolf." When "several sober, modest, and virtuous Women" swear in court that May "often" made lewd advances to them, Mather's warning to the Baptists that their impious rejection of his evidence would be "chastised by this very man's proving thro' the Vengeance of God, a blemish and a Ruine unto them" seems to be "now most remarkably coming to pass" (324). In the narrative, still under December 7, 1699, Mather solemnizes the Providential occasion by composing a sermon on Job 13:9, warning his great congregation *"that the Great God, who will not be mocked, will thoroughly discern, and terribly detect, those that go to mock Him."* The exemplary narrator does not neglect, in this moment of triumph, to set apart the Saturday before his sermon as a day of fasting "for secret Humiliations and Supplications" to avoid guilt for his "own former Iniquities" as "a *Mocker of God*" (325).

At this moment Mather brings into the narrative his most extensive discussion of the "Apostasy" represented by the Brattle Street Church. Preparing for his sermon on the Baptists' scandal was not, he says, the only reason for his secret fast "on the *Satureday* mentioned." He had also to pray for the "Courage, Patience, and Prudence" he would need to help defeat "the designs that Satan may have in the Enterprise" of the new church (325–26). Mather thus ties together his victory over the Baptists and his unresolved but probably unpromising combat against the renegade Congregationalists.

But Samuel May has not yet completed his usefulness in Mather's narrative. One of the few affirmative signs recorded about the ensuing winter is the publication of Mather's *A Warning to the Flocks,* his history of nine separate wolves in sheeps' clothing (329), and May suddenly appears again in a retrospective "Memorandum" dated May 11, 1700. Here Mather prepares for the denouement by noting that he "patiently committed the matter unto the Lord" and prayed for some new evidence that might confound "my Adversaries." Then, following a day of private thanksgiving dated May 28, in which "nothing remarkable occurr'd," another memorandum reports the ultimate discovery about "that vile Impostor." Letters from England in answer to Mather's own inquiry prove that Samuel May had forged a letter of recommendation from an English minister, that May was actually a brickmaker named Sam Axel, and that "after detection in Immoralities," Axel had deserted his wife and children in England and had brought with him to Boston "a whore . . . under the name of a Wife!" (350–51)

This conclusion to Mather's narrative of Axel/May not only justifies the unusual emphasis on an antagonist's name (during a year in which Mather's anxiety about his own family's good name has become acute); a very brief paragraph at the end of the last memorandum offers us a key to understanding great portions of Mather's "Reserved Memorials." The statement is so obviously conventional, and the adjective *marvellous* is so often repeated in these memorials, that we may easily make the mistake of dismissing it as merely perfunctory. "In receiving this Letter," Mather writes, "I received a marvellous Answer of Prayer. The Arrival of it, was highly seasonable, and serviceable" (351–52). Serviceable answers to prayer: there is the key.

My last example of Mather's narrative language will make the importance of prayer in these memorials especially clear, but we have already considered enough variations to put that final example in a perspective valuable for almost all the "Reserved Memorials." These memoirs record the private spiritual experience of a Christian who has resolved to celebrate and advance God's glory in the world. A very heavy proportion of all the entries concentrates on the spiritual exercises of days of fasting (especially Saturdays) or thanksgiving. Much of the external life of Boston and Christendom that enters these pages appears here as the occasion for those days of prayer. The repetition of marvelous responses to prayer should seem less tedious if we imagine ourselves within the system of belief rather than outside it. The accumulation of a great number of divine responses to prayer in one representative life may serve to extend God's glory by showing both the memorialist and prospective readers the variety and the meticulous care of Providence.

Nor should we underestimate the significance of those few entries that say "nothing remarkable" occurred on a particular day of fasting or in weeks intervening between dated entries. The days of prayer that get the most attention in Mather's "Reserved Memorials" are those in which something remarkable does occur—some methods of meditation or prayer that bring a new conviction of divine favor, a sign of divine reassurance, an "afflatus" or a marvelous answer. These phenomena range all the way from an extended prophecy, delivered by a shining angel, to the discovery of extraordinary relevance in the first passage the narrator's eyes light on when he opens the Bible at random.

In such "remarkables" or wonders, then, lies the same significance that anyone can see in the dozens of biographies in Mather's ecclesiastical history of New England: variety within uniformity. As almost all Mather's lives of the New England saints move from sin to justification to striving and suffering for the glory of God, yet with variations that demonstrate the range and intensity of that glory, so the succession of varying marvels in the "Reserved Memorials" constitutes a narrative of similar splendor. Sometimes, we must notice, the narrator acknowledges that his task is overwhelming even to a pen as indefatigable as his own: "My Life is almost a continual Conversation with Heaven," he writes during a crisis in 1713, "and more particularly, in my Attendence on the divine Institutions, my Intentions of Piety, and my Applications to Heaven, are so many and so various—it becomes impossible for me to keep Records of thousands of them" (2:267). Yet the accumulation of varied examples does form an impressive, if sometimes tediously predictable, narrative.

In that anachronistic critical term *predictable* lies one final admonition for the secular reader of "Reserved Memorials." We must try to imagine what an afflatus or a marvelous answer to prayer would do to us if we experienced it. In a sense the deep religious experience that Cotton Mather sought—"the inexpressible Irradiation from Heaven" (1:440)—is hostile to narrative, and not only because none but those who have the experience can comprehend it. Narrative wants variety, suspense, change, temporal sequence. Occasionally Mather can communicate a sense of the transcendent moment, as when he writes of a nocturnal vigil that he kept during his first wife's mortal illness, "If these be *Vigils,* I must (as far as the *sixth* Commandment will allow) have some more of them!" (1:422) But when he enters those moments themselves, the "irradiation" or the marvelous answer to prayer takes him into a realm outside narrative time. The hunger for more of these experiences stands opposed to variety or sequence except as a means to reproduce the transcendent condition. The marvel in the marvelous answer will usually seem perfunctory to us, unless we remember that the condition of "intimate Communions with Heaven" (1:441) is a state of bliss beyond further aspiration. We miss the point if we complain that it lacks variety.

My last example, then, follows prayer into the most intimate and painful relationships of Mather's domestic life. By the time he died at sixty-five, Mather had survived two of his three wives and thirteen of his fifteen children. From the death of his very first infant daughter at the age of five months in 1688, to the loss at sea of his beloved but exasperating son Increase in the last year of the "Reserved Memorials" in 1724, Mather records here their dying words (when he has them), his prayers, his hopes, his resignation, and his exemplary preaching at their funerals. His little Nibby, his "dear little Jerusha," his baffling Creasy, and the others all enter these pages by name when stricken or when any of them causes their representative father to take special care for their conversion. Here again wonders dominate much of the record, whether a Particular Faith precedes a surprising recovery or Mather's unaccountable omission of Mehetabel's name from his daily prayer is followed by the astounding news that the child had died an hour before the father began to pray (1:185–86).

The tension between Mather's affection for his family and his duty to resign his own will to God's makes these retrospective passages among the most passionately personal entries in the "Reserved Memorials." Mather's struggle to become the representative Christian obliges him to pray simultaneously for the recovery of his "desirables," his wife or child, and yet for the resignation to "sacrifice" them freely if God's will removes them from him. Readers who follow his persona through all these bereavements may notice a progression in his recorded efforts to become "a *weaned Christian,*" ready to answer when "called unto the Work of *Sacrificing*" (2:266) even as this Providential vocation begins to attain a variety rivaling that of the marvelous answers to prayer. When Mather's second wife and several of their children are dying during the epidemic of measles in 1713, he resolves to "give to the Town an Exemple of bearing Adversity after a suitable Manner, and of not Fainting in the Day of Adversity" (2:263). And when his "lovely [daughter] Nibby" lies dying a week after bearing her fourth child in 1721, Mather prepares to baptize the granddaughter with the name of Resigned on a Sunday afternoon. He records in his memorials two uses from the conclusion to his morning sermon: some Christians "fare the better for my Sorrows"; and (speaking of himself now in the third person as "a poor Servant of God" called to suffer) as long as he "knows he has a CHRIST concerned for him, and feels he has a CHRIST possessing of him, and conversing with him, none of all his Distresses prove too heavy for him. He don't sink under any Pressures, but can rise and soar and sing the Songs which God our Maker has given His children for whatever Night He will have to be passing over them." The child dies unnamed during the morning service, and the mother suffers "a long and an hard Death" two days later (2:648–49). Making these losses useful becomes the daily "Good Devised" in Mather's memorials for each day in the following week: praying for the widower and his children, setting aside a fast day for forgiveness of his own sins and the welfare of his surviving children, publishing two sermons about Nibby's death (2:649–50).

Mather was no less aware of these duties, doctrines, and sources of consolation when Nibby's mother and namesake, his first wife, died in 1702. What makes his narrative of that crisis, my fourth example, seem less submissive than the entries from 1713 and 1721 is the length of Abigail Philips Mather's mortal illness and the exhausting mystery of Particular Faiths. We know that he learned about Particular Faiths from his father, and that the two of them experienced separately the explicit divine promises that Increase Mather would be sent to London after all. Throughout the narrative of these months, which I believe was written at the end of the year, the representative persona's prayers for his dear consort's survival and for resignation to God's will are answered by thrilling assurances that she will recover. Thus prevented from simply resigning himself even as the medical evidence becomes incontrovertible, he seems to be called to record that evidence and yet to exemplify an irrepressible faith rather than a sacrificial submission. As the retrospective narrator who knows the outcome, he must portray the intensity of his persona's nocturnal vigils, his irradiations of conviction and his agonizing perplexity, the implicit arguments in his extended prayers, and his desperate search for signs of God's will. Yet he must try to puzzle out and explain the strange purposes God must have had in subjecting him to the excruciating combination of exhilarating, absolute assurance and then a shattering refutation of a Particular Faith.

Surely the writing itself constitutes a good part of Mather's therapy, as it often did. (Lydia George Mather, his third wife, knew where he was most vulnerable when she concealed and then scribbled over some of these records; in writing his way through that crisis, Mather resigns his precious memorials to God's will, as he has resigned his wives and children [2:583–85]). But if we recognize in the "Reserved Memorials" a deliberate version of a representative spiritual life, we should see here not chiefly an outburst of self-pity or pain. In addition to the grief, Mather writes, nothing so strange as the miscarriage of this Particular Faith has ever happened to him (2:451). His effort to reflect on the Providential meaning includes a good deal of deliberate rationalization as well as the portrayal of particular actions and characters—Abigail's dream of a formula to relieve one of her symptoms, her fear that she is tiring everyone out (but "I don't mean you, Mr. Mather!"), her dying words ("Heaven, Heaven will make amends for all"), the couple's mutual token of resignation by giving up the touch of their hands. Even if the rationalizing fails to convince a skeptical modern reader, it does represent some of the arguments that a beleaguered and bewildered Christian might use in similar straits (1:450–54).

Cotton Mather's "Reserved Memorials" represent an unusual challenge to the modern reader, not only because virtually every page confronts us with invitations or provocations to judge this figure who has been called "the Puritan you love to hate."[9] This collection of annual glosses upon discarded diaries needs to be read as a loosely cumulative, intermittently retrospective narrative celebrating the variety of wonderful providences granted to a representative Christian who struggles to record them even while he strives to see both his blessings and his extraordinary bereavements as equivalent revelations of God's will.

Notes

1. Worthington C. Ford's entire 1911–12 edition, out of print for some years, was reissued in the 1960s—with no acknowledgment of the Massachusetts Historical Society or of Ford's editorial work beyond his signed introduction—under the imprint of Frederick Ungar. More than one scholar has recently cited this edition as published in New York, with no date and no editor. Since the Ungar reprint is more widely available, I cite it here.

2. This long entry is dated Aug. 27 (1:69–73). Apparently, Ford did not notice the discrepancy in dates. Why would Mather, on Aug. 27, transcribe as an example of "Diaries then written by me" an entry written on the following day? If Mather himself did not simply err in recording the year or the day of the month, then he must have been writing this entry in his "Reserved Memorials" weeks after both of the specified dates had passed. The quoted words appear on pp. 71–72.

3. See W. R. Manierre, "A Description of 'Paterna': The Unpublished Autobiography of Cotton Mather," in *Studies in Bibliography* 18 (1965): 183–205.

4. Compare, for example, the entries for Oct. 29 and 30, 1681 (1:38–43), and the manuscript "Paterna," in the University of Virginia Library, pp. 38–40. See also Manierre, "A Description of 'Paterna,'" and Ronald A. Bosco's edition of *Paterna: The Autobiography of Cotton Mather* (Delmar, N.Y.: Scholars' Facsimiles and Reprints, 1976).

5. "Paterna," MS, p. 18.

6. Quoted from the opening pages of *Paterna*, in David Levin, *In Defense of Historical Literature: Essays on American History, Autobiography, Drama, and Fiction* (New York: Hill and Wang, 1967), pp. 39, 40.

7. In the narrative for 1693, Mather tells the story of his efforts to cure a possessed girl in Boston, and of Robert Calef's "most lying *Libel* to revile my Conduct in these matters" (1:172ff.). The date of Calef's "libel," in a letter challenging Mather's views on witchcraft, is Sept. 13, 1693. Subsequent allusions (1:177, 179) indicate that all this must have been written no sooner than Jan. 1694.

8. See David Levin, *Cotton Mather: The Young Life of the Lord's Remembrancer, 1663–1703* (Cambridge: Harvard Univ. Press, 1978), pp. 40–41.

9. See chapter 8 above, text at note 10.

10.

Edwards, Franklin, and Cotton Mather
A Meditation on Character and Reputation

When invited to discuss "Jonathan Edwards the man, the *character*" of the great theologian, I decided to approach the subject comparatively. Several scholars have written perceptively about Edwards's character.[1] I have learned, for example, from Richard Bushman's Eriksonian study, from Elisabeth Dodds's book on Sarah and Jonathan Edwards, and from Patricia Tracy's fine narrative of Edwards's career as a pastor. Perhaps we may understand Edwards and ourselves a little better if we reconsider some of the ways in which he resembles and differs from two other men who were celebrated—and maligned—in his day and who have become legendary in our own. I choose Benjamin Franklin and Cotton Mather not only because my courses in American literature often require me to discuss the writings of the three men, but also because Mather and Franklin live in our national myth and in our scholarship as memorable personalities.

Edwards and Franklin have often been compared as two geniuses of the American Enlightenment who represent divergent tendencies in Puritanism and in American culture.[2] Edwards represents aspiration toward union with the divine and toward establishing a firm metaphysical structure to support his Calvinist faith; Franklin embodies the Yankee's shrewd combination of self-knowledge and humor, applying his ingenuity to many kinds of social, ethical, and scientific problems

Reprinted by permission from *Jonathan Edwards and the American Experience*, ed. Nathan O. Hatch and Harry S. Stout (New York: Oxford Univ. Press, 1988), Copyright © 1988 by Oxford University Press, Inc. This essay was first presented at a conference on Edwards at Wheaton College, Ill., in 1984.

to show how character, personal wealth, and the commonwealth can all be improved. Franklin and Cotton Mather, too, have been instructively compared.[3] But Mather and Edwards have rarely been discussed together, even it has become customary to regard Mather as a man in whose mind the Enlightenment and Puritan orthodoxy struggled in ways that made him even more uncomfortable than his character makes some of us. I shall therefore highlight resemblances among the three men, but of course I do not claim that they were all alike, that we should pronounce the same judgment on them all, or that the differences among them are always less important than the similarities. I hope that the comparisons may help us to appreciate the nature of Edwards's individuality by explicitly recognizing some of our assumptions about how character should be defined and judged.

In these brief reflections on character and reputation, I shall probably seem to be spending more time on reputation than on the actual historical character; for I hope to show that current and traditional preferences have overemphasized peculiarities of personality, and that we have thus overlooked important qualities that all three characters share.

I should acknowledge that my own attitude is conditioned by years of sometimes embattled exposure to Cotton Mather, and that the best we can hope for in studying the past is to move closer to a just understanding. I do believe that individual character is not a mere figment or fictitious invention, and that our own historical circumstances—and comparisons of modern interpretations with the surviving seventeenth- and eighteenth-century evidence—can help us to restore to the individual portrait actual features that have been neglected or overlooked.

Edwards, Franklin, and Mather, although active and effective in some kinds of social affairs, are all known to us primarily through their writings. We read the character of each man in his prose style, and especially in the way he writes about himself in his diaries or autobiographical narratives. I suspect that one major reason why Edwards has enjoyed a much better press in modern scholarship than either Franklin or Mather is the directness, the relentlessly straightforward quality of his prose. Even when writing about his most intense spiritual experience, moreover, Edwards manages to seem detached if not impartial, describing phenomena in his soul or psyche without calling great attention to his personality.

Mather and Franklin, on the other hand, appear in their respective ways to be writing self-consciously, cannily, perhaps insincerely. I cannot agree with Edmund Morgan that Mather expresses "a false modesty about everything that he does."[4] Mather even introduces the most successful of all his books by refusing to say, "'Sorry 'tis no better.' Instead of *that*," he insists, "I freely tell my readers: I have written what is not unworthy of their perusal. If I did not think so, truly, I would not publish it."[5] Yet when Mather reports in his diary a vision promising that in imminent European revolutions against anti-Christian tyrants "sinful I shall be given a prominent assignment" and that "vast regions of *America*" will be introduced to knowledge of Christ by "poor, vile sinful me,"[6] not even the most sympathetic reader can miss the posing. Mather's awkward efforts to stifle or at least conceal his pride are defeated by his irrepressible delight. When Franklin opens his autobiography by admitting that one of his motives for writing is to gratify his vanity, and that he thanks Heaven for vanity, along with "the other comforts of life,"[7] many readers resist his effort to disarm them even as they perceive his joke. Franklin's humor, then, can be read as one more device of a manipulative personality, working his way with us while shutting us out from intimate knowledge of his true self.

Not even his famous rationalization of his pride can placate suspicious readers. When he tells his parable of the speckled axe, he is clearly ridiculing his own tendency to rationalize; his self-mocking irony is evident in the story of the man who decided that he "liked a speckled axe best," rather than just a sharpened edge, after the axe grinder agreed to polish the entire head if the customer himself would do the work of turning the grindstone (155–56). But every year several of my students who have no trouble perceiving Franklin's humor when he says that achieving true humility would amount to "a kind of foppery in morals" (156)—a condition in which he might have been proud of his humility—every year some of my ablest students protest that here again Franklin is trying to manipulate the reader. Against this effort some of them, and some older scholars, rearm themselves with a moral severity that one would have been more likely to expect from a Puritan than from a liberated modern scholar.

My purpose here is not to explain why that severity is visited on the head of Franklin, nor why so distinguished a scholar as Samuel Eliot Morison would say gratuitously that undergraduate life at Harvard must have returned to normal in 1674, "if that insufferable prig Cotton Mather"—then only eleven years old—"was being kicked about, as he so richly deserved."[8] Mather's latest biographer explains his own contemptuous judgment of Mather as an objection to insincerity when he coins the term "Matherese" to signify an ambiguous, self-deceptive language that professes friendship while revealing "a vengeful egotist nakedly transparent."[9] "This impossibly provocative fusion of the conciliator and the trouble-maker, of his goodwill and his rage," Kenneth Silverman writes, is what has "always made [Mather] seem at once splendid and contemptible" (256). And Edmund Morgan, in two essay-reviews in the last six years, has made it plain that what nauseates him is Mather's egomania, his trivializing of the divine, a gross confusion in which self-glorification is mistaken for, or misrepresented as, the glorification of God. When Mather professes—or at least tries—to "feel a secret Joy" in one of the most bitter disappointments of his life, "because I am thus conformed unto Him who was despised and rejected of Men," Morgan acknowledges the appropriateness of Mather's disappointment, that he "*was* the most eminent minister in New England" and therefore "an obvious candidate" for the presidency of Harvard. "But Jesus Christ he was not," Morgan says— as if Mather had seen no difference between being "conformed unto" Christ and being identified with Him—"and failure to become president of Harvard was not crucifixion."[10] I doubt if Morgan's judgment here would be modified if he had remembered that Cotton Mather, at the age of seven or eight, failed to understand why his father "seemed glad" to hear that young Cotton had been beaten for rebuking his playmates' "wicked words and ways," but that afterwards Cotton Mather came to appreciate the "Heavenly Principle" behind his father's reaction.[11]

This mixture of condescension and sarcasm might need more explanation if other scholars, from Robert Middlekauff and Sacvan Bercovitch to Richard Lovelace, had not been able (as I have been) to write about Mather without contempt.[12] What puzzles me is another question: How does Jonathan Edwards escape such disapproving language? Edwards, too, has been portrayed for two centuries as a prodigy who was well along in Latin studies by the time he was eight years old, and who wrote a fine essay on flying or sailing spiders when only eleven. But even before recent scholarship demonstrated that Edwards wrote that essay in his early twenties,[13] he was not portrayed as the kind of Infant Prodigy who deserved to be kicked about by normal school-mates. Only rarely has any portrait of his character included his report that "no *new* quarrel" has "broke[n] out betwixt me and any of the scholars" at Yale or his complaint against his classmates' "monstrous impieties and acts of immorality."[14] Nor, in the gravest disappoint-ment of Edwards's clerical life, his dismissal by the congregation he had served for twenty-three years, does his relentless farewell sermon provoke sarcastic disapproval of his vindictiveness—not even when he elevates himself (after a perfunctory disclaimer) to a close parallel with the prophet Jeremiah and the apostle Paul, nor when he repeatedly tells his opponents that Jesus Christ, "before the whole universe," will endorse Edwards's position in the Northampton controversy, and will judge the motivation of the pastor and every one of his critics, on the Day of Judgment.[15] In the same sermon Edwards warns a few who have begun to feel some religious awakenings that "the devil will undoubt-edly seek to make his advantage" of Edwards's dismissal, and he tells the young people that at the Judgment Day, "when we shall meet before Him," "God will approve and confirm" Edwards's warning "against frolicking (as it is called) and some other liberties taken by young people in the land" (196). Yet this mixture of admonition and self-justification is rarely represented as a trait of Edwards's character.

Edwards, moreover, was capable of writing the kind of private note that has damaged Cotton Mather's reputation. As Patricia Tracy has pointed out, Edwards resolved not to be envious at the time that his father believed one of Jonathan's cousins had been offered the cov-eted post in Solomon Stoddard's church. Jonathan resolved "always to rejoice in everyone's prosperity . . . and to expect no happiness of that nature as long as I live."[16] And when he sent off his essay on spiders to Paul Dudley, a fellow of the Royal Society, he cast his hope for publi-cation in the same kind of conventionally fulsome rhetoric, the same false modesty and elaborate decorum, that one finds in some of Mather's prose: "If you think, Sir," Edwards wrote, "that [my observations] are not worthy the taking notice of, with greatness and goodness overlook and conceal [them]"; and again, "Pardon me if I thought it might at least give you occasion to make better observations on these wonderful animals, that should be worthy of communicating to the learned world."[17]

Modern scholars may deplore Mather's willingness to blame the Devil for confusing the Lord's People with true and false accusations during the witchcraft craze in 1692; except in Robert Lowell's implicit criticism, I cannot remember reading any modern objections to Jonathan Edwards's comment, in his first Narrative of Surprising Conversions, on his uncle's suicide: "Satan," Edwards wrote, citing the same biblical text that Mather had used for a sermon on witchcraft, "seems to be in a Great Rage, at the Extraordinary breaking forth of the word of God. I hope it is because he knows that he has but a short time: doubtless he had a Great Reach, in this violent attack of his against the whole affair. We have appointed a day of Fasting in the Town this week, by Reason of this & other appearances of satans Rage amongst us against poor Souls."[18] It is not just the appeal to that biblical text, but the similar way of responding to threatening evidence, that links Mather's and Edwards's statements. Both admit that Satan has taken advantage of a crisis in which the respective minister has taken a controversial position. And in 1735 as well as 1692, for Edwards as well as Mather, blaming Satan for perverting the real meaning of the crisis serves only to verify the millennial significance of the episode.

Before returning more narrowly to the question of character, I would like to consider a few other parallels between Mather and Edwards. Edwards echoes Mather's *Magnalia Christi Americana* when he notes that the Reformation and the discovery of America were Providential steps toward "the glorious renovation of the world," which would "make way for the church's latter-day glory," beginning in America.[19] Edwards's xenophobic comments about the French in Canada during the Seven Years' War, cited in Sacvan Bercovitch's *The American Jeremiad*, do not differ markedly from Mather's strictures during the *Decennium Luctuosum*, the grievous decade of the 1690s. Both apocalyptic statements make partisan use of a millennial schedule. Although Edwards was capable, in *The Nature of True Virtue*, of recognizing in national loyalty an expanded form of self-love, his rhetoric in battle could echo the fiercest words of the seventeenth century. As Stephen Stein has noticed, Edwards predicted that "the saints," although forbidden ordinary revenge, would do "their utmost for the destruction of popery." The command in Revelation 5:6 to "Reward her even as she rewarded you" does not summon Christians to "revenge upon the persons of men," Edwards says, but followers of Antichrist "shall have that internal pains and torments of mind, that are like judgments that shall come upon them. Antichrist, as he is a body politic, shall forever die an eternal death. There may be papists, vagabonds that shall be the scorn of the world; but there shall never more be a popish polity." [20] The Roman church, Edwards says, is worse than Islam or Judaism; it is like "a viper or some loathsome, poisonous, crawling monster." [21]

Considerable evidence suggests that Mather was at least as effective as Edwards in pastoral visits and in supervising, disciplining, or instructing the young, and that Edwards's alienation from many of the young in his congregation, like his earlier troubles in supervising Yale undergraduates, was even more severe than Cotton Mather's. [22] Here we generally do recognize the contribution of Edwards's personality to the catastrophe of his dismissal. I refer not to the implicitly economic and political issues that Perry Miller and Ola Winslow, respectively, emphasized. [23] Those issues are large enough in their way to have a respectable place beside the questions of theology and church membership that preoccupied Edwards's majestic mind. No, it is Edwards's treatment of midwifery, secretly studied by children of church members, and the pregnancy of an unmarried young woman, whom Edwards commanded to marry the father of her child—it is these petty matters that Patricia Tracy has convincingly tied in a relatively new way to Edwards's character. [24]

The point of my comparisons of Edwards and Cotton Mather is not primarily to gain comfort from demonstrating that Edwards could sometimes be just as puritanically bad. Nor do I chiefly hope to use Edwards's faults as a lever for prying Mather's effigy loose from the gallery of monsters and restoring him to the human race. If we attend to the insights of Tracy and Bushman and to evidence that we judge similar traits and actions differently in Edwards, Franklin, and Mather, we may see reason to proceed cautiously when we build moralistic judgments into historical portraits. We may then be able to see other parallels in career and character, and to broaden our conception of character itself.

Consider the shape of the two careers. Each of these prodigious boys saw his father and a grandfather exercise strong authority in the respective congregations, and each of the young men joined a powerful progenitor as a colleague before entering the twenty-fifth year. At the age of twenty-six, each of them had to take charge of that progenitor's large congregation—Cotton Mather when his father went to England as agent of Massachusetts in quest of a restored charter; Edwards, when Grandfather Stoddard died. Both Edwards and Cotton Mather had extraordinary success in recruiting new church members in these early years, and as Mather's political and social influence flourished until the witchcraft trials, so Edwards enjoyed an extraordinary success in the revival of 1734–35. Stirred by millennial hopes, both Mather (at twenty-nine) and Edwards (at thirty-one) thought they had to face the perplexing, successful counterattacks of Satan—Mather in spectral evidence and Edwards in his despondent uncle's suicide. Mather knew from the beginning that spectral evidence was unreliable because the Devil could assume the shape of an innocent person, but he was convinced that some specters were agents of guilty witches. In the Great Awakening half a century later, Edwards struggled to define the distinguishing marks of true grace even as he had to admit that some of the marks were indistinguishable from satanic cheats, or self-delusion. Mather hoped that Boston might become, in 1697 and again in 1716, the new Jerusalem; Edwards hoped that the Great Awakening might be "the dawning, or at least a prelude," to the Millennium, which would probably begin in America, perhaps in the ideal Christian commonwealth that he was trying to achieve in Northampton.[25] Edwards, like Mather, wrote pamphlets against having "a heterodox minister settled amongst us."[26] And in their forties and fifties, both Mather and Edwards tried unsuccessfully to regain in recalcitrant congregations the heady influence they had enjoyed as young pastors. Mather, of course, was never dismissed by his congregation, but his disappointment was intensified by both the secession of a large group who formed a new church and a series of petty yet exhausting conflicts that stood in lugubrious contrast to the grand millennial battles of his twenties.

The great service that Patricia Tracy's book has done is to tie Edwards's character closely to historical circumstances. Her method is much more firmly rooted in quantitative evidence than my own study of Mather, but her results encourage me to see the value of comparisons across the generations. Tracy shows that Edwards was not above taking a self-pitying tone when he spoke at the ordination of Jonathan Judd, minister to the new congregation at Southampton. At the very time that he was fighting with his own congregation about salary, Edwards warned the new congregation not to pay their new minister "well for a while at first, while the relation between you and him is a new thing, and then afterwards, when your minister's necessities are increased, begin to fail, as it too frequently happens." Here, as Tracy notices, Edwards concedes that ministers "love to harp on this string" for obvious reasons of self-interest, but he promptly declares that he himself has not "been much in insisting on this duty in my own pulpit . . . ; and blessed be God that I have had no more occasion." Tracy suggests insincerity here, for he had occasion enough. But Edwards at least anticipates her objection. With characteristic rigor, he makes a logical distinction that includes a defiant appeal to his ultimate Authority. He dismisses as irrelevant "whatever any may judge of the secrets of my heart." The truth remains the truth: "it is enough for you to whom I have spoke it, that I have demonstrated that what I have delivered is the mind of God." Against such demonstrations, he warned the new congregation, there would always be some "anti-ministerial men," including church members, to whom it would seem "natural . . . to be unfriendly and unkind towards their own ministers, and to make difficulty for them." [27]

Does not Cotton Mather's desire to be conformed to the example of Jesus seem less peculiar when we remember what Jonathan Edwards, with pointed allusions to his own experience, told Jonathan Judd and the new congregation: that ministers "must suffer—even as Christ did, if necessary—to bring the Gospel to the pharisees"? [28] Is there any fundamental difference between Edwards's admonition about "anti-ministerial men"—or Thomas Shepard's axiom, "He that would live

godly must suffer persecution"[29]—and Mather's warning, written for
those who try to do good, and ridiculed by Edmund Morgan, "that a
man of *good merit*" may be treated as "a kind of *public enemy*"?[30] Is there
any major difference between Thomas Shepard's succinct command, in
the 1640s, "Suspect thyself much,"[31] and Cotton Mather's prescription
for responding to insults: "Be always really, heartily, inwardly *loathing
yourself*"?[32] Even if we did not have Richard Lovelace's excellent book
restoring Mather's writings to their theological context, the comparison to Edwards would supply a good perspective for Mather's pride.
Shepard, too, had recorded an almost identical response to the threat
of despair. When laboring under an intense awareness of sin, he said,
he had been given a divine message: "Be not discouraged therefore
because thou art so vile, but make this double use of it: (1) loathe
thyself the more; (2) feel a greater need [for] . . . Jesus Christ."[33]

And now that we have arrived at the central trait of pride, vanity,
self-identification with grandeur, let us compare our three representative figures—how they wrote about their own pride and how they say
that they tried to nurture or control it.

All three of these gifted men recognized their vanity and pride in
comments that were more than merely conventional, and they all resolved to control or at least disguise their feelings of superiority or
anger. Edwards resolved to substitute for his "air of dislike, anger, and
fretfulness" an "appearance of love, cheerfulness, and benignity."[34] In
an extraordinary passage that still perplexes my students, Edwards also
managed to discuss his pride in a way that can easily be misread as
blindly claiming (in Franklin's ironic words) to be proud of his humility—or proud of his awareness of his wickedness. A close reading of
the syntax—especially in the restored sentence that nineteenth-century
editors had deleted from Edwards's spiritual autobiography—shows
that Edwards does not claim actually to be the worst sinner in the
world. He only means to describe a feeling that he often has, especially
when other Christians try to express to him their sense of their own
unworthiness. Their expressions, he says, "may be suitable for them,"
but on these occasions (so I interpret the passage) "it *seems*" to Edwards
that "it would be a vile self-exaltation in me not to be the lowest in
humility of all mankind." And when "others speak of *their* longing to
be 'humbled to dust,'" Edwards says (though the italics are mine) he

thinks that he ought "to lie infinitely low before God." He sees the snare in such implicit competition—first when he attributes the apparent enormity of his sins not to his having "a greater conviction of sin than ordinary," but to his feeling that "I *am* so much worse, and have so much more wickedness to be convinced of." [35] I find it interesting that these statements come from one of the sentences that had been excised by nineteenth-century editors, not to be restored for modern discussion until Daniel Shea led us back to the text in Samuel Hopkins's biography. [36] Even without this restored sentence, however, Edwards demonstrates plainly that he sees the dialectical consequence of grace. The very paragraph that begins with his "greater sense of my universal exceeding dependence on God's grace and strength, and mere good pleasure, of late, than I used formerly to have"—that very paragraph ends with a startling confession: Although nauseated by "the very thought of any joy arising in me, on any consideration of my own amiableness, performances, or experiences, or any goodness of heart or life," he insists that he is "greatly afflicted with a proud and self-righteous spirit, much more sensibly than I used to be formerly. I see that serpent rising and putting forth its head everywhere, all around me." [37]

Those well-known lines about the spiritual dialectic between pride and humility have their institutional counterpart in a meditation that young Edwards wrote about a minister's power to do good—a statement that Patricia Tracy has used to foreshadow her narrative of Edwards's doomed effort to emulate his dominant grandfather's mastery of the congregation. Solomon Stoddard, we recall, was sometimes known as the Pope of New England. Here Edwards moves in his customarily methodical progress from step to step—from the pastor's administration of the sacraments, to his choice of who should receive the sacraments, and so to the extension of "my pastoral, or ministerial, or teaching power." If the people "are obliged to hear me," he says, only for ordinary reasons—"only because they themselves have chosen me to guide them, and therein declared that they thought me sufficiently instructed in the mind of Christ to teach them, and because I have the other requisites of being their teacher, then I have power as other ministers have in these days. But if it was plain to them that I was under the infallible guidance of Christ, then I should have more power. And if it was plain to all the world of Christians that I was under the infallible guidance of Christ, and I was sent forth to teach the world the will of Christ, then I should have power in all the world. I should have power to teach them what they ought to do, and they would be obliged to hear me; I should have power to teach them who were Christians and who not, and in this likewise they would be obliged to hear me."[38]

Professor Thomas Schafer has persuaded me that Patricia Tracy's reading of this meditation neglects the context, which remains unpublished. In this meditation and in others, Edwards has been discussing the function of ministers in general, and the power of "popes, bishops, and presbyters" as well. His use of the first person here, as elsewhere in the miscellanies on the same subject, may well be merely illustrative, using the pronoun "I" as we often use "you" or "one." Edwards is probably concerned in these months not only with the disciplinary struggles of his father in the congregation at East Windsor, nor especially with Grandfather Stoddard's unchallenged power in Northampton, but also with the defection of Timothy Cutler at Yale from the Congregational to the Anglican church. Surely Edwards meditates here on the nature of ministerial authenticity in any branch of Christianity. His theoretical extension of the young man's power into "all the world" may therefore have no connection to personal "dreams of unlimited power" or to a search for "solace" prompted by his father's weak control in East Windsor.[39]

Yet even if we reject such speculations, we cannot fail to see the competitive implication in this tradition of Christian teaching. One does not want to have teaching power "only as other ministers have in these days." "Difference of power" does exist, Edwards says, "amongst ministers, whether apostles or whatever." As Tracy clearly sees, the Puritan minister's obligation to have a true vocation, the source of true Christian authority, conflicts with his duty to be humble.

It is in the obligation to be at once proud and humble, distinct from counterfeit Christians and yet self-effacing, that the comparison of Edwards, Franklin, and Mather can be most illuminating. All three men worked out the ethical problem through some version of the doctrine of Christian calling, which both Franklin and Mather enunciate by repeating the biblical proverb (22:29) that says a diligent man will stand before kings. "Proud thoughts," Mather confessed in a private meditation, "fly-blow my best performances"; and in his warning that, should the Lord reject him after all, he would be "the direst example of a deluded and exalted hypocrite that ever was," he resolved to abhor himself even in his "enlargements and entertainments."[40] Like Edwards half a century later, Mather commanded himself to "walk softly and sorrowfully as long as I breathe on earth."[41] And just as Franklin would later compare his own methodical efforts at eliminating one fault at a time to weeding a garden, repeating his course in "The Art of Virtue" over and over again, so young Mather (though, of course, with none of Franklin's self-tolerant humor) perceived that his battle against pride and other sins would be perpetual: "Lord, I here take my *vow,* that I will never give Thee, or my own soul rest, until my dearest lust become, as bitter as death, as hateful as Hell unto me."[42]

We should not consider it accidental that Benjamin Franklin makes his general statement about vanity in the very first pages of his autobiography, or that humility is the last of his thirteen virtues and the only one (besides order) with which he reports that he had little success. Franklin's habit of humorous understatement introduces vanity not as a dear lust that must become as hateful as Hell to him, but as one of the comforts of life for which we should thank Heaven. He plainly says here at the outset that vanity often does considerable good, presumably by impelling men and women to achievements that benefit themselves and society. His doctrine of enlightened self-interest—seeing that one's own truest interest will ultimately coincide with virtue—implies a recognition of at least some utility in vanity. And his willingness to be content with the appearance of humility underlines the point. Not only will he refuse to abase himself in the extravagant language of Thomas Shepard, Cotton Mather, George Whitefield, Jonathan Edwards, and other Christians; Franklin really believes that vanity and ambition, if properly controlled, do considerable good.

What unites Franklin, Edwards, and Mather none the less is the intensity of their striving to drive their ambition or pride in ingenious efforts to do good in the world. All three men were proud and ambitious, and all three were impatient in the face of contradiction. All three were painfully sensitive to criticism; even if one rejects Melvin Buxbaum's or Bernard Bailyn's severe judgment of Franklin's behavior during the affair of the letters purloined from Thomas Hutchinson, one cannot miss the intensity of Franklin's pain and anger when he is forced to endure the abuse of Parliament and the press. Here Franklin seems almost Matherian in his resentment of libels against his virtue and his family name.[43] But it is in the young Franklin's concentration on ingenious ways to express his prodigious gifts, finding means to direct his ambition into acceptably virtuous forms, that he most clearly resembles Mather and Edwards. In the context of Edwards's and Mather's resolutions to try to subject their extraordinarily strong wills to the will of God, their passion to lie low before God and yet to be united to Him, Franklin's resolution to strive for humility by imitating Jesus and Socrates ought to seem less presumptuous (or less humorously ironic) than it did when it infuriated D. H. Lawrence.[44]

In narrating Mather's effort to control his stammer while he was still a young boy at Harvard, I remarked that the key to Mather's developing character was "not only the affliction, the anxiety, the incipient neurosis, but his mighty labor to make the most of it. Who," I asked, "can match the determination of the Puritan determinist?"[45] I believe that this determination, the power of this will to reconcile science and faith (gravely modified in Franklin, of course), ambition and humility, striving and resignation, self-examination and vigorous benefactions in the world—that the power of this will is more important to a comparison of the three men's character than Cotton Mather's shrillness, Franklin's worldly humor, or the emotional crises that Mather and Edwards suffered. Even in New England at the beginning of the eighteenth century, there was no natural law that tied every man's pride and ambition to virtue or to public service.

It should be no particular novelty to notice in the twentieth century that Cotton Mather and Jonathan Edwards both had to reconcile their own ambition with mixed feelings of rivalry and reverence towards their clerical fathers and grandfathers. And Benjamin Franklin tells us openly (if only to disarm us) that rivalry with his brother and resentment of real or imagined injustice led him to take questionable advantage of an opportunity to flee his apprenticeship.[46] Does psychoanalysis really oblige us to assume that the best way of resolving conflicting emotions is always to express our anger? I think not. Would Cotton Mather have been a better citizen, a less "odious," "contemptible," and "nauseating" human being, if he had let it all hang out instead of trying (at admittedly great cost) to become the best person he could be? If we notice that Edwards was at least as censorious with his congregation as Mather ever was with the Second Church in Boston, perhaps we won't scorn Mather's rebukes as vicious. Perhaps we will read character in the choice of virtue, service, and self-discipline.

Let us return to style. If we notice that Franklin, for all his delightful humor, was just as sensitive as Mather and Edwards to attacks upon his good name, and thoroughly glad to be honored, we ought to be able to report that Mather was delighted by his election to the Royal Society, rather than to say gratuitously, with his most recent biographer, that he was "giddy with delight."[47] But the differences in style and character will remain. Although they are not my chief subject here, I do want to say a few words about them before concluding.

Jonathan Edwards persuades me with the substance of his descriptions of his spiritual life that he lived as intensely, with highs and lows as exhilarating and depressing, as ever Cotton Mather did. Just imagine, for example, being present when Edwards could not bear the thought of being with non-Christians, or when he was overcome with loud weeping, or when he was moved to sing at length and to proclaim God's glory. Yet, except in the Applications of some of his revival sermons, his style expresses that emotion with rigorous control. The intensity of his will, the compulsive determination in his character, comes through to us in his relentless progression from one step to the next. In this character, then, many of us read the powerful intellect in the style—in which I include the quality of the mind, its capacity to order statements so that one seems inexorably to follow from its predecessor, as well as the clear diction and the rational tone. The self is expressed on the page, all right, but its intensity seems to be present almost objectively, in the form of irresistible argument.

It would be unjust to deny that Edwards was a much greater thinker than Cotton Mather, and I am convinced that the power and originality of Edwards's mind form an important part of his character. Yet I believe that in the rehabilitation (or what Donald Weber calls the recovery) of Jonathan Edwards during the last half century, one reason why many commentators have overlooked some of the less attractive traits and statements that I have dredged up here is respect for Edwards as a thinker. We need to preserve more room even in our scholarly images of the past for what James Baldwin calls "human weight and complexity."[48] By reviewing the unattractive and attractive resemblances among Edwards, Franklin, and Mather, we go beyond asking whether Mather's defects were monstrous. We remember that character is complex and that deliberate action, and qualities that memorable people share, may be as important to defining an individual character as the emotional quirks and diary entries that make him unique or the Oedipal impulses that move below his consciousness. Edwards, Franklin, and Mather, impelled to write voluminously and to strive ingeniously, ambitiously, resolutely for the public good or the glory of God, all lived by the word. They shared values and qualities of character that mark them as fellow American Puritans.

Notes

1. Richard Bushman, "Jonathan Edwards as Great Man: Identity, Conversion, and Leadership in the Great Awakening," *Soundings, an Interdisciplinary Journal* 52 (1969): 15–46; Elisabeth D. Dodds, *Marriage to a Difficult Man* (Philadelphia: Westminster Press, 1971); and Patricia J. Tracy, *Jonathan Edwards, Pastor: Religion and Society in Eighteenth-Century Northampton* (New York: Hill and Wang, 1980).

2. See, for example, Perry Miller, "Benjamin Franklin—Jonathan Edwards," in *Major Writers of America,* ed. Perry Miller, 2 vols. (New York: Harcourt Brace Jovanovich, 1962), 1: 82–98.

3. See, for example, David Levin, introduction to Cotton Mather, *Bonifacius: An Essay upon the Good* (Cambridge: Harvard Univ. Press, 1966); Phyllis Franklin, *Show Thyself a Man: A Comparison of Benjamin Franklin and Cotton Mather* (The Hague, Paris: Mouton, 1969); and Mitchell Robert Breitwieser, *Cotton Mather and Benjamin Franklin: The Price of Representative Personality* (Cambridge: Cambridge Univ. Press, 1984).

4. Edmund Morgan, "Heaven Can't Wait," *New York Review of Books,* May 31, 1984, p. 33.

5. Mather, *Bonifacius,* p. 13.

6. *The Diary of Cotton Mather,* ed. Worthington C. Ford, 2 vols. (Boston: Massachusetts Historical Society, 1912; rept. New York: Ungar, n.d.), 1:234.

7. *The Autobiography of Benjamin Franklin,* ed. Leonard Labaree (New Haven: Yale Univ. Press, 1964), p. 44.

8. Samuel Eliot Morison, *Harvard College in the Seventeenth Century,* 2 vols. (Cambridge: Harvard Univ. Press, 1936), 1:82–83.

9. Kenneth Silverman, *The Life and Times of Cotton Mather* (New York: Harper and Row, 1984), p. 255.

10. Morgan, "Heaven Can't Wait," p. 34. Cf. Edmund Morgan, "The Puritan You Love to Hate," *New York Review of Books,* Jan. 25, 1979, pp. 31–32.

11. Cotton Mather, "Paterna," MS in University of Virginia Library, pp. 3–4.

12. See Robert Middlekauff, *The Mathers: Three Generations of Puritan Intellectuals, 1596–1728* (New York: Oxford Univ. Press, 1971); Sacvan Bercovitch, "Cotton Mather," in *Major Writers of Early American Literature,* ed. Everett Emerson (Madison: Univ. of Wisconsin Press, 1972), pp. 93–149; and Richard Lovelace, *The American Pietism of Cotton Mather: Origins of American Evangelicalism* (Grand Rapids: Christian Univ. Press, 1979).

13. See *The Works of Jonathan Edwards: Scientific and Philosophical Writings,* ed. Wallace E. Anderson (New Haven: Yale Univ. Press, 1980), pp. 6–7.

14. Quoted in Alfred O. Aldridge, *Jonathan Edwards* (New York: Washington Square Press, 1964), p. 11.

15. "Farewell Sermon," in *Jonathan Edwards: Representative Selections,* ed. Clarence H. Faust and Thomas H. Johnson (New York: American Book Company, 1935), p. 188.

16. Quoted in Tracy, *Edwards,* p. 53.

17. *Edwards: Scientific Writings,* p. 32. Cf. Edwards's draft (p. 414): "If you think it *Childish* and consider the Rules of Decorum . . . with Greatness *and Generosity to look Down Pity and Conceal . . .* "

18. "Narrative of Surprising Conversions," in *Edwards: Representative Selections,* pp. 83–84. Robert Lowell's poem "After the Surprising Conversions" paraphrases Edwards's narrative, with ironic emphasis on Satan's alleged descent among the people of Northampton.

19. *The Works of Jonathan Edwards: Apocalyptic Writings,* ed. Stephen Stein (New Haven: Yale Univ. Press, 1977), p. 28.

20. Ibid., pp. 120–21.

21. Quoted by Stein, ibid., p. 111.

22. See, for example, David Levin, *Cotton Mather: The Young Life of the Lord's Remembrancer, 1663–1703* (Cambridge: Harvard Univ. Press, 1978), pp. 74–77, 90, 96–98, 113, 234–36, 271–73.

23. Perry Miller, *Jonathan Edwards* (New York: William Sloane Associates, 1949); and Ola E. Winslow, *Jonathan Edwards, 1703–1758* (New York: Macmillan, 1940). The two positions, in some respects antithetical to each other, are succinctly summarized in Tracy (who is, of course, arguing for her own position), *Edwards*, p. 183.

24. See, for example, Tracy, *Edwards*, pp. 190–92.

25. Jonathan Edwards, *Some Thoughts concerning the Present Revival of Religion in New England*, quoted in *Edwards: Apocalyptic Writings*, p. 26.

26. Quoted in Tracy, *Edwards*, p. 121.

27. Ibid., p. 156.

28. Paraphrased, ibid., p. 155.

29. Here Shepard is quoting the second epistle of Paul to Timothy (3:12), in the fifth sermon ("Few Are Saved") of *The Sincere Convert*, in *America in Literature*, vol. 1, ed. David Levin and Theodore L. Gross (New York: John Wiley and Sons, 1978), p. 129.

30. Here Mather is quoting "a late French author," in *Bonifacius*, p. 10. Morgan implies that Mather himself wrote it. See Morgan, "Heaven Can't Wait," p. 34.

31. See the fifth sermon, *American in Literature* 1:123.

32. Quoted in Morgan, "Heaven Can't Wait," p. 34.

33. Shepard, "Autobiography," in *God's Plot: The Paradoxes of Puritan Piety*, ed. Michael McGiffert (Amherst: Univ. of Massachusetts Press, 1972), pp. 44–45.

34. Quoted in Tracy, *Edwards*, p. 67.

35. Jonathan Edwards, "Spiritual Autobiography," *America in Literature* 1:333.

36. See Daniel B. Shea, *Spiritual Autobiography in Early America* (Princeton, N.J.: Princeton Univ. Press, 1968), pp. 206–8.

37. *America in Literature* 1:333.

38. Edwards, "Miscellanies," no. 40, quoted in Tracy, *Edwards*, pp. 64–65.

39. Tracy, *Edwards*, p. 65. Professor Schafer has graciously shown me his transcriptions of half a dozen miscellanies about these subjects, all apparently written in 1723, including at least two passages that clearly use the first person as an illustrative allusion to "anyone" or "one." I have quoted from his transcriptions with the permission of the Beinecke Library, Yale University.

40. See Levin, *Cotton Mather*, pp. 62–63.

41. Mather, *Diary* 1:43.

42. Ibid.

43. Melvin H. Buxbaum, *Benjamin Franklin and the Zealous Presbyterians* (University Park: Penn State Press, 1975); Bernard Bailyn, *The Ordeal of Thomas Hutchinson* (Cambridge: Harvard Univ. Press, 1974).

44. D. H. Lawrence, *Studies in Classic American Literature* (New York, 1923), pp. 12–13.

45. Levin, *Cotton Mather*, p. 37.

46. Franklin, *Autobiography*, p. 70.

47. Silverman, *Life and Times*, p. 254.

48. James Baldwin, *Notes of a Native Son* (Boston: Beacon Press, 1955), p. 172.

11.

Ordeal of a Loser

Thomas Hutchinson

Few characters in the Hall of American Infamy have come so close to unanimous election as the subject of this fine book. The wax figure of Thomas Hutchinson stands in the gallery beside those of Benedict Arnold and Aaron Burr. Although Hutchinson wrote an extraordinarily dispassionate defense of his conduct after he had become a hateful symbol to his countrymen, almost nothing in our historical literature before the 1890s goes beyond the few penetrating words of Hawthorne's "Legends of the Province House" in a sympathetic effort to understand Hutchinson's behavior during the 1760s and 1770s. Descended from Anne Hutchinson and related by his sister's marriage to the Mather family, Hutchinson understood very well two opposite routes to obloquy in New England, and before his own disgrace he expressed that understanding by writing the best eighteenth-century history of early Massachusetts. But his success as a merchant, his elevation to the highest governmental post in the colony, and his excellent comprehension of political theory and imperial law did not save him from an ordeal in which he came to resemble his fanatically wrongheaded great-great-grandmother and his sister's credulous father-in-law, Cotton Mather. In the name of prudence, reason, law, and patriotism Hutchinson insisted on declaring Parliament's right to tax the American colonies even while he argued intensely within the imperial government for forbearance. Then his political enemies published some of his confidential letters in a way that made him seem not only dogmatically legalistic

A review of *The Ordeal of Thomas Hutchinson,* by Bernard Bailyn (Cambridge: Harvard Univ. Press, 1974), reprinted by permission of the editors from *The Yale Review* 64 (1974): 118–22, copyright Yale University.

in defense of the British oppressors, nor only protective of the rich colonial offices that he and an extraordinary number of his relatives continued to hold, but also mendacious and treacherous toward his fellow citizens in Boston.

Hutchinson's ordeal, which Bernard Bailyn narrates with great sympathy and skill, reached its first degree when, during the Stamp Act crisis of 1765, a mob destroyed his beautiful mansion and scattered his precious historical papers in the mud; a second degree when he found himself reviled at home for collaborating in tyranny and rebuked in London for provoking the rebels to treasonous statements; and a third degree when, in exile, he lost all his treasured property in Massachusetts through confiscation and lost in London the attention and personal backing of the British patronage system on which he had relied in his loyalty to his conception of the law.

Bailyn has written a superb re-creation of Hutchinson's ordeal. From the night the mob bursts into Hutchinson's home in Boston to the concluding, moralistic letter in which Arthur Lee congratulates James and Mercy Otis Warren on their acquisition of Hutchinson's beloved country estate in Milton, the narrative moves from one disaster to another. The lucid, meticulous exposition of Hutchinson's political theory, his closely argued opposition to the Stamp Act, his disquisition on the separation of governmental powers, his ingeniously perceptive dialogue between Europa and America, and his earnest self-defense— Bailyn's fine representation of all these makes Arthur Lee's letter an admirably ironic conclusion to the entire narrative. A conscientious public official has been brought through ruin to a miserably waning life in exile, and the comment of his conquerors on his tragedy is as simple as the judgment of history by their descendants was to be for a century thereafter: "It has not always happened in like manner," Lee writes to the Warrens, "that the forfeited seats of the wicked have been filled with men of virtue. But in this corrupt world it is sufficient that we have some examples of it for our consolation."[1] That perfect word *consolation* shines in my memory long after I have read the subsequent, explicit judgment in Bailyn's epilogue and in "The Losers," his bibliographical essay on the treatment of Loyalists by historians.

Grateful though we must be for his remarkable achievement, Bailyn has not solved all the problems that confront the writer who tries to compose a sympathetic biography of so prodigious a loser. His chief difficulty is point of view. He writes so skillfully from Hutchinson's embattled perspective that he often screens the reader from awareness that other positions were intellectually and morally defensible. A number of passages do make Hutchinson's limitations unequivocally clear—his commitment to the tight network of his relatives in the government of Massachusetts, the "deepening self-delusion" into which his "acceptance of high office led him" and wherein he "became more and more tone deaf" at the very time that he needed to be more sensitive to his own difficulties and more responsive to the "inner meanings of the opposition voices" (170). Yet Bailyn's ear does not always function to distinguish his own judging voice from that of Hutchinson. He insinuates into the narrative and exposition of Hutchinson's ideas judgments of his own which seem to deny that there was any larger perspective than Hutchinson's: "Above all, he saw more clearly than any writer of the time that persistence in the claims of a moral basis for resistance must end in revolution—a revolution that history might justify if it succeeded, but not because it was in an objective sense more moral than the establishment it overthrew. For the relationship between law and morality, he saw, was ambiguous, and only success could be a final arbiter" (107).

Seeing is not a subjective act in that passage but an accurate perception of the way things are. A subtle shift in the meaning of "moral" between its first and second appearance and ambiguity in the phrase "history might justify" add to the reader's perplexity. One cannot be sure here whether the main subject is the validity of "history's" reasons for judging, the way historians ought to judge, or the meaninglessness of judgment in the face of irreversible fact. One can agree that the relationship between law and morality is ambiguous without abandoning the effort to approach moral judgment "in an objective sense." If that effort has any value, one might more fairly consider the issue not between "the establishment" and "the revolution" but between a colonial system and an independent republic. Is there no moral difference?

The technical difficulty becomes substantive in other passages as well. Portrayed almost exclusively in the most vehement attacks upon Hutchinson, complex figures such as John Adams and Benjamin Franklin usually seem in this book to be simply partisan, whereas

Hutchinson's invocations of law often call upon principle. And so, although Bailyn, of course, knows and sometimes explicitly says that Hutchinson completely misunderstood the depth and complexity of the opposition, when he declares in the epilogue that Hutchinson was "more intelligent, tolerant, experienced, and perceptive—and less sanctimonious by far—than most of those who opposed him" (377), one is provoked to reflect not only that a dozen or so of those opponents were similarly superior to most Loyalist leaders but also that this book gives inadequate emphasis to the crucial superiority in the few opponents who were more intelligent, tolerant, and perceptive than Hutchinson. Only in one fine passage which shows Benjamin Franklin advising Lord Dartmouth to do absolutely nothing about the Massachusetts General Assembly's declaration of virtual independence can Bailyn's readers see the evident superiority of Franklin's insight (214). Even when Hutchinson struggles for survival and exoneration by courting favor in London during the Revolution, Bailyn's sensitive delineation of his plight screens the reader from an adequate view of the opposition and the issues. That excellent passage traces the careful line that Hutchinson tried to walk between being accepted by the highest royal officials and seeming to approve the detested Coercive Acts against his people back in Boston, but Bailyn seems to believe Hutchinson's behavior was damning evidence only for "those who wished to see it that way" (318). Was it only the distortions of his correspondence, only misreadings out of context that condemned him, and never the substance correctly understood? Hutchinson deserves our sympathetic understanding, and history can scrupulously afford to distinguish between loyalty to the system and positive approval of its injustices. It ought also to distinguish between showing why a man acted as he did and implying that there was no other way for him to act. Much as he wished to do otherwise, Hutchinson did choose as absolutely as his opponents chose.

Technically as well as substantively, nonetheless, there are numerous triumphs in Bailyn's *Ordeal*. Among the most remarkable is his consistently implicit invocation of our contemporary experience through deft exposition. The unauthorized publication of Hutchinson's confidential letters reminds us (130–31) of the dean of the Harvard Faculty of Arts and Sciences who was similarly mistreated in 1969 and of the later controversy over Richard Nixon's White House tapes. Bailyn also brings the view of the American Revolution from England aptly into line with some perceptions of the American crisis over Southeast Asia in 1970. Hutchinson's problems came to seem unimportant in England, Bailyn shows, because "the great issues had become immediate and practical problems of conducting a land war three thousand miles from Europe and in the face both of a military foe that fought tenaciously in unorthodox ways and of a political opposition at home that was tireless, brilliantly articulate, and convinced that the war was an abomination being poorly fought against a people whose worst crime was to have struggled for the rights of men" (343–44). In that fine passage and in others Bailyn indicates in the narrative what he has candidly remarked in the preface: that the plight of a conservative administrator "in a time of radical upheaval" has a new opportunity to be observed with sympathy among scholars who recently tried to defend besieged universities (vii).

Note

1. Bernard Bailyn, *The Ordeal of Thomas Hutchinson* (Cambridge: Harvard Univ. Press, 1974), p. 374.

12.

Francis Parkman's *The Oregon Trail*

When I borrowed George Bancroft's *History of the United States* from the Harvard College library in 1946, just one hundred summers after Francis Parkman's celebrated adventure on the Oregon Trail, I found Parkman's signature boldly inscribed inside the cover of the third volume (1840). In that volume, at the age of seventeen or eighteen, Parkman had read Bancroft's narrative of the heroic French Jesuits in seventeenth-century Canada and of René Robert Cavelier de La Salle, whom Bancroft portrays as the kind of doomed Byronic figure that would later dominate Parkman's *La Salle and the Discovery of the Great West*. Parkman decided in 1841 to write the history on which he expended forty years' labor. He can hardly have overlooked Bancroft's extended reflections on the intellectual powers and cultural rigidity of North American Indians, for he had been passionately devoted for several years to vigorous action in the woods and mountains of New England.

The intensity of that commitment, evident in the epigraph Parkman chose for his first book, argues for personal and cultural sources deeper than the experience of reading one volume of history. Bancroft deserves special notice only because of the link between two of Parkman's passions: devotion to the wilderness and dedication to a particular subject in American history. Before he ever ventured west of St. Louis, Parkman knew that he wanted to observe "savage" life in the wilderness and to write the history of what he then called "the old French war." [1] Committed to the literary life of Unitarian New England gentlemen scholars even as he rather casually studied law at Harvard, Parkman had gone off on a physically demanding expedition in each summer of his college years, and he had published five narratives of

Introduction to the Viking Penguin edition of *The Oregon Trail* (New York, 1982), reprinted by permission of the publisher.

those travels in the *Knickerbocker Magazine*. He remembered twenty years later that "a new passion [had] seized him" during his mid-teens, and that it had "soon gained full control over the literary pursuits to which he was also addicted."[2] Just as he would later chide his hero, General James Wolfe, for failing to perceive that "the hero is greater than the poet," so in his forties he insisted that his own youthful ventures had relied "less on books than on such personal experience as should, in some sense, identify him with his theme."[3] His thoughts of "the forest," he said, had "possessed his waking and sleeping dreams, filling him with vague cravings, impossible to satisfy."[4] And during his senior year at Harvard, two years before he headed west for St. Louis and the Oregon Trail, he had suffered a nervous collapse which suggests that neither side of his paradoxical commitment had full control over the other.

Parkman's fear of becoming an invalid or an idle New England gentleman had endeared Byron to him long before he put Byron's revulsion from sickening decay on the title page of *The Oregon Trail:*

> Let him who crawls enamor'd of decay,
> Cling to his couch, and sicken years away;
> Heave his thick breath, and shake his palsied head;
> Ours—the fresh turf, and not the feverish bed.[5]

Parkman would identify himself on that title page as Francis Parkman, Jr., the young man of action who would not follow Francis Parkman, Sr., into the Unitarian clergy, nor other models into the law, but who would demonstrate his respectful allegiance as a writer.

Except for five years on his grandparents' farm in Medford, which gave him freedom to hunt in the wild woods of the Middlesex Fells, Parkman's boyhood resembled that of his most privileged contemporaries. Like many of them, he felt the weight of his New England heritage as both a gift and a challenge. Through his mother he was descended from John Cotton, an eminent minister of the founding generation in the 1630s and 1640s. Parkman's paternal grandfather, one of the richest merchants in Boston, had left a fortune large enough not only to let the next generation of the family live comfortably on a clergyman's modest salary, but also to let grandson Francis obey a literary vocation without much anxiety about income. The Reverend

Francis Parkman, moreover, was a protégé of the great William Ellery Channing and was pastor of the New North Church. Young Francis attended the Chauncy Hall School for four years and entered Harvard College in 1840. He persevered in spite of an apparent breakdown in 1843 that forced him to take an extended leave for a seven-month trip to Europe. Elected to Phi Beta Kappa, he went from the college to the Harvard Law School and graduated in 1846, only to suffer a recurrence of eye trouble that gave him an excuse for his adventure on the Oregon Trail.

Whatever the sources of Parkman's physical or emotional ailments, which he first experienced as "a painful beating of the heart,"[6] later as a weakness with symptoms of dysentery, later still as a terrible pressure on the brain and threats of blindness, and finally as a nearly crippling arthritis, Parkman struggled against the menace of incapacity for nearly sixty years. As a youth he drove himself to develop endurance in the mountains of New Hampshire and the wilds of Maine. As a resolute historian he sometimes had to employ readers to help him when his eyes were too weak for research and writing, and he was sometimes allowed to work for only a very brief time each day. His nine-volume history of British and French exploration and conflict stands therefore as a memorable personal victory.

Parkman could not have known how remarkably critical the year of his western adventure would be to the future of his country, and at the age of twenty-two he was not sufficiently prescient to know that several of the men he met in St. Louis would become major figures of the westward movement. But he did plan to meet in St. Louis several French survivors who had known the sachem Pontiac, the central figure in the first of Parkman's projected histories. From one of these men, Pierre Chouteau, Parkman's interview in St. Louis yielded valuable information about the circumstances of Pontiac's death.

Although Herman Melville, in an otherwise splendid review, complained that Parkman or the publisher had seductively added "California" to the title of *The Oregon Trail* in 1849, the year of the Gold Rush, the new trails on which Parkman and his companions set out in 1846 did include the name of California. The California and Oregon trails coincided for more than a thousand miles before they separated.

(Melville implicitly conceded the point, but said this was also the route to Bombay, and that a writer who had stopped on the eastern slope of the Rockies ought not to say he has followed the Bombay Trail.) Parkman did meet some members of the tragic Donner party, and yet another group that was trying to find a more direct route to California. After his two-week sojourn among the Ogillallah Sioux, he headed south and then east along the Santa Fe Trail to Westport, Missouri.

The date of Parkman's adventure is of central importance from a literary as well as a historical point of view. A number of excellent contemporary writers, not all of them known to Parkman, were turning their adventurous experience into literary art. Richard Henry Dana, Jr., narrated the experience and pleaded the cause of ordinary sailors in *Two Years before the Mast* (1840). Washington Irving followed his famous books on travels in England and Spain with narratives from his tour of the American West in *A Tour on the Prairies* (1835). And in the very year of Parkman's journey to the West two of the best American writers of the century occupied themselves with the literature of personal experience in nature: Herman Melville published *Typee,* a narrative based on his weeks among cannibals in the Marquesas Islands; and Henry Thoreau, in residence at Walden Pond, was already recording his experiment in confronting the essential facts of life—the experiment on which he would report a few years later in one of our great books, *Walden; or, Life in the Woods* (1854).

Every one of these books profits from a commitment to study the manners of others, to report on a life close to nature, and to use the author's new perspective as a means of revealing new truths about American civilization. Melville's protagonist is surprised to learn that a society of cannibals lives without internal strife because it lives without money, and he concludes that "white civilized man" (observed through his historic influence on primitive cultures in the Marquesas and Sandwich islands) is "the most ferocious animal on the face of the earth."[7] Henry Thoreau, hoeing beans near Concord, Massachusetts, hears the music of a military band and comments not about life in the Sandwich Islands but about Americans who are "said to live in New England."[8] And Frederick Douglass, recently escaped to the North and still subject to recapture, publishes in 1845 a forthright declaration of his equality and a challenging analysis of American slavery and liberty in *The Narrative of Frederick Douglass, an American Slave, Written by Himself.*

Francis Parkman begins his journey, then, in 1846, a time of great literary concern with American character, in the year Bernard De Voto later called the Year of Decision. Parkman's adventure coincides with the opening of the war between the United States and Mexico. In the West he meets emigrants bound for the Pacific Coast and persecuted Mormons (whom his first version of this narrative calls "a horde of fanatics")[9] on their way to Utah. Before returning east to the "settlements," he meets soldiers both going to and returning from Mexico. The whole country seems at times to be full of movement toward the West. For better or worse, American destiny seems manifest. The Indian nations and the buffalo, wandering together across the Great Plains, are doomed.

Parkman, of course, already knew before setting out for the West that the Indians' way of life was doomed. His entire book, like many others of the time—from James Fenimore Cooper's romances to Parkman's own later histories—is steeped in nostalgia for a primeval world that is fated to change drastically. Parkman arrives not only prepared to study strange manners and natural phenomena but also convinced that they will very soon disappear. "My business," he says in the preface to a later edition, "was observation, and I was willing to pay dearly for the opportunity of exercising it" (xi).

The Oregon Trail is therefore filled with pictures that express a remarkable intensity, as if the narrator were at once resolved to suffuse his life with experience and to preserve the experience in images against the immediate threat that similar experience will no longer be possible. He must see the Indians before their way of life vanishes. He longs to experience the buffalo hunt, an Indian war, the summer migration of an Indian village. He rejoices to hear that the Dahcotah (Dakota) nation plans war against the people called Snakes, and he is deeply disappointed when he misses the action. Struck with a debilitating illness, he acts out what might be considered an allegory of his entire scholarly life as he defies sickness and forces himself onward over a vast landscape in a desperate effort to find the Sioux in their genuine martial condition. Ill and alone at that point, he wanders over dry hills and plains in futile search of a large Indian army. With him he carries three books—the Bible, the works of Shakespeare, and the works of Byron—but it is only the last of these that he mentions reading during his long adventure. Lonely endurance in the face of hardship is his test of manhood.

Yet even as he bears his literary culture with him, Parkman is committed to correcting its erroneous versions of actual experience. His dissent from idealized pictures of American Indian life has been noticed ever since Herman Melville singled it out in one of the first reviews, but Douglas Anderson and Melody Graulich have recently shown in independent studies that Parkman was one of a number of factual writers who set out to correct eastern misconceptions of the West.

The excellent pictures that result from these attitudes express some of the best qualities of romantic writing in nineteenth-century America. Among contemporaries only Thoreau and Melville can match the exactness of Parkman's pictures: the prairie teeming with animal life; snakes, owls, prairie dogs, wolves, antelope; a bullfrog, a turtle, and snakes in a pond; the "level monotony of the plain" (61) when it is empty and Parkman can see "not a tree nor a bush nor a living thing" (78); the moon rising in a prairie sky; a group of "squalid" Indians with shaved heads and leading their "meagre little horses" laden with buffalo meat (62); a wagon train seemingly motionless ("the tall white wagons and the little black specks of horsemen" in the "tall rank grass" of the prairie [65]); a sudden prairie thunderstorm turning the woods purple and leveling the tall grass; ox-wagons fording a treacherously swift stream; "a long procession of buffalo . . . walking in Indian file, with the utmost gravity and deliberation," on the crest of a distant hill (67).

In depicting the buffalo, Parkman takes care to communicate the experience of wild terrain, as well as the massive numbers of buffalo, before he concentrates on what it is like to shoot a single buffalo bull. On his first hunt, for example, he follows his guide through the tall, rank grass toward the base of the hills:

> From one of their openings descended a deep ravine, widening as it issued on the prairie. We entered it, and galloping up, in a moment were surrounded by the bleak sand-hills. Half of their steep sides were bare; the rest were scantily clothed with clumps of grass, and various

uncouth plants, conspicuous among which appeared the reptile-like prickly-pear. They were gashed with numberless ravines; and as the sky had suddenly darkened and a cold dusty wind arisen, the strange shrubs and the dreary hills looked doubly wild and desolate. [66]

In almost every chase, with Indian hunters and with his few traveling companions, Parkman reminds us of the immensity of western space, the changeable terrain, the correction of illusion as one rides at full speed over rough but seemingly level ground and then suddenly loses perspective when the land dips between two hills. Repeatedly the chase takes the hunter miles away from his companions, and he must find his solitary way back to camp after a lonely separation, sometimes overnight.

This kind of experience leads Parkman to anticipate some of the techniques of impressionism, as in the passage just quoted, and it also leads him to stress the versatility of human vision. The painter's eye, restricted a moment ago by the sudden entry into the ravine, can now, in the open country, hold in view a massive number of animals:

> We had gone scarcely a mile when we saw an imposing spectacle. From the river bank on the right, away over the swelling prairie on the left, and in front as far as the eye could reach, was one vast host of buffalo. The outskirts of the herd were within a quarter of a mile. In many parts they were crowded so densely together that in the distance their rounded backs presented a surface of uniform blackness; but elsewhere they were more scattered, and from amid the multitude rose little columns of dust where some of them were rolling on the ground. Here and there a battle was going forward among the bulls. We could distinctly see them rushing against each other, and hear the clattering of their horns and their hoarse bellowing. [331–32]

From that distant perspective Parkman takes us with him in chase of the herd until, "half suffocated by the dust and stunned by the trampling" sound, he gives a sharp impression from the center of the mass as the herd rushes into the ravine: "Suddenly, to my amazement, the hoofs were jerked upwards, the tails flourished in the air, and amid a cloud of dust the buffalo seemed to sink into the earth before me" (333). Herman Melville quoted that passage in his review of *The Oregon Trail*.

The climactic picture of the buffalo is a clear portrait of an individual creature confronted by Parkman the lone hunter, who lies in wait by a river and watches buffalo come to drink. Except for a few more adjectives and some uncertainty about point of view, Parkman anticipates here both the literary method and the attitude toward nature of Ernest Hemingway. As the hunter waits beside a stream, a bull steps out from the grass on the other side and

> bends his head to drink. You may hear the water as it gurgles down his capacious throat. He raises his head, and the drops trickle from his wet beard. He stands with an air of stupid abstraction, unconscious of the lurking danger. Noiselessly the hunter cocks his rifle. As he sits upon the sand, his knee is raised, and his elbow rests upon it, that he may level his heavy weapon with a steadier aim. . . . The bull, with slow deliberation, begins his march over the sands to the other side. He advances his foreleg, and exposes to view a small spot, denuded of hair, just behind the point of his shoulder; upon this the hunter brings the sight of his rifle to bear. . . . The spiteful crack of the rifle responds to his touch, and instantly in the middle of the bare spot appears a small red dot. The buffalo shivers; death has overtaken him, he cannot tell from whence; still he does not fall, but walks heavily forward, as if nothing had happened. Yet before he has gone far out upon the sand, you see him stop; he totters; his knees bend under him, and his head sinks forward to the ground. Then his whole vast bulk sways to one side; he rolls over on the sand, and dies with a scarcely perceptible struggle. [342–43]

The same kind of pictorial skill helps Parkman give his human pictures a depth not merely visual but also historical. At the very beginning he shows us a remarkably varied collection of people preparing to leave the frontier settlements. (Melville, who would later set the scene of *The Confidence-Man* on a steamboat headed down the Mississippi River, praised in his review Parkman's description of the mixed crowd aboard one on the Missouri.) When Parkman arrives at Fort Laramie after weeks of hard riding and walking, he encounters a migrant Indian village and a large group of emigrants heading west. He depicts the emigrants as "a crowd of broad-brimmed hats, thin visages, and staring eyes. . . . Tall awkward men, in brown homespun; women with cadaverous faces and long lank figures, came thronging in together, and, as if inspired by the very demon of curiosity, ransacked every nook and corner of the fort" (106). Parkman shrewdly notices the indiscriminate thoroughness of their invasion, the depth of their anxiety and mistrust for strangers, and their bewilderment before the immensity and desolation of the country through which they slowly travel: "They seemed like men totally out of their element; bewildered and amazed, like a troop of schoolboys lost in the woods" (106). He catches the determination, the unpreparedness, and the misery of these migrant families in one symbolic picture that makes them the last pilgrims in a three-hundred-year-old westward movement. He notices along the trail beside the river Platte

> the shattered wrecks of ancient claw-footed tables, well waxed and rubbed, or massive bureaus of carved oak. These, some of them no doubt the relics of ancestral prosperity in the colonial time, must have encountered strange vicissitudes. Brought, perhaps, originally from England; then, with the declining fortunes of their owners, borne across the Alleghanies to the wilderness of Ohio or Kentucky; then to Illinois or Missouri; and now at last fondly stowed away in the family wagon for the interminable journey to Oregon. But the stern privations of the way are little anticipated. The cherished relic is soon flung out to scorch and crack upon the hot prairie. [82–83]

The pictures of migrant Indian villages have the same strong historical quality, but here Parkman does not need to comment so explicitly on their symbolic meaning. From his first encounter outside Fort Laramie through his sojourns among the Ogillallah and among the Dahcotah in the Black Hills, he gives us numerous pictures of the nomadic village that travels all day, establishes itself quickly in tents at evening, and then disappears in the morning as fast as these fated Indians and the buffalo on which they thrive will disappear from the face of the Great Plains. Throughout his description of Indian customs and manners, the suddenness of their arrival and departure, with imagery of swarms, reinforces our sense of their impermanence.

Yet Parkman's tone in describing Indian life rings with the condescension that Melville recognized as the genteel New Englander's conception of progress. As Parkman moves among the Indians he sounds very much like Tommo, the narrator of Melville's *Typee,* but unlike Melville's narrator Parkman never learns to respect the people whose life he observes. He speaks in the tone of the civilized easterner observing inferior beings, and his language is full of allusions to savages, superstition, cutthroats, half-breeds. When concentrating on the ugliness or harshness of Indian life, he creates vivid, often comic pictures which many readers have welcomed as a correction of sentimental fiction about the Noble Savage. Consider, for example, his description of an eighty-year-old Ogillallah squaw:

> The moving spirit of the establishment was an old hag of eighty. You could count all her ribs through the wrinkles of her leathery skin. Her withered face more resembled an old skull than the countenance of a living being, even to the hollow, darkened sockets, at the bottom of which glittered her little black eyes. Her arms had dwindled into nothing but whip-cord and wire. Her hair, half black, half gray, hung in total neglect nearly to the ground, and her sole garment consisted of a remnant of a discarded buffalo-robe tied round her waist with a string of hide. Yet the old squaw's meagre anatomy was wonderfully strong. She pitched the lodge, packed the horses, and did the hardest labor in the camp. From morning till night she bustled about the lodge, screaming like a screech-owl when anything displeased her. [140–41]

Here and in more pleasant delineations of Indian clothing and customs Parkman gives us vivid information from an uncomprehending outsider whose self-criticism never extends beyond good-humored reminiscences of the discomforts of travel. He is a faithful reporter and a brave man, but limited by a very narrow conception of Indian culture. He can describe an Ogillallah hero who looks like "an Apollo of bronze" and speaks in the "deep notes of an organ"; but he must remind us that "after all [the hero] was but an Indian" (149–50).

Douglas Anderson has wisely pointed out that this passage is often quoted out of context (as I myself have done), that Parkman goes on to give a splendid picture of Mahto-Tatonka's respected ceremonial function within his community, and that in the first published version (printed in the *Knickerbocker Magazine*) the long paragraph concludes with a resonant declaration which was deleted from all subsequent editions:

> Truly it is a poor thing, this life of an Indian. Few and mean are its pleasures. War without the inspiration of chivalry, gallantry with no

sentiments to elevate it. Yet never have I seen in any Indian village on the remote prairies such depravity, such utter abasement and prostitution of every nobler part of humanity, as I have seen in great cities, the centres of the world's wisdom and refinement. The meanest savage in the Whirlwind's camp would seem noble and dignified compared with some of the lost children of civilization. [10]

Yet despite his conventional judgment that many civilized men in Rome, Liverpool, and New York were even more degraded than savages, Parkman gives us in *The Oregon Trail* an ill-comprehended experience of Indian hospitality, the nomadic life, and Indian religion. In these pages Indian thought, like Indian conversation, seems empty, to be judged by the standard of technological and Unitarian progress. "They were thorough savages," Parkman says of the Ogillallah. "Neither their manners nor their ideas were in the slightest degree modified by their contact with civilization. They knew nothing of the power and real character of the white men, and their children would scream in terror when they saw me. . . . They were living representations of the 'stone age'" (189).

It is just after his introduction to Ogillallah life that Parkman predicts the decline of the buffalo and therefore the ruin of the "large wandering communities who depend on them for support. . . . The Indians will soon be abased by whiskey and overawed by military posts; so that within a few years the traveller may pass in tolerable security through their country. Its danger and its charm will have disappeared together" (190). Parkman understands the direction of history but not the nature of Indian life. For him that life exists chiefly as danger and charm, as experience and image but not as value.

In this regrettable limitation, as in his strength, Parkman represents American literary culture in his time, although Melville, Thoreau, and a few others would have dissented. The western Indians in those days were often a genuine threat to any stranger moving across the landscape, but Parkman seems unable to connect the Indians' hostility with the threat posed to their life by white migration. He cannot transcend the invaders' point of view. He repeatedly comments on the need to treat Indian offenses severely in order to avoid contemptuous attacks in consequence, and although he never does encounter real danger from Indians, he describes many near-misses and narrates several tales of murder.

Faithful nevertheless to his primary duty as observer, Parkman achieves in *The Oregon Trail* one of the liveliest accounts we have of life in motion on the Great Plains. He does not underestimate the misery caused by insects, oppressive heat, violent storms, runaway horses, disagreeable companions, and enervating illness. His portrayal of a starving black man who has wandered for thirty-three days on the prairie, barely subsisting on crickets and lizards, gives us a view of loneliness that is just as powerful as Melville's portrayal of the madness caused by solitary immersion in the vast calm of the Pacific Ocean. Even in some of the descriptions of his own loneliness, when his illness is most distressing, Parkman lets us experience both the misery and the heroism attendant on adventure in the West.

Here, as I have already suggested, Parkman's narrative tends toward allegory, for in his great histories he was to spend the rest of his life in a literary quest for genuine historical Indians, and was to fight against an illness more completely debilitating than those that afflicted him during this journey. Among all the motley characters in *The Oregon Trail,* Parkman is almost unique in his capacity to understand the historical significance of the experience. Both the merits and the defects of his reflections on actual Indian life owe something to his interest in legendary Indians, and when he encounters the grandsons of Daniel Boone among the bands of emigrants, he is alert to the legend of the frontiersman. In the characterization of his guide Henry Chatillon, Parkman finds legend justified by reality.

Henry Chatillon is an illiterate hero, schooled in the ways of the Indian and the prairie, possessed of "a natural refinement of mind"; his face is "a mirror of uprightness, simplicity, and kindness," and he has a naturally shrewd perception of character (12–13). When Parkman meets him Chatillon has just returned to St. Louis after four years in the Rockies, and he is prepared to set forth again almost immediately. He has fought the grizzly bear, he is thoroughly at home among the Indians, and he is loyal to his Indian wife, whose grievous death occurs during the narrative. Parkman depicts him only a few times, but with unforgettable effect when Chatillon moves easily among a herd of buffalo, who "seem no more to regard his presence than if he were one of themselves" (345). He regards the buffalo as "a kind of companions," and he tells Parkman that he never feels alone when they are around him (346). Like Cooper's Leatherstocking, he cannot abide the wanton shooting of wild creatures. He acts most forcibly in Parkman's narrative as the virtuous antagonist of a self-indulgent soldier who has joined the party for the ride back to the settlements.

The return to those secure communities is for Parkman a return from the "arid deserts, meagerly covered by the tufted buffalo-grass," through Arcadian plains "carpeted with rich herbiage sprinkled with flowers," to the green prairies "of the poet and novelist" (376–77). As Parkman expresses relief over his return to the settlements, he remains true to the call of the wilderness, to which he looks back regretfully. It is Henry Chatillon, at the end of the book, who represents that attraction in the final paragraph. Parkman depicts him there in plain city clothes that express his "native good taste"; and we are asked at the end to imagine him riding the gift horse of Shaw, Parkman's comrade, and firing Parkman's rifle in the Rocky Mountains (381). There, in Parkman's fancy, Henry Chatillon rides as a living testimony to the possibility of mediation between the doomed past and the inevitable future; and Parkman heads east on railroad coaches and steamboats to memorialize that possibility in a book.

Chatillon thus resembles not only Cooper's Leatherstocking, whose virtues he embodies, but also Melville's Bulkington, the sailor in *Moby-Dick* who, having just returned to New Bedford from a three-year voyage, immediately embarks on another. Chatillon cannot stay long in the settlements; he must return to the mountains. And the overwhelming effect of Parkman's book is an impression of the grandeur in which men like Chatillon and more uncouth, typical trappers live their exciting, dangerous, hardy lives. Sometimes the empty prairie is "an impersonation of Silence and Solitude" (184). Once, at sunset, it looks like "a turbulent ocean, suddenly congealed when its waves were at the highest, and it lay half in light and half in shadow as the rich sunshine, yellow as gold, was pouring over it. The rough bushes of the wild sage were growing everywhere, its dull pale-green overspreading hill and hollow" (185). Soon afterward, the hill country nearby is filled with violent action as Ogillallah hunters kill buffalo with bow and arrow, and Parkman gives us a memorable view of some young men cracking huge buffalo thighbones and devouring the marrow. It is the rich, wild variety of life and the vast size of the continent that Parkman celebrates in dozens of landscapes, portraits, catalogs. He brings experience to his eastern readers, and he also brings them a joyful report of the great country over which the invasion, with more of his cheers than his regrets (and regardless of both cheers and regrets), inexorably moves.

The consequences of his heroic journey may be properly said to have remained with Parkman for the rest of his long life, for he was never again thoroughly free of sickness, and he was even forced by his damaged eyesight to dictate much of the narrative when he first composed it (following the journal he had kept and letters he had written home) for the *Knickerbocker Magazine* (1847–49). His permanent place in American letters may well have been established by this book of his youth, but he returned often to this summer's experience in the great histories that form his major achievement. Over the next forty-five years he composed his narrative history of *France and England in North America,* celebrating the achievements and sufferings of explorers, missionaries, and soldiers in the centuries from the first French settlements to the Anglo-American conquest of Canada in 1763. As he struggled to complete that history, the American frontier was extended to the Pacific Coast. Parkman died in 1893, at just about the time the official report by the United States Census stated that the frontier no longer existed.

Notes

1. Howard Doughty, *Francis Parkman* (New York: Macmillan, 1962), p. 50.

2. Francis Parkman, autobiographical letter, in Charles-Haight Farnham, *A Life of Francis Parkman* (Boston: Little, Brown, 1900), p. 319.

3. Francis Parkman, *Montcalm and Wolfe,* 2 vols. (Boston, 1894), 2:286; Farnham, *Parkman,* p. 320.

4. Ibid.

5. Byron, *The Corsair,* Canto 1:27–30.

6. Farnham, *Parkman,* p. 133.

7. Herman Melville, *Typee: A Peep at Polynesian Life,* ed. Harrison Hayford et al. (Evanston and Chicago: Northwestern Univ. Press, 1968), p. 125.

8. Henry D. Thoreau, *Walden; or, Life in the Woods* (Boston, 1894), p. 2.

9. See Francis Parkman, *The Oregon Trail,* 4th ed. (1872; rept. Boston, 1894), p. 37. In the fourth edition, the original wording of the *Knickerbocker* articles has been softened to "large armed bodies of these fanatics," but the preface refers again to "polygamous hordes of Mormon" (p. x).

10. Douglas Anderson, "The Explanation of the West: Exploration, Expectation, and Uncertainty from Lewis and Clark to Frederick Law Olmsted" (Ph.D. diss., Univ. of Virginia, 1980), pp. 181–82.

13.

James Baldwin's Autobiographical Essays

The Problem of Negro Identity

The world and James Baldwin's place in it have changed drastically since the publication of *The Fire Next Time* a year ago. Baldwin, it is true, had already published in the *New Yorker* and the *Progressive* the essays that have since won phenomenal sales in book form. But the Birmingham riots had not yet occurred. Baldwin had not made the electrifying speaking tour that hit western universities and towns with the force of an old-fashioned revival. Nor had he received the full-scale, public analysis that has since been accorded him by such divergent journals as *Life, Encounter,* and *Dissent.* Medgar Evers had not been shot. The Birmingham children had not been murdered in their Sunday school. President Kennedy was not only alive but subject to the criticism of spokesmen like Baldwin who (along with the madness of segregationists) later persuaded him to speak to the entire country on the moral issue of racial discrimination.

Now, of course, Baldwin has come to represent for "white" Americans the eloquent, indignant prophet of an oppressed people, a voice speaking in print, on television, and from the public platform in an all but desperate, final effort to bring us out of what he calls our innocence before it is (if it is not already) too late. This voice calls us to our immediate duty for the sake of our own humanity as well as our own safety. It demands that we stop regarding the Negro as an abstraction, an invisible man; that we begin to recognize each Negro in his "human

Reprinted from the *Massachusetts Review* 5 (Winter 1964): 239–47; this paper was first presented to the section on Literature and Society at the annual meeting of the Modern Language Association, December 1963. The word *Negro* was then generally accepted as a proper term, the equivalent of African American in 1991.

weight and complexity";[1] that we face the horrible reality of our past and present treatment of Negroes—a reality we do not know and do not want to know.

This message has always formed the core of Baldwin's autobiographical writings, those essays that have made *Notes of a Native Son, Nobody Knows My Name,* and *The Fire Next Time* more successful than his fiction. It is a message that seems to me undeniable, in spite of logical difficulties and fluctuations of attitude over a discouraging fifteen years of accelerating conflict and creeping progress, and it is a message that seems now almost too urgent to allow the presumption of literary analysis and historical qualification. Yet Baldwin has made his desire "to be an honest man and a good writer" (9) the central metaphor through which to express, in his autobiographical writings, his spiritual quest and his evangelical plea to our society. Moreover, this patently topical subject requires us to look with Baldwin at several issues in American and other history and to consider him in relation to writers who seem as remote as Cotton Mather.

The word "identity" recurs over and over again in Baldwin's autobiographical essays. The essential question, for himself and for the American audience that he assumes is white, is: Who am I? or: How can I be myself? In his answers to these questions we see the strength that places several of Baldwin's autobiographical essays among the best in American literature; we must see there also several inconsistencies and errors that may be the inevitable price of his method.

As he has rearranged them, without regard for chronology, in his books, these essays give great importance not only to the question of identity but to Baldwin's recurrent answer: I am a writer. His resolution to be an honest man and a good writer concludes the autobiographical preface to *Notes of a Native Son.* This book tells us at what cost in experience and self-analysis Baldwin arrived at so abstract an acceptance of his humanity. Being a writer meant coming to terms with his condition as native son, first as the individual son of his individual father, then in the ironic sense conveyed by Richard Wright's novel, and finally, with the perspective of his European experience, in reluctant but unqualified acceptance of his complex fate as an American Negro, this new man, "as American as the Americans who despise him, the Americans who fear him, the Americans who love him"

(173)—a man with a peculiar status and a peculiar mission to speak in the Western world at a time when it is imperative to know that "this world is white no longer, and it will never be white again" (175).

The obligation to find a voice with which to speak one's message to the Western world is familiar to students of American religion and American autobiography. It did not begin with Richard Wright or with naturalism. Baldwin seems aware of the relationship between his religious experience and his new obligation as the Writer when he recounts his last conversation with his father in the superb narrative essay that gives *Notes of a Native Son* its title. Here, as later in *The Fire Next Time,* Baldwin describes his religious conversion as an adolescent and his youthful success as a preacher. Then he recalls that his father, an unsuccessful preacher who hated white people and deeply suspected the son's literary ambitions, had once suddenly asked him: "You'd rather write than preach, wouldn't you?" And he recalls that his answer was "Yes" (108). He does not pursue the relationship so emphatically as I shall follow it, but it seems clear to me that in his work the writer's mission is very much like the young preacher's, except that the nature of the truth has changed. Released from the beliefs that distorted his view of reality, he can now bear faithful witness to the truth that he believes we all need to see. He can use his special powers to convey some sense of experiences that, like grace, can be known only at first hand: the discovery of color and of the society's war on anyone who resists its racial categories; the discovery of one's own rage, of hatred for one's persecutors, one's black father's powdered corpse, one's own color; the resolution to transcend one's hatred. Baldwin's function as a writer is to make us see, and he shocks us with abrupt reversals of our usual point of view—as the first black man, a veritable Gulliver, ever to enter a cold, white Swiss village; as a half-frozen worshiper on Christmas Day in a solitary cubicle in a French prison, "peering through a slot placed at the level of the eye, at an old Frenchman, hatted, overcoated, muffled, and gloved, [who preached] . . . in this language that I did not understand, to this row of wooden boxes, the story of Jesus Christ's love for men." When Baldwin is "chilled by the merriment" with which Frenchmen who have subjected him to great misery endeavor to warm him, he reminds us of Henry Thoreau. In a "deep, black, stony, and liberating way," he tells us, his own life began the day he endured this merriment, for he learned then that "the laughter of those for whom the pain of living is not real . . . is universal and never can be stilled" (158). Here he reminds us of enthusiasts like Thoreau and Melville and Edwards and Hooker, who persisted in seeing the convicting reality that others would not see.

Throughout *Nobody Knows My Name* and *The Fire Next Time,* the role of the writer as the center of identity remains important. The writer, rather than the statesman, is our most important means of reopening communication between the Old World and the New, Baldwin tells us in the opening essay in *Nobody Knows My Name,* and in this volume he moves as a critical observer through Europe and America, reporting on a conference of African writers and artists, on visits to Harlem and the Deep South, and on his personal relationship with Richard Wright and Norman Mailer.

In *The Fire Next Time,* the main essay brings religion back into the center of autobiographical concern. Here Baldwin describes his early life in Harlem, his conversion, and his successful performance as a preacher in "the church racket."[2] The experience, of course, is the uniquely harrowing experience of the son of a Negro minister in the ghetto, but his discovery of inadequacies in the Christian God and the Christian people who dominated his childhood differs little from the same discovery in other self-taught American writers: Benjamin Franklin, Thomas Paine, Herman Melville, Mark Twain. Having become a writer, having learned to use the warfare between rage and intelligence that he says destroys many American Negroes, Baldwin goes in this autobiographical narrative on a mission to Elijah Muhammad, leader of the Black Muslims, and the second half of the narrative sets off against the first another religious effort to diminish him by capturing his allegiance. Elijah Muhammad sees that Baldwin wants to become himself, but the Muslim meaning for that phrase simply substitutes one kind of racial power for another. When the prophet asks Baldwin, the former Christian, "And what are you now?," Baldwin replies: "'I? Now? Nothing.' This was not enough. 'I'm a writer. I like doing things alone.'" Then, as in the account of his earlier conversion (and Martin Luther's supposed account of his conversion), Baldwin the narrator adds: "I heard myself saying this" (84).

The writer has won by his experience a place that is separate from both groups, Christians and Muslims. To the presumably white audience he shows the "hypocrisies," as he calls them (61), of Christianity, and he forces us to see that there is much in the Muslim movement to tempt him or any Negro. Yet he cannot be himself unless he faces his American past, his African past, and his indissoluble relationship to his countrymen and the world. He steps forward at the end to apply the lesson for all of us, speaking in the first person plural for "relatively conscious whites and relatively conscious blacks, who must . . . insist on, or create, the consciousness of others." He demands that we recognize our past and our unique opportunity to abandon the fiction that this is a white nation, and thus "to achieve our country" (119). He calls this achieving our identity, our maturity as men and women. Like many a preacher before him, he admits that we are merely a handful. No matter, he concludes. We must "dare everything" or face the prophetic warning: "*God gave Noah the rainbow sign, No more water, the fire next time*" (120).

In this brief study of the writer's mission in Baldwin's autobiographical essays I have understated his awareness of complexity in human personality and history. The perceptive sensibility of the writer stands in these works for his commitment to respect that complexity. He wants, I believe, to represent the lonely individual trying to achieve dignity in the modern world. Becoming himself requires him to accept with pain the hatred that he has felt for his father, for white men, and for himself. The effect of the entire series is a powerful, if gloomy, reassertion of the American idea—the very notion of the union of the human race that such patriots as George Bancroft celebrated long ago. And the idea gains great force from Baldwin's emphasis (often in Christian language that burns deep) on the Negro's awareness that Americans have so consistently betrayed the principle. Through these narratives the Negro becomes, in one of the least felicitous of Baldwin's phrases, "*the* key figure in this country" (*Fire* 108). One reason, of course, is that American treatment of the Negro will test the country's worthiness to survive in a world no longer white. But another, more important to the development of an honest man and a good writer, is that the Negro himself must overcome immense pressures and temptations if he is to transcend the fact of color, the hatred of whites, the restricting bitterness that might keep him from achieving what Baldwin calls his identity. The writer uses his experience as an American Negro to tell us crucial truths about ourselves and all men.

It seems to me that Baldwin accomplishes this task most effectively in several of the brilliant autobiographical essays in *Notes of a Native Son*. Especially in the title essay, one of the best autobiographical narratives in our literature, he gives us a sharp sense not only of the pain but of the vigorous diversity of Negro life in America. Even when he is describing the signs warning of the Harlem riots of 1943, signs that reveal a growing union of resentment against the mistreatment of Negro soldiers, he communicates this variety. He is not picturesque or sentimental; he never lets us forget his belief that before reaching puberty every Negro native to this country has been irreparably scarred by the conditions of his life; but he paints a memorable picture of the disparate groups gathering in the streets, and his recognition of the differing responses of "race" men and prostitutes and sharpies and churchly women and newspaper editors keeps us in touch with the human beings to whom our innocence does so much damage.

In almost every essay, however, and especially when he writes about our obligation to face the facts of the past, Baldwin's didactic purpose and his predicament as an American Negro force him to ignore his conviction that color does not matter. They force him to ignore the weight and complexity of human beings. Although he shows magnificently that he knows better, his method leads him to write of Negroes as if they were all of one mind and culture, and of whites (or groups of whites) as if they belonged uniformly to another. The uncertainty of method appears most openly in the midst of a superb piece called "The Harlem Ghetto," when Baldwin, having explained the hostility that many Harlem Negroes feel toward Jewish shopkeepers, doubts that "any real and systematic cooperation can be achieved between Negroes and Jews." So sweeping is the generalization, so seriously has he taken his labels, that he feels compelled to enter a qualification familiar to racists who are quick to reassure one about some of their best friends: "This is in terms of the over-all social problem," he says, "and is not meant to imply that individual friendships are impossible or that they are valueless when they occur" (69). Here the writer seems to have forgotten that the only possible kind of friendship in a tragic world is individual friendship and that systematic cooperation can hardly occur between groups that have no existence except through the irrational, unsystematic exclusions of others.

The problem is most serious in Baldwin's discussion of the Negro's past, and it is especially serious because he calls us to face the past honestly and to resist the temptation to invent a false one. When criticizing Richard Wright and when reporting on a conference of Negro and African artists, Baldwin sees plainly the vast difference between Africans and American Negroes; nor does he fail to notice that much of the language, psychology, moral attitude in which Richard Wright's eloquent *Black Boy* protests Western injustices comes from forces that "had nothing to do with Africa."[3] The value of the Negro's special experience, Baldwin perceives, is its double-edgedness, the Negro's separateness from both Europe and Africa. He even goes so far as to contend that the only thing all Americans have in common is their having no identity other than the identity being achieved on this continent.

Yet the "I" in these essays often proclaims an undefined African heritage "that was taken from him, almost literally, at one blow" (169). He proclaims what seems to me a specious distinction between the experience of African immigrants, uniquely horrible though that has been, and the experience of all other immigrants. He tells us that a man called Baldwin enslaved him and forced him to kneel at the foot of the cross. He tells us that the most illiterate Swiss villager is related, in a way he himself can never attain, to Dante, Shakespeare, and Michelangelo, and that the cathedral at Chartres and the Empire State Building say something to Swiss villagers (or would if the villagers could ever see them) that these buildings cannot say to him. When he enters a Swiss village, he says, he finds himself among a people whose culture "controls" him, has even in a sense "created" him. "Go back a few centuries," he says, "and they are in their full glory—but I am in Africa, watching the conquerors arrive" (164–65). The same difficulty persists in a more positive way when at last he affirms his American identity and praises the sturdiness of the "peasant" stock from which he descends: "I am one of the first Americans to arrive on these shores" (*Fire* 112).

The fallacy here lies deep in the method and in the historical assumptions. We must be prepared to accept it as an expression of one sensitive Negro's response to his predicament, and perhaps as a polemical answer to condescending views of the Negro's past; but we must reject it when, as in the examples I have just cited, Baldwin seems to offer the argument as truth. For our purposes it will suffice to outline the logical and historical difficulties. The method ignores, first of all, a major truth demonstrated by Melville J. Herskovits and others, that the African Negro's culture was not destroyed by the shock of enforced emigration and slavery.[4] Moreover, as Baldwin himself seems to recognize elsewhere, the choice of genealogical identity for an American can lead (by the methods used here) to strange problems. Where do the descendants of mixed races or nations go in this atavistic game? My own children (if I may use an autobiographical example) can choose to be in their glory in Germany or Denmark or among seasick Protestants on the Mayflower—or else among Jews in Romania or Russia. Unless he subscribes to a more exclusively genetic theory of culture than he has specified, Baldwin must find it hard to believe that Western culture controls him any more than it controls millions of other Americans who have no African ancestors.

Surely the way in which Baldwin is related to Shakespeare and Dante is more important than the way an illiterate European is related to either of them—more important, too, than the way Baldwin is related to the man in Africa watching the conquerors arrive. The Bible he uses so magnificently is not someone else's Bible but his Bible, and he is not the creature but the master of the language he uses. The American Negro's past to which he calls our attention is much more complex than the demands of Baldwin's autobiographical and polemical techniques have sometimes allowed him to admit; and so is the past of American whites. It will not weaken the force of Baldwin's indictment to recognize that, as early as 1781, the slave owner Thomas Jefferson wrote a warning as ominous as *The Fire Next Time*. There is no attribute of the Almighty, Jefferson wrote, that could lead whites to expect divine support in the conflict Jefferson considered inevitable unless slavery could be abolished. Nor can we take any comfort from the knowledge that our national imperviousness to the Negro's humanity has resisted the wit of a Benjamin Franklin and the eloquence of a Henry Thoreau. Baldwin, however, would honor us all without compromising himself in the slightest degree if he would accept his identity as an original American writer whose autobiographical work has established its place in a tradition that begins with Bradford, Woolman, Franklin, Edwards, Emerson, and Thoreau.

Notes

1. James Baldwin, *Notes of a Native Son* (Boston: Beacon Press, 1955), p. 172.

2. James Baldwin, *The Fire Next Time* (New York: Dial Press, 1963), p. 43.

3. James Baldwin, *Nobody Knows My Name* (New York: Dell Books, 1961), p. 37.

4. See, for example, Melville J. Herskovits, *The Myth of the Negro Past* (Boston: Beacon Press, 1941), and Sterling Stuckey, *Slave Culture: Nationalist Theory and the Foundations of Black America* (New York: Oxford Univ. Press, 1987).

Part Three

Fiction and History

14.

American Fiction as Historical Evidence

Reflections on Uncle Tom's Cabin

The historical document known as Uncle Tom's Cabin illustrates a truth that has been known to American historians ever since Washington Irving published Knickerbocker's *History of New York:* that contemporary experience of historians alters the evidence they study. My earliest recollection of that humbling but challenging truth is a high school history teacher's warning in 1939 that we ought not to choose *Uncle Tom's Cabin* as collateral reading, because (he said) Mrs. Stowe depicts slave owners and slavery too critically. Thirty years later I find that my most difficult problem as a teacher centers on the same book, which many students now reject as James Baldwin rejected it, for combining sentimentality and racial condescension with vindictive stereotypes in a way that deserves the scornful title, "Everybody's Protest Novel." Some of my students declare that Mrs. Stowe "knows nothing about black people," and that for knowledge of conventional characters we might as well read instead a few original radio scripts for *Amos 'n Andy.* One graduate student in history insists that Mrs. Stowe practices cruel deception by inventing the loving family of Uncle Tom and Aunt Chloe, because the Moynihan Report, Stanley Elkins's book on *Slavery,* and a number of other sociological projections depict the slave family as matriarchal. A few students, whose feelings I respect, find it unbearable to read seriously beyond the obvious signals that this is a book written for an Anglo-Saxon Us (however culpably aggressive) about an intellectually and energetically inferior (albeit an admirably patient

Reprinted by permission from the *Negro American Literature Forum* 5 (1971): 132–36, 154; this paper was first read to the joint meeting of the American Studies Association and the Modern Language Association, December 1970.

and peaceful) African Them. Whatever the context, a sensitive young reader must develop an extraordinary capacity for detachment in order to read beyond the narrator's many variations on this kind of statement: "Now there is no more use in making believe be angry with a negro than with a child; both instinctively see the true state of the case, through all attempts to affect the contrary." [1]

Against most of these limited readings I have appealed to a small group of excellent critical essays about *Uncle Tom's Cabin*—commentaries by Edmund Wilson, Charles Foster, Kenneth Lynn, Alice Crozier, Cushing Strout, and Howard Mumford Jones—because all these writers acknowledge the book's literary value as well as its documentary importance for American literary and social history, and they all recognize some connection between the documentary importance and Mrs. Stowe's literary skill. I have also appealed to historical authorities, including a not wholly facetious declaration by Kenneth Stampp that *Uncle Tom's Cabin* is one of the best books ever written about American slavery. And now some genuinely new historical research has put new life into the old book. Professor Herbert Gutman has blasted the foundations of the matriarchy by demonstrating that in all parts of the United States, during the last years of slavery, black children, whether slaves or free, were just about as likely as lower-class white children to grow up in two-parent households. And he has demonstrated that black Americans emerged from slavery with the two-parent, patriarchal household as the norm of family life. Gutman's full study has not yet been published, but in a recent issue of the *New York Review of Books* Eugene Genovese has built a long speculative essay on Gutman's fine work and on insights that were already explicit in the novels, psychiatric studies, and histories of Albion Tourgee, Ralph Ellison, Margaret Walker, Robert Coles, and C. L. R. James. Genovese asks us to study Afro-American strengths and human triumphs under American slavery, as well as the suffering and degradation.

With such encouragement, I confess that my interest in romantic histories and historical romances leads me to read *Uncle Tom's Cabin* as a romance of manners written by an extremely perceptive, intelligent woman. As we read it retrospectively, aware of subsequent history and literature, we see not only Mrs. Stowe's anticipation of other authors' themes, character types, and issues, but also her remarkable understanding of them. If God did write the book for her, as she is said to have claimed years afterward, he made more use of her social intelligence than her emphasis on his inspiration would seem to allow, and he let her see how to make the sentimental romance an especially appropriate instrument of that intelligence. I should like to concentrate my remarks on what Mrs. Stowe saw truly about the nature of her society, and how she strengthened her book with some of her most valuable perceptions. But first let me acknowledge gratefully my debt to the literary critics I have already mentioned. They all pay intelligent attention to Mrs. Stowe's sharp criticism of both North and South and to the central importance of passionate feeling, motherhood, and the family in her condemnation of slavery; Mrs. Crozier and Kenneth Lynn write especially well about the romance; Charles Foster, whose study is the most admirably thorough, writes an excellent commentary on Mrs. Stowe's perceptive sympathy, evidently indebted to Charles Dickens and O. A. Brownson, for all "The Laboring Classes"; Cushing Strout writes especially well about Mrs. Stowe's millennial hope, the nature of her racial condescension, and her confusion about African colonization, a confusion in which he sees "enormous documentary value." Edmund Wilson sees in the book "a whole drama of manners and morals and intellectual points of view."[2] Howard Jones refuses to patronize Mrs. Stowe's Christianity.

It seems to me likely that the extraordinary popular success of *Uncle Tom's Cabin* may owe as much to the book's intellectual power as to its strong sentiment. Whether or not my conjecture persuades you, the examples I am about to discuss ought to demonstrate that a sentimental romancer in the early 1850s explicitly delineated relationships that we too often credit to the original discovery of recent historians. When properly understood, moreover, the literary genre in which she cast her reflections proves capable, despite its obvious weaknesses, of expressing an admirably complex statement of American social contradictions. I cannot give here all the evidence to justify my admiration for the book, but the argument can safely rest on the following discussion of manners, Christianity, and nonviolence. I shall spend most of my time on manners.

Mrs. Stowe sees the complexity of American slavery, and she makes admirable use of literary and racial stereotypes to reveal it. Her opening scene confronts us with three male characters, a gentleman, a vulgar slave trader, and a black child (Harry) whom the planter calls Jim Crow and commands to dance for the two men. The child dutifully plays the comic role of Jim Crow. He obeys a command to imitate "old Uncle Cudjoe with the rheumatism" and "Elder Robbins reading a psalm" (1:16–17), whereupon the trader decides to buy the child, along with Uncle Tom, the best hand on the plantation. One feels an unsettling ambiguity about Mrs. Stowe's attitude during this and the subsequent episodes that set the entire plot in motion, for she evidently prefers Mr. Shelby's gentlemanly manners to the bluntness and the social presumptuousness of Haley, the trader, and she apparently believes that black children were born to dance. Her triumph is nonetheless clear. She shows us that the gentleman and the trader were bound together in selling and buying black talent, black childhood, black joy. Later on, she gives the repulsive trader the line that explicitly identifies the two classes with each other: when Shelby's son condemns Haley for "buying men and women, and chaining them like cattle," Haley replies: "So long as your grand folks want to buy men and women, I'm as good as they is; 'tain't any meaner sellin' on 'em than 't is buyin'" (1:152). Even more brilliantly, moreover, Mrs. Stowe's dramatic action highlights one major function of the grand folks' superior manners: to protect gentlemen from direct recognition of the brutal reality that makes them as mean as traders. Mrs. Stowe may prefer the gentleman to the slave trader, but when Haley understandably complains that Eliza's escape has cheated him out of his investment in her son, Shelby demands that he "observe something of the decorum of a gentleman" in the presence of Mrs. Shelby (1:68); and when Haley persists, Shelby retreats into an even more pompous declaration that the family honor has been impugned. The pomposity is as unmistakably there in his language as in some of the preposterous diction that William Faulkner later gave Thomas Sutpen in *Absalom, Absalom!* The threat of a challenge cows the vulgar trader. So much for the function of honor. Haley's only revenge is to pronounce the ugly truth to young George Shelby and to elicit in reply a vow that George will never buy or sell people. Only a few hours after his father's threatening appeal to honor, George admits to Haley that for the first time in his life he feels ashamed to be a Kentuckian.

Manners function in the same intricate way among the black characters. A century before Stanley Elkins, Mrs. Stowe echoed Frederick Douglass's argument that plantations like Simon Legree's brutalized field hands, if not in the way of Nazi concentration camps, which weren't yet available, then at least in the way of English and American factories. But she avoids Elkins's erroneous claim that male self-respect was virtually impossible because there was no black male authority. Even on Legree's plantation and especially on the property of Uncle Tom's other two owners Mrs. Stowe creates a variety of functions and degrees of authority, rivalry, respect. Uncle Tom is not merely Mr. Shelby's best hand, "a large, broad-chested, powerfully-made man, of a full glossy black," with a "truly African face" that expresses grave and steady good sense along with benevolence (1:40–41). He is also the central authority among Shelby's slaves, the leader of prayer meetings, the wise man consulted in crises. When he decides to let himself be sold rather than run away, he offers as his explicit reason the given condition on which the plot originally moves: that if he doesn't go with Haley the entire plantation and all the slaves will go to Haley by default. Tom does follow this argument with an appeal to true honor (as distinct from Shelby's class honor), and he soon insists on the kind of Christian forgiveness and trust in Providence with which his name is unpleasantly associated in our language; but in this context it is especially important to notice that both these appeals follow from the inevitable condition—either he goes or everyone goes—and that even in his most magnificent insistence on forgiveness he is in absolute command of his cabin. Aunt Chloe expresses the fiery response of intelligent human nature, blaming Mr. Shelby, begging her "old man" to flee (1:64), and wishing all slave traders in hell: "lor, if the devil don't get 'em, what's he good for?" (1:86). But Tom is in command, and his wife defers to his forgiveness, his misplaced faith in Shelby, and his practical good sense of the common danger. This is a patriarchal, two-parent household, and the young children in it know that the father who loves them enough to weep at the prospect of leaving them is strong enough to enforce his domestic authority.

There is no need or time to discuss here the entire range of black characters on the several plantations, from the hired-out mechanic and inventor George Harris and Eliza, his serving-maid wife, to Legree's slave drivers and the various antecedents of Faulkner's Dilsey who preside over the Kentucky and New Orleans kitchens. I do need to say a few words about Sam and Andy, the two slaves whose adroit bungling, manipulation, and psychology delay Haley long enough to insure Eliza's miraculous escape across the Ohio. Mrs. Stowe's clumsy efforts to condescend into the comically political mind of Sam are technically and racially embarrassing, but she carries off his actions and his treatment of the master class with brilliant success. She shows Sam and Andy elaborating the kind of role in which Haley had originally found Eliza's little boy so adaptable. These grown men, however, use the role assigned to them by white men; they use it to thwart a white man's will and to play off one master against another. In a burlesque of Anglo-Saxon bustle and efficiency they deftly mismanage the chase as white stereotyping says that a black man would, and in the same way they trick Haley into commanding them to take the wrong road. At the end their loud, ambiguous laughter completes the burlesque; we hear some of their actual, unmistakable words, but Haley hears the laughter that masks even as it expresses their contempt (96). It is the same laughter that makes young Thomas Sutpen want to strike out at the fantastic balloon-face in Faulkner's *Absalom, Absalom!*, and Haley reacts with a foreshadowing of Sutpen's anger.

In praising Mrs. Stowe's portrayal of Sam and Andy, I don't mean to contradict my students' judgment that Mrs. Stowe had little understanding of black people. I do believe that she understood a great deal about people's relationships with one another and about how conventional literary characters and sociological stereotypes or roles express genuinely human qualities. Topsy's perception of Miss Ophelia's revulsion from the physical touch of black people, and Topsy's willingness to adapt to the expectations of her owners, are deeply true even though the characterization often seems to me hopelessly limited (in a way that Eva St. Clare's is not) by Mrs. Stowe's inability to write from inside the black child's mind. For me it is the functioning of manners that overcomes the faults. The white characters discuss Topsy in her presence as if she were not there, and her alert response reveals the depth of their misunderstanding and the intelligence of her own observation. For me this kind of relationship does more than the most fervently explicit pleas to establish Mrs. Stowe's genuine appreciation of her central contention: that black men and women are thoroughly human.

In view of this purpose, as several critics have seen in different ways, Mrs. Stowe's heavy emphasis on sentiment is itself an intelligent comment on her society. The Ohio senator's wife who shelters Eliza and her son in defiance of the Fugitive Slave Law exemplifies the critics' judgment when she appeals to a mother's feelings against her husband's cautious reasoning on "great public interests": "I *hate* reasoning, John—especially reasoning on such subjects" (1:122). Earlier, when Mrs. Shelby learns that Eliza's son and Uncle Tom must be sold to save the rest of the estate, she reminds her husband that her "common sense" has always told her slavery could come to no good (1:58). By calling your attention to the pervasiveness of reasonable analysis that underlies this appeal to universal sentiment, I hope to give a clearer idea of the book's sociological range and historical insight. Repeatedly Mrs. Stowe shows us a situation in which logic has gone wild. Like the creator of Jason Compson, she has an astonishingly fine ear for the language of racism and the fundamental contradictions embraced by men who must defend slavery. She begins with our old friend Haley, who argues with unexpected persuasiveness that it is more humane not to bring up slaves to expect humane treatment. "You mean well by 'em," he concedes, "but tan't no real kindness, after all . . . I think I treat niggers just about as well as it's ever worth while to treat 'em" (1:22). Mrs. Stowe makes devastating use of other slogans. "It's a free country," declares George Harris's owner when the man to whom George has been hired out tries to dissuade him from spitefully demoting George to field labor; "It's a free country. The man's *mine,* and I do what I please with him" (1:31). When reminded of George's laborsaving invention the same man replies that it is just like "a nigger" to invent something that will avoid work. "They are all labor-saving machines themselves, every one of 'em!" (1:29). Americans in the free states praise Hungarian rebels as heroes but hunt fugitive southern slaves for bounty, dead or alive. Even Augustine St. Clare, the most intelligent commentator and to my mind the finest characterization in the book, fails to see until Uncle Tom forces him to see the logic of all his own thorough arguments against slavery, for St. Clare is astonished and hurt to learn that Tom would rather be free than owned by the kindest master. In the end, then, we observe Simon Legree, who claims to run his plantation merely on the economic principle that it is cheaper to work slaves into the ground and then buy new ones than it would be to care for individual health and welfare. Legree contradicts his own principle by beating poor Tom to death—supposedly in order to preserve his authority, but the action, like the entire system, is essentially self-defeating.

In the face of such reasoning Mrs. Stowe implies that the only reasonable hope lies in a primary appeal to feeling and common sense. For thirty years before the composition of *Uncle Tom's Cabin,* romances had often opposed the natural hearts of heroes and heroines against the formal restrictions of civilized law and historical tradition. Whether or not *Uncle Tom's Cabin* helped to cause the Civil War, the author does in effect foresee the catastrophe. In her last direct address to the reader, she insists that "there is one thing" besides prayer "that *every* individual can do" to oppose slavery: "they can see to it *that they feel right*" (2:317). She entreats her readers to "*feel* strongly, healthily, and justly, on the great interests of humanity" against "the sophistries of worldly policy" (2:317). Her last warning is biblical, apocalyptic, but also worldly wise. Years of wrath were coming.

As every reader must quickly perceive (among the white characters, at least), it is the women in the book who most clearly represent the supremacy of right feeling. But it would be a mistake to assume that the women's authority rests on sentiment and intuition alone. Here again Mrs. Stowe's sharp observation of manners penetrates so deeply beyond the obvious contrasts that defects in characterization are overcome by social understanding. Mrs. Shelby's rebuke of her husband brings out woman's role among American aristocrats and businessmen. Both the husband and the wife see that woman is the moral authority and that, in effect, her moral purity is maintained by ignorance and irrelevance. Both Shelby and the Ohio senator leave moral and religious questions to their wives, and thus declare that in the real world moral and religious questions are unimportant. What I want to stress here is a perception of Mrs. Stowe's that is rarely noticed. Repeatedly in this book, the women with the most powerful moral sentiments also develop extremely intelligent arguments. Mrs. Shelby points the lesson when she says that she *could* understand her husband's affairs if he didn't keep her in such ignorance of them; and it is she and Aunt Chloe who eventually begin to execute reasonably practical plans for redeeming Tom. Aunt Chloe gives Tom a series of unanswerable arguments to show that Mr. Shelby doesn't deserve Tom's loyalty, and little Eva herself—too often dismissed in our day as "sugary confection"[3]—sees that her father's desire to shield her from knowledge of miserable suffering is a selfish way of defending the cruel system. She ought to know the real horrors, she insists, and she ought to feel about them. She sees, beyond his childish assurance that his kindness will protect his slaves, the need for a system that won't depend on one man's kindness.

With Eva, then, we come to the question of Christianity. I pass over the central function of Tom's and Eva's piety; it is no less important for being obvious, but in this final set of examples I wish to show the primacy of Mrs. Stowe's social intelligence even on the one subject that is closer to her heart than the domestic sentiments of women. She knows that Uncle Tom is "a moral miracle" (1:305). She shows us in the opening pages her awareness that true Christianity often plays into the hands of the exploiters. We are told explicitly that Tom's extraordinary trustworthiness—or at least Shelby's extraordinary financial trust in him—began just after Tom's conversion at a camp meeting. "Why, last fall," Shelby says to Haley, "I let him go to Cincinnati alone, to do business for me, and bring home five hundred dollars. 'Tom,' says I to him, 'I trust you, because I think you'r a Christian—I know you wouldn't cheat.' Tom comes back, sure enough; *I knew he would.*" Haley, too, says that he values religion in a nigger, "when it's the real *article*" (1:14–15). This kind of perception, so economically dramatized and so heavily freighted with commercial diction, goes a long way toward authenticating Mrs. Stowe's conception of Tom's saintly resistance to Simon Legree. I assent to her conception of the moral miracle because she knows that trustworthiness is valued by genuine Christians and commercial exploiters of the genuine article. She knows that the moral miracle brings a high price in the market because he is not only strong but obedient. And she highlights his most saintly qualities by contrasting them in action to equally powerful black rejections of Christian principles. I have already mentioned Aunt Chloe's passionate refusal to forgive Mr. Shelby and her desire to send all slave traders to the devil. In the same spirit George Harris renounces the country, the race, and for a time the God of his father and, though white enough to pass, wishes he himself were "two shades darker, rather than one lighter" (2:300). And when Tom refuses to help Cassy murder Simon Legree, because (he says) "The Lord hasn't *called* us to wrath. We must suffer, and wait his time"—then Cassy replies with the powerful arguments that our outraged contemporaries have so often used in recent years:

> "Wait! . . . Haven't I waited?—waited till my head is dizzy and my heart sick? What has he made me suffer? What has he made hundreds of poor creatures suffer? Isn't he wringing the life-blood out of *you?* I'm called on; *they* call me! His time's come, and I'll have his heart's blood." [2:251]

Tom, of course, wins that argument, but we must remember that Mrs. Stowe wrote both speeches. Speaking in her own voice, after all, our author has directly warned us several hundred pages earlier that "you [like the slave trader] can get used to such [horrible] things, too, my friend; and it is the great object of recent efforts to make our whole northern community used to them, for the glory of the Union" (1:189). If we read only Uncle Tom's appeal to Cassy, we will tend to agree with some of the most disgusted of my students about the book; if we read only Mrs. Stowe's remarks about the horrors, we may adopt my high school teacher's opinion. To see the richness of the historical evidence in *Uncle Tom's Cabin,* as in less topical works of fiction, we must study the complex reality of the whole book.

Notes

1. Harriet Beecher Stowe, *Uncle Tom's Cabin; or, Life among the Lowly,* Introduction by Howard Mumford Jones (Columbus, Ohio: Charles E. Merrill, 1969), 1:112. This is a photographic copy, in one volume, of the first, two-volume edition.

2. Alice Crozier, *The Novels of Harriet Beecher Stowe* (New York: Oxford Univ. Press, 1969); Kenneth S. Lynn, *Visions of America* (Westport, Conn.: Greenwood Press, 1973); Charles Foster, *The Rungless Ladder: Harriet Beecher Stowe and New England Puritanism* (Durham: Duke Univ. Press, 1954); Cush-

ing Strout, *The Veracious Imagination* (Middletown, Conn.: Wesleyan Univ. Press, 1981); and Edmund Wilson, *Patriotic Gore* (New York: Oxford Univ. Press, 1962).

3. Strout, *Veracious Imagination,* p. 60.

15.

Modern Misjudgments of Racial Imperialism in Parkman and Hawthorne

I

Sensitivity to Anglo-American racial prejudice in our own time has led modern scholars to new understanding of some nineteenth-century issues and texts, including Herman Melville's *Typee,* "Benito Cereno," and *The Confidence-Man,* but it has also tempted some of us into anachronistic error. Let an embarrassing blunder on the first page of Francis Jennings's *The Invasion of America* stand as an admonition to us all. Preparing us to consider the European invasion from the native American's point of view, Jennings declares not only that most nineteenth-century American writers were misled by ethnocentric prejudice, but also that the historian Francis Parkman falsified the record deliberately. Anyone who pursues the documentation for this charge through an article by Francis Jennings and into Parkman's *Montcalm and Wolfe* will be surprised to discover that Jennings achieved an awkward poetic justice by misrepresenting Parkman's book.[1]

Jennings claims to have proved that much of Parkman's distortion was deliberate. If we used Jennings's own standard of judgment, however, we would have to decide that he himself had deliberately misrepresented Parkman. In both men the fault seems to me instead to be clearly intellectual rather than moral. Each one reads his evidence partially as he moves toward his narrative or argumentative purpose. Few readers who attend closely will decide that mid-twentieth-century

Reprinted by permission from the *Yearbook of English Studies* 13 (1983): 145–58, a special issue on "Colonial and Imperial Themes."

standards are materially higher than Parkman's or that we should take Jennings's advice to discard *Montcalm and Wolfe*.

In "A Vanishing Indian" Jennings does show that Parkman over-states the role of Frederick Post, a Moravian missionary, in English negotiations for peace with the western Indians in 1758—partly be-cause Post himself exaggerated it. The rest of Jennings's argument is questionable or patently erroneous. He charges Parkman with conceal-ing evidence that Indians, and especially one Pisquetomen, were the really important English emissaries. Parkman, he says, sends Post forth alone among hostile savages without admitting that friendly savages have guaranteed Post's safety, and without emphasizing the French ar-my's instigation of a conspiracy to kill Post. Let this passage represent Jennings's argument:

> In Parkman's account, the menace to Post is an undifferentiated forest rabble; Indians are "seized" with wild emotions, unpredictable, irratio-nal, melodramatic. Parkman reported accurately that Post was con-ducted to Fort Duquesne in order that the Indians there might hear the peace message; he wrote that Post protested in vain—words used also by Post—but he omitted the continuation in Post's sentence; "they . . . said that I need not fear the French, for they would carry me in their bosoms, i.e., engage for my safety." [311]

This critique is impressive until one reads Parkman himself. Jen-nings's error is surprisingly simple. He has worked so hard to note Parkman's every modification of the eighteenth-century record that he neglects to read Parkman accurately. He tells us that Parkman's entire account of Post's "journey outward is contained in one sentence, 'The Moravian envoy made his way to the Delaware town of Kushkushkee, on Beaver Creek, northwest of Fort Duquesne . . .'" (309). The elision here is Jennings's work. Consider now the six sentences from *Montcalm and Wolfe* on which Jennings has based the lines that I have just quoted.

> The Moravian envoy made his way to the Delaware town of Kush-kushkee, on Beaver Creek, northwest of Fort Duquesne, where the three chiefs known as King Beaver, Shingas, and Delaware George re-ceived him kindly, and conducted him to another town on the same stream. Here his reception was different. A crowd of warriors, their faces distorted with rage, surrounded him, brandishing knives and

threatening to kill him; but others took his part, and, order being at last restored, he read them his message from the Governor, which seemed to please them. They insisted, however, that he should go with them to Fort Duquesne, in order that the Indians assembled there might hear it also. Against this dangerous proposal he protested in vain. On arriving near the fort, the French demanded that he should be given up to them, and, being refused, offered a great reward for his scalp; on which his friends advised him to keep close by the camp-fire, as parties were out with intent to kill him. [2:145–46]

Parkman, then, is not the only historian capable of deleting inconvenient clauses from the documents that he quotes, and it is clear that Jennings excels him in making Indians vanish. It is true that Parkman sometimes represented Indians as an undifferentiated rabble, but in this episode he clearly portrays them as friends and threatening dissenters. The friends, who receive Post kindly and protect him, win out. In a subordinate clause of the critique Jennings does concede that Parkman "acknowledged the French price on Post's head," but actually Parkman places the French demand for Post at an emphatic point in his narrative. He does not portray Post as dependent on "the whim of capricious and untrustworthy beast-creatures," as Jennings says he does, but as an emissary among Indian friends. In the next two paragraphs Parkman argues both that the Indians' own division led them to act against their people's true interest, which lay with the French, and that the Delawares' response was "worthy of a proud and warlike race."

Today, even as in the old times of heroic narrative, it is easy to read one's notes in accord with one's thesis. The erroneous historian is not necessarily dishonest, and neither minor errors nor large prejudices necessarily invalidate a historian's work. Parkman's narrative of Lovell's Fight, although written fifty years after Nathaniel Hawthorne's story "Roger Malvin's Burial," may help us to evaluate similar but more difficult questions of judgment in recent commentary on Hawthorne's story.

II

The central issue in historical interpretations of Hawthorne's story is the significance of the introductory paragraph. "Roger Malvin's Burial" belongs to the early group of tales that Hawthorne had hoped to publish as a collection about colonial New England. Here, as in "Alice Doane's Appeal," "My Kinsman, Major Molineux," "The Gentle Boy," and (a few years later) "The Maypole of Merrymount" and "The Gray Champion," Hawthorne begins with a historical commentary that establishes a context, and perhaps a tone, for his provincial tale. Half a century ago modern scholars followed Hawthorne's direction to his historical sources, but not until 1964 did Ely Stock open the wide gate of ironic interpretation.[2] Let us begin with the facts.

Lovell's Fight, the skirmish in which Reuben Bourne and his prospective father-in-law, Roger Malvin, have been wounded before Hawthorne's narrative begins, occurred in 1725, precisely a century before Hawthorne graduated from Bowdoin College and began to read and write about the New England past. To mark the approach of the centennial several works, including two poems by Hawthorne's classmate Henry Wadsworth Longfellow, were published in the 1820s, and G. Harrison Orians, David S. Lovejoy,[3] and Ely Stock have identified particular phrases and incidents on which Hawthorne surely relied. One nineteenth-century account, for example, based on a hundred-year-old narrative, describes a wounded lieutenant who survived for two or three days only to see that some wild cranberries, found by him and a comrade, spilled out through his abdominal wound. Only at Lieutenant Farwell's "earnest entreaties," a phrase that one finds in Hawthorne's narrative of a virtually identical debate, did Farwell's faithful companion agree to leave him to perish, and not until the reluctant survivor had "taken Farwell's handkerchief and tied it to the top of a bush that it might afford a mark by which his remains could the more easily be found." Hawthorne also borrowed that handkerchief for his story, transforming it into his guilty protagonist's own bloody bandage, symbol of his unredeemed vow to return and bury the doomed comrade.[4]

John Lovell (Lovewell in earlier spelling) organized and led a party of thirty rangers authorized "to kill and destroy their enemy Indians" and to receive a daily subsistence from the Massachusetts legislature, along with large bounties for "the scalps of male Indians old enough to fight."[5] In January 1725 the force had grown to eighty-seven men, recruited from five towns, and after nearly a month of fruitless searching to the north they surprised a raiding party of ten warriors from Canada, asleep in their wigwams on a February night, and killed them all. In mid-April, then, Lovell set out with a new force of forty-six men, which soon shrank to thirty-four after one of the men fell ill and a small group was left to guard him at a makeshift fort near Lake Ossipee.

The main force was lured into an ambush by a Pigwacket brave, whom the twenty-one-year-old chaplain, a Harvard graduate, scalped after an exchange of fire that left Captain Lovell and the Pigwacket mortally wounded. The Pigwacket force, reported to have numbered from "forty to eighty men," seemed at first to be overwhelming; one of the Massachusetts soldiers, Benjamin Hassell, fled at once to the new fort at Lake Ossipee, where he told such a catastrophic story that the surgeon and the guards abandoned the fort, helping their ailing comrade back to the town of Dunstable. But Lovell's ambushed men, though outnumbered and robbed of their packs, fought for ten hours, until the Pigwackets withdrew at nightfall. Twelve of the colonists were mortally wounded and eleven of the twenty survivors, including Jonathan Frye, the scalping chaplain, were seriously hurt.

One of the two surviving lieutenants was too badly wounded to be moved. He asked to have his gun loaded so that he might kill another Indian before being scalped upon the Pigwackets' expected return the next morning, and his request was granted. He was left there alone in the darkness, and his comrades tried to make their way through "the snarl of underbrush" toward the fort at Lake Ossipee. Soon four more of the wounded men, including Chaplain Frye and Lieutenant Farwell, were abandoned "with their consent" (*HC* 1:256) and with a promise that a rescue party would be sent out for them as soon as help could be found at the fort. The fort, of course, was empty, having been "shamefully abandoned," Parkman says (*HC* 1:256), and the eleven who reached it found only some bread and pork and a note on birch bark saying that they and all the other colonists involved in the fight had been killed.

Of course, the eleven were in no condition to keep their promise to the four they had left in the woods. In smaller groups they straggled into Dunstable between May 13 and May 15, five to seven days after the fight. Their four wounded comrades tried to return, too, after it had become clear that no rescue was likely, but Chaplain Frye soon had to lie down. Eleazer Davis, one of the two who eventually did reach the settlements, reported that Frye had begged him and the others to press on: "Tell my father that I expect in a few hours to be in eternity, and am not afraid to die." They did leave him alone, and, as we have seen, Davis later obeyed Lieutenant Farwell's earnest entreaties to go on alone after Farwell had to stop. Davis found his way after eleven days to the fort at Lake Ossipee and then, three weeks after Lovell's Fight, to the town of Berwick. Josiah Jones spent fourteen days in the woods before he "arrived, half dead, at the village of Biddeford" (*HC* 1:257).

When the small group who had abandoned the fort arrived in Dunstable on the eleventh, a troop of militia was sent out to rescue wounded survivors and pursue the Pigwackets. Hassell, the man who had fled, was too ill to guide them, "or pretended to be so," but another man "who had just returned offered to go in his place" (*HC* 1:258). This party did find the bodies of twelve colonists near Lovell's Pond and a shallow grave in which a warrior named Paugus and two other Pigwackets were buried.

III

Hawthorne's story itself has virtually nothing to do with Lovell's Fight, but it does focus intense light on the genesis of guilt in Reuben Bourne's anguishing decision to abandon a wounded comrade, his prospective father-in-law, in the wilderness. Eighteenth-century and nineteenth-century accounts of Lovell's Fight, moreover, provide a number of actions that might well have drawn Hawthorne's sensibility to questions of guilt, shame, and moral ambiguity. Not only in Lieutenant Farwell's earnest entreaties to Eleazer Davis but in several other incidents, too, the record calls our attention to abandonment. Benjamin Hassell runs away when the Pigwackets ambush Lovell's men, and later he refuses to guide the rescue party to Lovell's Pond. The surgeon and the guards at the fort on Lake Ossipee abandon their post when Hassell tells them of the disaster. Lieutenant Robbins is left with a loaded gun to die near the unburied bodies at Lovell's Pond. The four wounded men who cannot continue are left in the woods, with a promise of rescue, as the stronger survivors press on to the fort. Chaplain Frye is left alive and dying by Davis, Farwell, and Jones. Presumably after they have somehow been separated from Jones, Davis leaves Farwell alive but dying.

Here then we can see ample reason for Hawthorne's statement in the introductory paragraph that readers familiar with this celebrated episode will recognize some of the incidents even though he has substituted fictitious names. We can also see in these facts several candidates for identification as the circumstances to which Hawthorne's introduction alludes. Let us reconsider that entire opening paragraph.

> One of the few incidents of Indian warfare naturally susceptible of the moonlight of romance was that expedition undertaken for the defence of the frontiers in the year 1725, which resulted in the well-remembered "Lovell's Fight." Imagination, by casting certain circumstances judicially into the shade, may see much to admire in the heroism of a little band who gave battle to twice their number in the heart of the enemy's country. The open bravery displayed by both parties was in accordance with civilized ideas of valor; and chivalry itself might not blush to record the deeds of one or two individuals. The battle, though so fatal to those who fought, was not unfortunate in its consequences to the country; for it broke the strength of a tribe and conduced to peace which subsisted during several ensuing years. History and tradition are usually minute in their memorials of this affair; and the captain of a scouting party of frontier men has acquired as actual a military renown as many a victorious leader of thousands. Some of the incidents contained in the following pages will be recognized, notwithstanding the substitution of fictitious names, by such as have heard, from old men's lips, the fate of the few combatants who were in a condition to retreat after "Lovell's Fight." [6]

All the published commentary since 1964 has followed Ely Stock in reading this paragraph as Hawthorne's ironic dissent from the prevailing celebration of Lovell's Fight. [7] The moonlight of romance becomes necessary, in that reading, to casting certain circumstances judicially into the shade, and those circumstances are not the ones on which we have just focused our dim flashlight, but the motives and brutal conduct of Lovell and his men. One commentator has called Hawthorne's introductory paragraph "sarcastic,"[8] and all have emphasized the bounty offered for Indian scalps, or some other features of that brutal warfare: the surprise killing of the ten sleeping Indians in their wigwams, the presence of an armed chaplain in Lovell's band. Although each of the studies has its own thesis, the most recent article can stand for the others on this issue. John Samson refers to Roger Malvin and Reuben Bourne as "less-than-heroic Indian fighters limping back from an unsuccessful Sunday scalping session" (459). After that pejorative description of the central characters and the expedition, no reader will be surprised by Samson's answer to the question that he next asks us to consider: "why Roger and Reuben were there—why there was a Lovell's Fight in the first place." He admits that Massachusetts sought "to protect its borders against Indian incursions," but neither he nor the other recent commentators mention the policy of New France in Governor Dummer's (sometimes called Lovell's) War. "In securing its land as disreputably as the mother country," Samson says, "Massachusetts is echoing the British policy of [James II in] 1687 and becoming every bit a tyrannical imperialist herself—an irony Hawthorne certainly must have noticed" (459). By the end of the argument, Samson has placed quotation marks around *protect;* Reuben Bourne's "bloody bandage, acquired scalping Indians to 'protect' the frontier, is a travesty of American values and a monument to hypocrisy. America, in pursuing the material land, has forgotten what the land symbolized" (461).

The chief defect in all these historical commentaries on Hawthorne's story is the narrowness of the context in which they set Lovell's Fight. Implicitly or explicitly they all ask (with Samson) why Roger Malvin and Reuben Bourne were there, but they do not ask why the Pigwackets were there. Even Robert Daly, who presents the most thorough and accurate summary of the episode, calls Lovell's Fight "the culmination of a dirty little scalp-hunting expedition" (105), and he leaves the uninformed reader free to believe that the ten Indians killed in Lovell's successful raid at night were peaceable men asleep in wigwams on their own land. He tells us that Lovell and his men cashed in the ten scalps taken in this raid, but neither he nor any other modern commentator mentions the new French blankets and rifles captured from the same murdered Indians, a war party fitted out in New France for a raid on Anglo-American settlements.[9] Francis Parkman's history will help us to understand the significance of the historical context.

Parkman, too, reports that Lovell and his men "were much like hunters of wolves, catamounts, or other dangerous beasts," that their chaplain "carried a gun, knife, or hatchet," and that "not one of the party was more prompt [than Chaplain Frye] to use them" (*HC* 1:250–52). But Parkman has carefully placed his scalping chaplain and the entire episode in a balanced comedy of grisly deceit. In his narrative Lovell's Fight serves primarily as an interesting example of the war that New France and New England fought while technically at peace, for nearly a decade after the Treaty of Utrecht. The Anglo-American forces capture letters from Governor Vaudreuil of New France commissioning Father Sebastien Rale, a Jesuit priest among the Abenakis, to continue fomenting raids on English houses, and when Vaudreuil indignantly protests the murder (or, as Lieutenant Governor Dummer of Massachusetts calls it, the death "in the heat of action") of Father Rale, Dummer not only cites Vaudreuil's own letters praising Rale's "incendiary" activities, but also deplores an Indian war party's scalping of an English minister in Rutland.

Parkman, of course, has little sympathy for benevolent views of Indian culture. His narrative of these events explicitly declares that few frontiersmen, exposed to actual raids, expressed the kind of solicitude for the natives that some people secure in Boston or London were free to venture, and his account of the Abenakis' shifts under the suasion of Father Rale and the English is marred by gratuitous pronouncements about supposed racial defects. Yet even in a paragraph that begins by declaring that "the wild Indian is as unstable as water," this ethnocentric historian gives historical action a convincing complexity that is lacking in the modern condemnations of Hawthorne's "scalphunters." Parkman demonstrates, for example, that an Abenaki group called the Norridgewocks had sought peace with the English settlers until Father Rale (according to one of Rale's own captured letters) persuaded them to begin killing the Englishmen's cattle and burning English haystacks. Parkman's New Englanders believe that specific purchases and the Plymouth Company's seventeenth-century charter give them title to the land, and he has reminded us that Indians believe the land belongs inalienably to the entire nation, so that no chiefs ever had the right to sell permanent title. "Yet afraid as the Indians were of another war," Parkman admits, "Rale could scarcely have stirred them to violence, but for the indignities put upon them by Indian-hating ruffians of the border, vicious rum-selling traders, and hungry land-thieves." The English governor, moreover, has not kept his promise to build trading posts in which the Indians would be treated fairly (*HC* 1:222–23).

The complexity of Parkman's comedy is delightfully intricate. He shows us that both the Norridgewocks and the New Englanders disagree vehemently among themselves. Governor Shute is unable to build the promised trading posts because the jealous Massachusetts legislature will not appropriate funds for them. The Norridgewocks embarrass Father Rale by leaning toward an accommodation with the English, but Rale and Governor Vaudreuil call in the aid of converted Indians from Canada, besides lavish supplies of ammunition and fire-arms, and the Norridgewocks and other Abenakis are persuaded to renew and intensify the raids. Governor Shute, "in defiance of every Indian idea of propriety," blusters through a hilarious dialogue with a Norridgewock chief, outraging propriety with constant interruptions and by addressing all his remarks to the interpreter rather than to the chief, who perseveres in rigorous politeness to address the governor until provoked by a final insult to walk out, "leaving behind an English flag that had been given" him (*HC* 1:216–18). The Massachusetts Assembly "absurdly" tries "to counteract the influence of Rale" (who has 6,000 livres a year to spend on arms and supplies) "by offering £150 a year in their depreciated currency to any one of their ministers who would teach Calvinism to the Indians." Against the country minister who accepts this impossible assignment, Rale pits not only the knowledge and affection that he has earned in decades among the Abenakis, but also more than a hundred pages of his polemical Latin (*HC* 1:220–21). And as quotations from Governor Vaudreuil's and Father Rale's letters accumulate in Parkman's text, openly telling the French ministry that "we must let the Indians act for us" to prevent English settlement on Abenaki lands, the Massachusetts House of Representatives votes to offer a reward of £500 in depreciated currency for the death of Rale; but the governor and Council refuse to approve the measure. A raid on Norridgewock by Colonel Westbrook and 300 men captures the incriminating letters of Rale but also provokes retaliation that burns the village of Brunswick. Governor Shute prepares for a decisive campaign, only to be outraged by the Assembly's insistence on the power to recall his commander from the field for interrogation. As Shute leaves for London in virtual secrecy, then, the undeclared war is carried on by Lieutenant Governor Dummer as Indian war parties burn farms and murder families, including the minister of Rutland, and New Englanders kill at least one squaw, twenty-six fleeing men, and, in a last raid on Norridgewock, Father Rale himself (*HC* 1:231–37).

Parkman's Father Rale is no martyr but a political and military agent, representative of the spiritual change that Parkman highlights in the Canadian missions since the days of Father Jogues and other seventeenth-century martyrs. Yet Parkman carefully distinguishes his own judgment from that of the

> border settlers, who saw in [Rale's death] the end of their troubles. In their eyes, Rale was an incendiary, setting on a horde of bloody savages to pillage and murder. While they thought him a devil, he passed in Canada for a martyred saint. He was neither the one nor the other, but a man with the qualities and faults of a man,—fearless, resolute, enduring; boastful, sarcastic, often bitter and irritating; a vehement partisan; apt to see things, not as they were, but as he wished them to be; given to inaccuracy and exaggeration, yet no doubt sincere in opinions and genuine in zeal; hating the English more than he loved the Indians; calling himself their friend, yet using them as instruments of worldly policy, to their danger and final ruin. In considering the ascription of martyrdom, it is to be remembered that he did not die because he was an apostle of the faith, but because he was an active agent of the Canadian government. [*HC* 1:239]

Parkman, then, narrates Lovell's Fight because it was "too noted in its day, and too strongly rooted in popular tradition, to be passed unnoticed." In the year after Rale's death and the breaking of the Norridgewocks, this celebrated episode also comes to illustrate in personal detail the nature of the wars and skirmishes that make up the bulk of

Parkman's half century of conflict. The Pigwackets are a division of a Sokoki tribe among the Abenakis, settled deep in the wilderness "on the upper waters of the Saco," and Parkman says that they would have been safe for "some time longer if they had not taken up the quarrel of the Norridgewocks and made bloody raids against the English border" (*HC* 1:248). Although Parkman's Lovell is not closer to the moral condition of George Washington than Parkman's Father Rale was to that of the Jesuit martyrs, the search for Indian warriors' scalps does not begin until two men in Lovell's town of Dunstable have been "carried off" in a raid by the Pigwackets, who then also kill eight or nine of the neighbors sent out to rescue the two captives. Some reports say that Josiah Farwell, Lovell's brother-in-law, was the only one of the ten to survive. It is this disaster in the autumn of 1724 that provokes Lovell, Farwell, and Jonathan Robbins to volunteer to spend a year hunting "their enemy Indians" if the legislature will show them "Encouragement suitable" (*HC* 1:249). As Nathaniel Hawthorne knew long before Parkman based his account on some of the same sources, these men who were hunting scalps were also hunting the killers of their neighbors and friends. Yet none of the recent commentaries on "Roger Malvin's Burial" represent scalp hunting as morally any more complex than abstract Indian hating and simple greed.

IV

In the literary world of Scott, Carlyle, and Macaulay, of Washington Irving, William H. Prescott, and George Bancroft, no comment on history was more common than the claim that a subject was worthy of romance.[10] Hawthorne used *romance* as a favorable term to describe his own early work,[11] and of course he associated both imagination and moonlight with the artist's true perception rather than with the silliness of moonshine. Since advocates of ironic readings have relied heavily on Hawthorne's declaration that "the open bravery displayed by both parties was in accordance with civilized ideas of valor" and that "chivalry itself might not blush to record the deeds of one or two individuals," we must reconsider those lines before turning to the central issue.

The "open bravery" rests on historical testimony. The Reverend Thomas Symmes, on whose narrative of 1725 Hawthorne and most historians relied, claimed that survivors of Lovell's Fight had stressed the Pigwackets' unusually open way of fighting, after the original surprise of their ambush. Although one twentieth-century investigator has questioned Symmes's reliability because Symmes may have changed the date of Lovell's Fight from Sunday to Saturday in order to protect the memory of Chaplain Frye against imputation of Sabbath breaking, her challenge to the affidavit signed by two of Lovell's men and by the only officer who survived rests on an inference that I find highly questionable.[12] Hawthorne's syntax characteristically seems almost to court equivocal readings, so that once we have begun to suspect irony we cannot infallibly prevent the skeptical from giving cynical emphasis to the word *civilized,* but the tone of the whole story may combine with Symmes's affidavit from Ensign Wyman to restrain less suspicious readers.

Similar information may also detoxify a clause that looks as ironic (especially when removed from the context) as "chivalry itself might not blush." In a judicious footnote Parkman reports the "more than doubtful tradition" of a single combat between John Chamberlain and a "war-chief" named Paugus, who met unexpectedly, when, it is said, they both went to a nearby brook to clean their guns (*HC* 1:258–59). Twentieth-century investigators have questioned whether Paugus was a Pigwacket or even a chief, but all contemporaneous accounts, including the ballad that gave Ensign John Wyman credit for killing Paugus, report that it was the death of this chief that moved the victorious Pigwackets to withdraw before they had killed all of Lovell's men. And, of course, the story of Lieutenant Robbins's request to have his gun loaded before being left to face the returning Pigwackets has chivalric analogues.[13] It seems reasonable to conclude, then, that Hawthorne's allusion to chivalry is merely a conventional reminder, like many similar lines in Joel Barlow, Washington Irving, James Fenimore Cooper, George Bancroft, and (later) Herman Melville, that unlettered woodsmen or captains of whalers might deserve the literary attention that has traditionally been reserved for royalty and chivalry. In that context we should not feel obliged to read ironically Hawthorne's accurate report that "the captain of a scouting party of frontier men has acquired as actual a military renown as many a victorious leader of thousands."

The central issue is Hawthorne's judgment of Anglo-American presence and expansion on the land. The only explicit statement on this question in "Roger Malvin's Burial" declares: "The battle, though so fatal to those who fought, was not unfortunate in its consequences to the country; for it broke the strength of a tribe and conduced to peace which subsisted during several ensuing years." Hawthorne knew that the end to that temporary peace, and at last the Old French War of the 1750s, had deep causes not only in Anglo-American greed but also in Franco-American policy. And of course he knew that doubts about Anglo-American title to the land had figured in American literature ever since the days of Roger Williams. In Hawthorne's own childhood the question had been raised unanswerably in Diedrich Knickerbocker's hilarious rehearsal of the right by discovery, the right by civilization, and the right by extermination, and more recently Cooper and Bancroft had struggled to find literary formulas to justify the accomplished, if in some ways regrettable, fact of conquest.[14] Balancing his recurrent allusions to the burning of Indian villages when he sums up the sins of the Puritans (as in "Young Goodman Brown," for example), Hawthorne consistently accepts the inevitability of Anglo-American conquest and endorses its benefits.[15] Tempted, in "The Old Manse," to follow his discovery of an arrowhead into a sentimental meditation that revives the vanished "Indian village and its encircling forest," he wonders "whether it is a joy or a pain, after such a momentary vision, to gaze around in the broad daylight of reality and see stone fences, white houses, potatoe fields, and men doggedly hoeing in their shirt-sleeves and homespun pantaloons." Then he draws back abruptly: "But this is nonsense. The Old Manse is better than a thousand wigwams."[16] He has been no more successful than Irving and Cooper at deriving the right of conquest, but he would not wish Concord, or the historic honeymoon cottage in which he wrote some of his best work, or that work itself, to have had no existence.

Similar judgments are evident in "Main Street" (1849) and "The Gray Champion" (1835), but perhaps the best single authority for challenging the ironic interpretation appears in *Famous Old People* (1841), the second of three brief historical narratives for children, which are

republished together as *The Whole History of Grandfather's Chair.*
Grandfather's narratives and judgments often oblige the children to
recognize some of the moral complexity in human affairs, but I cannot
recall a single passage in which Grandfather's judgment is uttered ironically. His description of the American version of Queen Anne's War
stresses the destruction wrought by the French and Indians:

> In the course of it, New England suffered much injury from the French
> and Indians, who often came through the woods from Canada, and
> assaulted the frontier towns. Villages were sometimes burnt, and the
> inhabitants slaughtered, within a day's ride of Boston. The people of
> New England had a bitter hatred of the French, not only for the mis-
> chief which they did with their own hands, but because they incited
> the Indians to hostility.
> The New Englanders knew that they could never dwell in security,
> until the provinces of France should be subdued. [17]

Hawthorne knew as well as Parkman that the history of French
and English competition in North America had been a bloody one, and
he knew the outlines of Father Rale's military activities. [18] Even in the
history that he wrote for children, he presents so gloomy a succession
of wars that one sensitive child wishes "our forefathers could have kept
the country unspotted with blood." Grandfather concurs, but when the
same child questions whether the mothers of slain soldiers would have
seen generosity in the two hundred chests of Spanish dollars that Parliament sent to Massachusetts in payment for the conquest of Louisbourg, Grandfather gives Hawthorne's complex judgment: "Every
warlike achievement involves an amount of physical and moral evil, for
which all the gold in the Spanish mines would not be the slightest
recompense. But, we are to consider that this siege was one of the
occasions, on which the colonists tested their ability for war, and thus
were prepared for the great contest of the revolution. In that point of
view, the valor of our forefathers was its own reward" (119).

In "Old News" (1835) Hawthorne had expressed in his own voice
a similar judgment of the victory at Louisbourg. He, like Grandfather,
wanted the reader to remember the possibility of "a truer glory" than
even the military honor of General Wolfe, the hero who was killed
while conquering Quebec. [19] But before we accept a recent critic's ar-

gument that Roger Malvin's Christian name alludes to diabolical deception (as in Roger Chillingworth and in one of folklore's names for the Devil), we should remember Hawthorne's high praise for the actual Roger Conant, first settler on the site of Salem, "this good yeoman" who in "Main Street" is honored by some of Hawthorne's most approving rhetoric.[20] Conant belongs to "that class of men who do not merely find, but make, their place in the system of human affairs; a man of thoughtful strength," he plants "the germ of a city."[21]

V

We are all inclined to associate our favorite writers with judgments of which we approve. Although scalp hunting and bounties are as repulsive to me as they are to any of Hawthorne's recent critics, I find it hard to imagine that the subtle moral intelligence evident in Hawthorne's exposition of Reuben Bourne's multiple motives would have overlooked the genuine moral ambiguities in Lovell's expeditions. I see no clear evidence that Hawthorne regarded Roger Malvin and Reuben Bourne as greedy or bloodthirsty Indian fighters, nor any that Reuben's fifteen-year-old son Cyrus has ever fired at a human being, even in self-defense. Reuben Bourne's guilt begins not in scalp hunting but in his awareness of mixed motives for what the narrator clearly says is "a justifiable act."[22] Hawthorne, I believe, saw heroic qualities in the survivors' ten-hour stand against an equal or superior force that had already mortally wounded Lovell and all but one of his lieutenants; heroic qualities, too, in the wounded survivors who urged their comrades to abandon them, as Malvin commands and then "wiles" Bourne to do. Neither the phrase "moonlight of romance" nor even the "circumstances cast judicially into the shade" persuade me that Hawthorne's opening paragraph invites us to see Lovell's Fight and Reuben Bourne's blighted life in ironic condemnation of Anglo-American lust for land. The historical setting does serve to remind us that American history, like all moral experience, should be read with critical sympathy. When Hawthorne recommended that a "dark, funereal stone" be erected on Gallows Hill to commemorate "the errors of an earlier race, and not to be cast down, while the human heart has one infirmity that may result in crime," he did not object to the memorial column on Bunker Hill; that battleground was "the height which our fathers made sacred with their blood, poured out in a holy cause."[23] He did not call Lovell's Fight a holy cause, nor did he condemn it. He found in its aftermath material for a superb study of ambiguous guilt, prevarication, and compulsion.

Notes

1. See Francis Jennings, *The Invasion of America: Indians, Colonialism, and the Cant of Conquest* (Chapel Hill: Univ. of North Carolina Press, 1975), p. 1; Jennings, "A Vanishing Indian: Francis Parkman versus His Sources," *Pennsylvania Magazine of History and Biography* 87 (1963): 306–23; Francis Parkman, *Montcalm and Wolfe,* 2 vols. (Boston, 1892).

2. Ely Stock, "History and the Bible in Hawthorne's 'Roger Malvin's Burial,'" *Essex Institute Historical Collections* (hereafter cited as *EIHC*), 100 (1964): 279–96.

3. G. Harrison Orians, "The Source of Hawthorne's 'Roger Malvin's Burial,'" *American Literature* 10 (1938): 313–18; David Lovejoy, "Lovewell's Fight and Hawthorne's 'Roger Malvin's Burial,'" *New England Quarterly* 27 (1954): 527–31.

4. The quotation by Lovejoy ("Lovewell's Fight," p. 530) is taken from *Collections, Topographical, Historical, and Biographical,* ed. John Farmer and Jacob B. Moore, 2 vols. (Concord, Mass., 1823), 2:306. It comes from an article by J. B. H. (probably Joseph Bancroft Hill, says Lovejoy). Lovejoy points out that Hawthorne's Roger Malvin uses the phrase: "Tell my daughter . . . that . . . you . . . left me only at my earnest entreaty."

5. Francis Parkman, *A Half-Century of Conflict,* 2 vols. (Boston, 1893), 1:249 (hereafter cited as *HC* in the text).

6. Nathaniel Hawthorne, "Roger Malvin's Burial," in *Mosses from an Old Manse,* ed. William A. Charvat et al. (Columbus: Ohio State Univ. Press, 1974), pp. 337–38.

7. See Edwin Fussell, *Frontier: American Literature and the American West* (Princeton, N.J.: Princeton Univ. Press, 1965), pp. 75–77; Diane C. Naples, "'Roger Malvin's Burial'—A Parable for Historians?" *American Transcendental Quarterly* 13 (1972): 45–48; Robert Daly, "History and Chivalric Myth in

'Roger Malvin's Burial,'" *EIHC* 109 (1973), 99–115; and John Samson, "Hawthorne's Oak Trees," *American Literature* 52 (1980): 457–61.

8. Fussell, *Frontier,* p. 75.

9. See Parkman, *Half-Century* 1:253.

10. For one of many summaries of such comparisons, see David Levin, *History as Romantic Art: Bancroft, Prescott, Motley, and Parkman* (Stanford, Calif.: Stanford Univ. Press, 1959), 3–23.

11. See Nathaniel Hawthorne, *The Snow Image and Uncollected Tales,* ed. William A. Charvat et al. (Columbus: Ohio State Univ. Press, 1974), p. 4.

12. Fannie Hardy Eckstorm, "Pigwacket and Parson Symmes," *New England Quarterly* 9 (1936): 378–402. Since Robert Daly accepts Eckstorm's argument and applies it to "Roger Malvin's Burial," it needs to be dealt with here. Both Eckstorm and Daly interpret as a thorough disclaimer a qualification in the survivors' affidavit. Ensign Wyman and two other men signed "An Attestation": "We whose names are hereunto subscribed, having had the preceding narrative read to us (though we can't each of us indeed attest to every particular article and circumstance in it), yet we can and do aver that the substance of it is true, and are well satisfied with the truth of the whole." Daly and Eckstorm concur in arguing that, since "these three men had never been out of sight and hearing of one another they all must have known the same things and should have been able to take their oath to anything that happened." But surely every man engaged in a ten-hour battle will see and hear some things differently from his comrades' experience. Only a resolute skepticism will read so innocuous a qualification as part of "a conscious artifice intended to deceive, and therefore formally a lie, quite comparable to" Reuben Bourne's prevarication in Hawthorne's story (see Daly, "History and Chivalric Myth," p. 109).

13. One of Daly's most interesting arguments concerns Hawthorne's application of chivalrous standards to judge Reuben Bourne's desertion of Roger Malvin. See Daly, "History and Chivalric Myth," pp. 112–14. On Paugus, see Eckstorm, "Pigwacket and Parson Symmes," p. 389.

14. Washington Irving, *A History of New York, from the Beginning of the World to the End of the Dutch Dynasty,* by Diedrich Knickerbocker (New York, 1812), b. 1, chap. 5; James Fenimore Cooper, *The Pioneers* (New York, 1823); George Bancroft, *History of the United States from the Discovery of the Continent,* 10 vols. (1834–74), vols. 1 and 3. Bancroft's first volume was not actually published until after "Roger Malvin's Burial."

15. Hawthorne, "Young Goodman Brown," in *Mosses from an Old Manse,* p. 77.

16. Hawthorne, "The Old Manse," ibid., p. 11.

17. Nathaniel Hawthorne, *True Stories from History and Biography,* ed. William A. Charvat et al. (Columbus: Ohio State Univ. Press, 1974), pp. 94–95.

18. Hawthorne read about Father Rale in Thomas Hutchinson's *History of the Province of Massachusetts Bay* (see the modern edition, edited by Lawrence S. Mayo, 3 vols. [Cambridge: Harvard Univ. Press, 1936], 2:164–66, 197–200, 222–23, 234–37). Hawthorne refers explicitly to Rale in a notebook entry about "A Bell's Biography" (see *Hawthorne's Lost Notebook, 1835–1841,* ed. Barbara S. Mouffe [University Park and London: Penn State Press, 1978], p. 29). First published in 1837, "A Bell's Biography" describes sympathetically the death of an unnamed priest who resembles Father Rale, but Hawthorne points out that some of the Indians assembling at the church "bore flaxen-haired scalps at their girdles, as if to lay those bloody trophies on Our Lady's altar" (*The Snow Image,* p. 105).

19. Hawthorne, *The Snow Image,* p. 144, and *True Stories,* p. 133.

20. Hawthorne, *The Snow Image,* p. 53. Robert Daly sees the sinister allusion in Roger Malvin's name (see Daly, "History and Chivalric Myth," pp. 103–4).

21. *The Snow Image,* pp. 52–53. Robert Daly perceives similar qualities in Richard Bourne, portrayed in Hutchinson's *History of Massachusetts,* and he argues that Hawthorne intended an ironic contrast between the actual Richard Bourne and the fictitious Reuben Bourne (see Daly, "History and Chivalric Myth," pp. 104–6).

22. Hawthorne, *Mosses from an Old Manse,* p. 349.

23. Hawthorne, "Alice Doane's Appeal," in *The Snow Image,* p. 280.

16.

The Province of Historical Criticism

Historical Fact in Hawthorne and Colacurcio

As readers of his painstaking articles had every reason to expect, Michael Colacurcio's *The Province of Piety* makes an extraordinarily thorough case for treating Nathaniel Hawthorne's historical fiction as moral history—fiction that is at least as serious about history as it is about morality. Colacurcio gives us 522 pages on "Moral History in Hawthorne's Early Tales" and 137 pages of endnotes which conduct a generous colloquy—generous in both spirit and space—with the published commentary of other scholars and critics. In both text and notes, moreover, Colacurcio demonstrates his own knowledge of Puritan and Unitarian theology, and he often succeeds in demonstrating that Hawthorne's knowledge went far beyond the mechanical facts that mere source hunting might discover. In these pages Hawthorne becomes not merely a perceptive anticipator of Perry Miller but an ironic observer who was bound to "deconstruct" the self-deceptive lies that his contemporaries connived with their dead ancestors to tell about the pieties of early New England. It is what Hawthorne and Colacurcio say about early New England that should make this book especially interesting to readers of *Early American Literature*.[1]

It has always been foolish, if comforting for ignorance, to argue that the history in "The Gentle Boy," "Young Goodman Brown," "The Maypole of Merrymount," and *The Scarlet Letter* is irrelevant to the central meaning of the fiction. *The Province of Piety* makes such a claim demonstrably untenable. Colacurcio is at his best when he highlights Hawthorne's religious language, and political diction when it refers to specific historical issues: "visible sanctity" in the empty church in Bos-

Reprinted by permission from *Early American Literature* 20 (1985): 164–72.

ton when Robin Molineux peers through the window; the "congregated mirth" of the mob in the same story. Whether or not we can read Hawthorne intelligently or profitably without knowing the history of colonial New England, Colacurcio proves that we will read Hawthorne more intelligently if we take the trouble to see the range and depth of his historical judgment. To interpret Hawthorne's historical tales, Colacurcio declares in one of his broadest claims, "is to deconstruct, one by one, the various chapters of an emergent American mythology" (130). "Ignorance of the facts is no excuse [for misreading Hawthorne's historical fiction]," he says, "even if we should know all the hermeneutical rules in the world" (117).

Yet much of the historical interpretation in this learned book depends on a special reading of "the facts." Colacurcio's own theory surely acknowledges that interpretations of history may be just as partial as interpretations of irony. We have "no perfect litmus test for detecting irony on the tongue of the speaker," he says; irony "always exists (or not) pretty much in the ear of the listener. But in the end most of us will think better of Hawthorne's intelligence if he does not quite mean *all* that his 'narrator' says" in "The Gray Champion" (209). Notice here the appeal to what most of us think. Implicitly relativistic, it not only seems to assume here that most of us want to think better rather than worse of Hawthorne's intelligence; it also implies a valid modern consensus about the moral significance of American history in the seventeenth and eighteenth centuries.

Twice before, as a reviewer of excellent books in these pages, I have asked readers to believe that a few brief lines of praise are not merely ceremonial, that the approval must not be overshadowed by my several pages of detailed dissent. Here again I feel obliged to explain my dissent more fully than my praise and to declare my gratitude for much that *The Province of Piety* has taught me about theological and other historical issues in some of Hawthorne's best (and some of his neglected) tales and sketches; and about the development of his narrative and historical techniques.

Let us begin the dissent with "The Gentle Boy," with the text as our central issue. Colacurcio argues persuasively that Hawthorne delineates equivalent moral blindness in enthusiastical Quakers and persecuting Puritans, but in this configuration he chooses to set what he calls the "cold" piety of Tobias Pearson's conscience against the truly charitable heart of Dorothy Pearson. In this reading Tobias Pearson becomes a weak representative of "the Puritans," whom Colacurcio says that Hawthorne represents as, "essentially, rationalists of the scholastic sort" (169); and the gentle boy's Quaker mother, who has left her natural duty in search of an enthusiast's martyrdom, stands opposite, not to Dorothy Pearson alone, but to the too calculating piety of Tobias: "In the historic world of Tobias Pearson and Quaker Catherine, . . . the two great Commandments [to love your neighbor as yourself and to love God with all your might] have come apart" (182).

To find support in the text for this reading of what he calls "the theology of 'The Gentle Boy'" (189), Colacurcio deconstructs the scene in which Tobias decides to take into his own home the child (Ilbrahim) whom he has found weeping on a fresh grave below the gallows, only a few hours after the child's Quaker father has been hanged. In Hawthorne's text Ilbrahim's wails, coming from the desolate place just after Tobias has heard the autumn wind "moaning" through the pines, sound "more mournful than even . . . the wind." Twice Hawthorne tells us not that these are recognized as a child's cries, but that they sound "*like* the wailing of a mortal," and "*like* the wailing of a child" (my italics). Only after he has "struggled against superstitious fears" associated with the age and the place does Tobias reason that "some infant, *it may be,* has strayed from its mother, and chanced upon this place of death. For the ease of mine own conscience I must search this matter out" (70–71; my italics).

In the Colacurcio version that last sentence of Hawthorne's is quoted in isolation to prove that "Tobias's charity is cold and slow indeed. One can scarcely imagine his words in the mouth of the Good Samaritan of the New Testament, whose motive we must suppose is love of neighbor rather than 'ease of conscience'" (164). When we turn to the Christian parable (Luke 10:30–37), we must notice that the Samaritan has no reason to doubt he has encountered a real man, robbed, beaten, and left half-dead. The Colacurcio version of "The Gentle Boy" does not tell us Tobias decides "the voice is most likely mortal," that he must strain his eyes to see whether anybody at all is there "in the dim moonlight," or that the objectionable reasoning has occurred before Tobias knows he has heard the cries of a real child. In

Hawthorne's text "the Puritan" lays his hand on the child's shoulder as soon as he reaches him, and addresses him "compassionately." He immediately promises to find the boy's home and deliver him to his mother. When the boy reveals his strange name and declares that his home is here at the grave, Tobias does wonder whether this is an apparition rather than a human child, but he quickly decides that the child is human, and he quickly offers to give him "a warm supper and bed" in the Pearsons' own home. If it is "religious prejudice" that makes "the Puritan" drop the child's hand upon learning of his Quaker identity, Hawthorne's text shows us that it is the Puritan's version of Christianity that quickly overcomes the prejudice: "'God forbid that I should leave this child to perish,' said he to himself. 'Do we not all spring from an evil root? Are we not all in darkness till the light doth shine upon us? He shall not perish, neither in body, nor, if prayer and instruction shall avail him, in soul.'" And when the child declares that his father's grave will be his home, Tobias (designated once again as "the Puritan") exclaims: "No, child, no; not while I have a roof over my head, or a morsel to share with you!"

Within a few minutes, then, Tobias has resolved to take the waif to his own home; and before his charitable wife can express any reaction at all to the child, her Puritan husband has first commanded her to "be kind" to "the little outcast, whom Providence hath put into our hands," and then announced his "resolution to feed and clothe" the boy "as if he were his own child."[2] Hawthorne's text will not support Colacurcio's claim that Dorothy Pearson, "completely free from explicitly doctrinal encumbrances," acts "out of simply natural or maternal benevolence in agreeing to care for the child" (167). She does not act at all until her husband, whom she is bound to obey, commands her to be kind. Only at this point does Hawthorne's text say that "Dorothy was gifted with even a quicker tenderness than her husband." Omitting the key word "even," the Colacurcio reading treats Dorothy's charity as truly Christian, hearty, "incarnational," but neglects to report her immediate approval "of all [her husband's] doings and intentions"—including his "resolution . . . to counteract the pernicious errors hitherto instilled into [the child's] infant mind."

From here on, the Colacurcio reading assumes that the coldness and slowness of Tobias Pearson's charity have been established. Toward the end of a long exegesis, when he declares that "the tale's most central concern . . . is the social fact and religious meaning of Tobias Pearson's decision to adopt Ilbrahim," Colacurcio can refer casually to "the original 'Puritan' slowness of that action" (191). Only a few literal-minded readers may remember, after twenty-odd pages of wide-ranging analysis and speculation, that the original charge of coldness and slowness, weakly founded as it is, says nothing about Pearson's decision to adopt the child, but refers only to his reason for investigating the nature of the sound borne to his ears by the wind in the darkness. Even the kindness of Luke's Good Samaritan was content to leave the injured man at an inn and to pay his expenses. It is hard to believe that Hawthorne, or "most of us," would judge as cold and slow a character's decision to adopt as his own a child he has known only a few minutes or hours.

The point of my objection here goes beyond the dangers of partial reading or special pleading. The virtues of Colacurcio's work may make the fallacies unusually hard to detect. His oversimplifications and inaccuracies are imbedded in an extremely complex disquisition that seems to insist on finding the time to consider all reasonable interpretations. One of the great pleasures of reading him is that of engaging in a leisurely, subtle discussion. His learned analyses of many moral issues in Puritan and Romantic literature make it hard to believe that he will oversimplify other issues. Yet *The Province of Piety* treats the historical judgments of both Cotton Mather and George Bancroft, on various crimes of the Puritans, as much more simple than they were. It assumes most of us agree that Mather's biography of Sir William Phips was "outrageously celebrative" (60) and that Phips's religious conversion was not only conveniently timed but (like his alleged patriotism) probably fraudulent; that Perry Miller's judgment of the Mathers' conduct in the witchcraft crisis was just; that Samuel Sewall's confession of error in the judgment of the witches was nobly motivated; that George Burroughs (the one person whose conviction for witchcraft Increase Mather explicitly endorsed, because it met Mather's criterion requiring two credible witnesses to overt acts) was condemned largely on spectral evidence; that zeal to protect the rights of Englishmen was not a genuine motive in the revolution against Governor Andros in 1689; and that the American Revolution was not a "majestic" but an ordinary event in human history.

In presenting the early Hawthorne as virtually the sole deconstructor of pious lies about the sins of the fathers, Colacurcio also neglects such unsettling predecessors as Diedrich Knickerbocker on the right of conquest, James Fenimore Cooper on the murderous partisans of the American Revolution in *The Spy* (and on the hypocritical third-generation Puritans in *The Wept of Wish-ton-Wish*), and (again) Washington Irving on "Philip of Pokanoket" in *The Sketch-Book*. These texts make one doubt the claim that Hawthorne's contemporaries "had not yet learned to tell the unlovely truth about their national experience" (121).[3]

Most of these dismissive simplifications enter *The Province of Piety* in support of the claim that Hawthorne was deeply critical rather than ambivalent toward Puritanism, and nowhere more ironically critical of self-deceptive lies about Puritan crimes than in "The Gray Champion" and "Roger Malvin's Burial." The problem is at least partly rhetorical. The argument for reading "The Gray Champion" as an ironic attack upon New England's mythologizing begins speculatively enough. But along the way our guide to the moral history adopts an ironic tone himself. In mid-argument he does throw one bone to the beleaguered colonists: "Of course the political situation [under Andros in 1689] is not, in all literal fact, a very happy one!" (211). But the cancellation of the charter, the persecution of Congregationalists in England, the pursuit of the regicides in New England, the beheading of a New England woman's mother by the authorities in England—these facts do not enter the ironic exposition. Hawthorne's attack on mythologizing appears here to be not an insistence on a historical reality that includes respect for the Puritans' complex position, morality, perplexity, but the demolition of straw men. The "schizoid phantasm of Dr. Cotton Mather" and the "Puritanic paranoia" of *The Wonders of the Invisible World* typify the heightened rhetoric of a paragraph in which Colacurcio argues that "something left out of" Hawthorne's text is "an absence that is palpably present." For the moment no longer speculative, this paragraph calls "The Gray Champion" an "utterly ironic tale" (216). The exposition seems to assume that our knowledge of the complex history of Massachusetts entitles us, in support of Hawthorne's dissent from the pious judgments of his contemporaries, to enter summary judgments of our own.

The most severe of those judgments, and the most prejudicial selection of historical facts, color the powerful essay on "Roger Malvin's Burial." Hawthorne's target in that story is identified as "the most debased form of literary lying" (119). Long before beginning his 12,000-word essay on the story, Colacurcio has already referred to Lovewell's Fight as "a dirty little bounty-hunting expedition" (78), and that judgment governs his entire account. His brilliant analysis of Reuben Bourne's moral regression from the self-deceptive desertion of Roger Malvin to the self-destructive manslaughter of his only son stands in astonishing contrast to the "social" interpretation that follows. One wonders how the subtle moral intelligence that has just traced Reuben Bourne's miserable course with insight and sympathy could have produced the prejudicial narrative of Lovewell's Fight on which the ironic interpretation must be based. The Colacurcio version does not report that Pigwacket warriors had kidnapped two of Lovewell's neighbors, or that eight of the ten men sent out to rescue those two were ambushed and killed, or that the sleeping Indians killed in a midnight raid by Lovewell's men were not peaceable natives in their own village but a Canadian raiding party newly supplied by the French.[4] It is in discussing this episode that Colacurcio rules out ignorance of the facts as an excuse for misreading, and he repeatedly deplores "the dismal facts of the historical situation" (118), "the altogether unlovely facts of the case" (118), "the Lovewell farce" (120). "Once we [readers] remember these facts," he writes, "we instantly know how to proceed" (118). We attribute to Hawthorne a condemnation of "imperialist expansion [bought] at the price of a carnage originally inspired by intentions equally materialistic and altogether less grand" (119).

This is not the place to rehearse the entire debate over Hawthorne's allegedly ironic introduction to "Roger Malvin's Burial." One can argue for an ironic reading even after acknowledging the facts that the Colacurcio version neglects. But the historical facts and motives are much too complex to justify our instantly knowing how to proceed. The original motives of Lovewell's men, in response to the Pigwacket raid, were perhaps neither imperialistic nor materialistic. "The facts" about which Hawthorne may have waxed ironic should include the French decision to wage war on the Anglo-American settlements in a time of formal peace. A long essay celebrating Hawthorne's moral complexity ought not to be morally simplistic.

It is on questions concerning "our national conscience," and in pursuit of Hawthorne's irony, that *The Province of Piety* oversimplifies, and usually in the first half of the book. Colacurcio does eventually acknowledge "Hawthorne's sense that the ugly realities of Indian warfare . . . were somehow inevitable. The point," he says, "was not at all to repudiate America," nor was it "to *hate* America. . . . The point was simply to *understand* it" or "to see, and in fiction to show, where the available and growing national 'story' was dangerously wrong" (156–57). But in concentrating on the "ugly realities," "unlovely facts," and "past ugliness" in his pursuit of irony, and in neglecting other facts, Colacurcio's explications leave the impression that both he and Hawthorne consider the essential facts ugly. He concedes grudgingly that "one or two individuals" in Lovewell's Fight "probably did act bravely in a basically depraved situation" (119), whereas the historical record gives us reason to delete the word "probably" and raise the number to fifteen or twenty.

One odd consequence of all this emphasis on ugliness and irony in "The Gray Champion," "My Kinsman, Major Molineux," and "Roger Malvin's Burial" is neglect of a recurrent historical fact linking the fictitious Reuben Bourne to Lovewell's Fight. Not once but several times, the historical record tells us that actual men had to make the same decision with which Hawthorne's tale begins. They had to decide whether to perish with a wounded comrade who was unable to travel, or leave him to die alone. Nothing in the eighteenth-century record (partial though that, of course, may be) indicates moral disapproval or doubt about the grim choice to save the lives that could be saved. The "scalping chaplain," one of those left to die alone, does order his companions to leave him and one may thus infer their reluctance, but we hear nothing of their remorse or of recrimination from others. These facts seem to me at least as relevant to the moral history in "Roger Malvin's Burial" as the presumably sanctimonious decision of pious eighteenth-century narrators to change the date of Lovewell's Fight from Sunday to Saturday. Like young Goodman Brown's apparent ignorance of original sin, Reuben Bourne's remorse over his decision, and his fiancée's insistence on knowing whether he had given her father a decent burial, might both be anachronistic interpolations for the storyteller's nineteenth-century moral and psychological purpose. Or Hawthorne's revision of this part of the record might express one more particle of the "unlovely truth" that Colacurcio says Hawthorne's contemporaries (as well as their eighteenth-century predecessors) had not yet learned to tell about their national experience. Unmentioned, along with the unlovely flight of a coward who actually refused to guide a rescue and burial party to the site of the disaster, these actual precedents for Reuben Bourne's original decision are not present in *The Province of Piety* to complicate or impede the argument for irony.

My emphatic dissent qualifies, but does not deny, the magnitude of Michael Colacurcio's achievement. I agree heartily that we should use our best understanding of New England history to deepen our understanding of Hawthorne and his fiction. Colacurcio's massive study, more powerfully than any other single work I know, advances our understanding of Hawthorne's development and practice as a historical writer. Damaged by an insistence on irony and by an ideological or ethical severity that seems to be at least partly responsible for neglect of some important historical facts, *The Province of Piety* nonetheless gives us excellent, revised versions of Colacurcio's exhaustive articles on "Young Goodman Brown" and "The Minister's Black Veil." It also presents an eloquent, witty defense of historical criticism. And even in the chapters to which I have taken exception, the moral and literary analysis is often admirably perceptive. The value of this book, like the events and issues we have considered here, is more complex than applause or dissent can fairly express.

Notes

1. Michael J. Colacurcio, *The Province of Piety: Moral History in Hawthorne's Early Tales* (Cambridge: Harvard Univ. Press, 1984). See John P. McWilliams, *Hawthorne, Melville, and the American Character* (Cambridge: Cambridge Univ. Press, 1984).

2. In the original version published in *The Token,* a passage about the mother's tender feelings intervenes between Tobias's command and his announcement of the adoption, but the passage was deleted when Hawthorne revised the story for *Twice-Told Tales.*

3. The contemporaries referred to here are not the celebrated writers but the mass audience of magazine readers. But many of those readers made up the very audience that had welcomed *The Spy, The Pioneers,* and *The Sketch-Book. The Pioneers* is relevant here because the paragraph from which I have just quoted declares that one of the truths Hawthorne's audience had not yet learned is Thomas Hutchinson's pronouncement (in Colacurcio's paraphrase): "True heroism lies not in combat and conquest but in the foundation of flourishjng towns and colonies." Colacurcio does cite *The Deerslayer* on racial prejudice, but only to emphasize its belated appearance in the 1840s (560n.53).

4. I refer here only to the main text. A note does add that my own article supplies "the appropriate reminder of French and Indian guilt" (560n.47). Neither French nor Indian behavior enters into the representation of the historical facts in Colacurcio's analysis of moral history in "Roger Malvin's Burial." See above, chapter 15.

17.

Innocents Abroad

From Mark Twain and Henry James to Bellow, Malamud, and Baldwin

The tradition is complex, as a number of scholars have shown.[1] Acknowledging that complexity, I shall concentrate on continuities and differences between the three contemporary writers and the tradition, trusting you to remember that I know I am selecting one refrain that has been sounded ever since the first English settlement of Massachusetts 365 years ago. At first innocence means simplicity without the defects of naïveté. The refrain sets bishops and archbishops of England and the Continent against true believers who try to restore the primitive liberty, order, and beauty of the earliest Christian churches. In a new seventeenth-century exodus the Lord's People flee England for the New Canaan, to escape the "vile ceremonies" that Satan's followers have "foisted in" upon the church.[2] William Bradford's history of Plymouth Plantation and Thomas Hooker's *Survey of the Summe of Church-Discipline* profess to use a "plain style" of writing, and Thomas Hooker defensively invites those English readers who "covet more sauce than meat" to "find cooks to their mind." His book comes "out of the wilderness," he says; planters, who have enough trouble keeping warm, will "leave the cuts and lace to those that study to go fine."[3]

We see this attitude in an even more secular context 150 years later, when Joel Barlow writes a brilliant mock-epic poem upon finding cornmeal mush, or hasty pudding, at an inn in the French Alps. He scorns both "the vicious rules of Art" and "the thin diluted soup" that he associates with French cuisine. The planting, harvesting, grinding,

Reprinted by permission from *RANAM* 18 (1985): 163–82.

and eating of the plain corn become a pastoral celebration of his provincial American republic in Connecticut. Here the provincial American poet who boasts that "all my bones were made of Indian corn" demonstrates his mastery of the mock-epic form, the heroic couplet, and some of the classical allusions in the learned work of English wits.[4] The same double-edged message lies concealed in the honorific initials O. S. M.—One of the Swinish Multitude—that Philip Freneau attached to one of his pseudonyms as a satirical retort to Edmund Burke's criticism of popular revolution.[5] The message reverberates in Washington Irving's mock-heroic *History of New York*, which ridicules European historiography, and it reverberates yet again when Mark Twain, exhausted by his Italian guide's endless repetition of Michelangelo's name, declares that he never felt so soothed as he did on learning—yesterday—that Michelangelo is dead.[6]

Between the Napoleonic Wars and the First World War American literature generally represents Europe as the country of the past: not only, in Nathaniel Hawthorne's words, *Our Old Home*,[7] but the repository of the tradition of the race. Europe is a museum. There the American visitor can see accumulated triumphs in the visual arts, triumphs achieved before Europeans were aware that the New World exists. In this good way, but also with consequences more corrupt, Europe was the country of the senses. Through millennia of conflict, intrigue, plague, and slaughter, Europeans had come to know about sin, defeat, betrayal, and compromise. Romantic historians in the United States traced the course of human Progress as the course of Liberty, from Greece and Rome, through the German forest, through the northern Netherlands (in their rebellion against Spain), through England to North America. In politics Liberty advanced from the ceremonial tyranny of feudalism and monarchy toward the plain American republic; in religion, from ceremonial Catholicism, with its tolerance of pagan festivals, toward austere Unitarianism—in both politics and religion, away from ceremonial and legalistic forms toward simplicity, away from conventional, embellished surface toward the simple essence.[8] Washington Irving, with none of his former irony, congratulates the historian John Lothrop Motley in 1856 for having fulfilled "the high calling of the American press—that rising tribunal before which the whole world is to be summoned, its history to be revised and rewritten, and the judgment of past ages to be cancelled or confirmed."[9] And, of course, Mark Twain, near the end of the century, depicts a simple Connecticut Yankee whose common political sense, literacy, and technology make him superior to the bogus magic of the wizard Merlin and to all the knights of Arthurian England. Here again, as in the plain diction of Bradford and Hooker in the seventeenth century, the criticism is not only moral but also literary. Mark Twain's Yankee burlesques both the repetitive battles in medieval romance and the nostalgic sentimentality of some nineteenth-century Romantics and Victorians who idealized the good old days of chivalry. His target here resembles the ideas of the poet E. A. Robinson's Miniver Cheevy:

> Miniver loved the Medici
> Albeit he had never seen one;
> He would have sinned incessantly
> Could he have been one.[10]

The ambiguity of the Connecticut Yankee's own destructive violence— even the gruesome conclusion, when he electrocutes the massed chivalry, 25,000 knights who have marched against his anachronistic republic—complicates but does not cancel his rejection of European history. There were two reigns of terror, he says, the one we know by that name in the few months of the 1790s and another that lasted for centuries.[11]

Whether in history, in art, or in politics, the innocent character here sees things directly, with his own uninstructed eye. Huckleberry Finn reports that Bunyan's masterpiece *The Pilgrim's Progress* is a book "about a man that left his family, it didn't say why."[12] Mark Twain concedes that Leonardo's *Last Supper* was once a pretty picture, but by the time he sees it, it is too dim to be beautiful[13] (he would have been happy to know that in our time it would be successfully cleaned). The Connecticut Yankee sees a house full of pigs where his guide insists that they are ladies under enchantment, and he tries to learn how a man encased in armor can scratch, or wipe his nose, or expel a fly that has entered through a breathing vent in his visor.

Henry James's American innocents are even more complex than those of Mark Twain, but in some of his best works on the European theme James plays variations on a theme that Mark Twain and many predecessors had sounded: the contrast between being and doing. In that juxtaposition Europe often represents being, not primarily because Europeans seem to care more than practical Americans care about ends, but rather because Europeans are over there across the Atlantic and are not caught up in the life of American commerce—or perhaps, because those Europeans who are caught up in the getting and spending are not the main subject of the American visitor's interest. Christopher Newman, the self-made millionaire in James's *The American,* says that he has long since learned in America how to make himself felt,[14] and that he has come to Europe to learn how to feel. Characteristically here, the European is wrapped in tradition, convention, complex associations of family and class, whereas the best American (as Yvor Winters remarked long ago)[15] is set down in Europe without such baggage, as if free to make independent moral choices. In *The American, The Portrait of a Lady,* and *The Ambassadors,* for example, the central character, in contrast to some other Americans and Europeans, is free, open, not rigid; willing and even eager to learn from European art, manners, experience. Although sometimes awkward and self-deluding, this American is able to move easily, with the natural grace of a classless gentility, in aristocratic salons in Europe. His moral triumph—even the coarse Christopher Newman's triumph—comes through in a scene that shows both his new perception of complex European manners and his ability to behave impeccably.

The classic statement of independent or transcendental selfhood comes from Isabel Archer, James's heroine in *The Portrait of a Lady,* when she dissents from an expatriate American's declaration that we are all made up of conventions and appurtenances, and that even our clothes express our essential selves. Isabel insists that neither the consequences of her taste, nor any material thing, can adequately represent her.[16] And although this young American woman, "affronting her destiny," is "ground in the very mill of the conventional,"[17] James persuades me to believe in the value of her remarkable self. Her portrait is not complete until we have seen that her perceptive powers have been admirably developed. We see the full range of that development in her celebrated review of her wretched marriage, in her discovery that a minor lapse in manners reveals the true relationship between her husband and Madame Merle, and in the conventional skill with which

Isabel manages her dramatic confrontation with each of those two who have ground her in the mill.

Lambert Strether's case in James's *The Ambassadors* is even more complex than Isabel Archer's. From the very first scenes, nonetheless, Strether's consciousness defines Europe as the land of sensory experience, and virtually the first sense of which his arrival in Europe makes him conscious is a sense of escape from the "cold thought" of Massachusetts.[18] In the end we see, of course, that an insistence on rectitude and duty remains an essential part of his identity, but his very notion of rectitude has been transformed by his insistent abandonment of himself to sensory impressions of Paris, of a beautiful French lady, and of the French landscape. In all these characters of Mark Twain and James, moreover, innocence means not only simplicity and relative purity but also a costly naïveté that fails to perceive, or sees belatedly, the value and complexity of European customs.

Now of course American writers in the nineteenth century did express some interest in contemporary European events, the major revolutions, wars, and other political struggles. But American literature, in that period, expressed very little concern with the life that most Europeans were actually living at the time. A rough generalization about the changes between the turn of the century and the decades just after World War II must emphasize a radical shift in temporal emphasis. As the United States becomes a world power, as American life is again directly affected by European events, especially in World War I, writers seem more ready to treat Europe as contemporaneous. Yet even in the 1920s and 1930s issues of art persist. Writers and fictional characters come to Europe to explore European forms, to escape from American money grubbing. T. S. Eliot and Ernest Hemingway learn from Ezra Pound or Gertrude Stein, and Hemingway declares that his plain prose is American; he dismisses Hawthorne and other nineteenth-century predecessors, except for Mark Twain, as English colonials even while he delights in learning from James Joyce and from the paintings of Goya and Cézanne.

Whether or not they stressed the French connection, as Wallace Stevens did, or declared an American separatism with William Carlos Williams or Van Wyck Brooks, all these writers felt themselves to be personally born into the Franco-Anglo-American tradition. Even in the

first four decades of this century, therefore, one obvious, central distinction between these writers and their black or Jewish countrymen is
simply that for the blacks and the Jews the old genealogical relationship has disappeared. As early as the first generation of Jewish-
American writers around 1920—Abraham Cahan or Anzia Yezierska,[19]
for example—the very definition of Europe has changed. And in our
contemporaries who are the main subject here, I believe that this fundamental change persists. No longer does "Europe" mean only France,
Italy, Spain, Germany, the Netherlands, and England. Central and
eastern Europe, including Poland and Russia, enter. Bernard Malamud
even writes an entire novel, *The Fixer,* about an early anti-Semitic trial
in Russia. And in the fiction of the last forty years the Holocaust of
the War against the Jews not only replaces but dwarfs the Spanish
Inquisition, the French Reign of Terror, and World War I as proof of
Herman Melville's statement (1846) that "the white civilized man" is
"the most ferocious animal on the face of the earth."[20]

In the rest of this essay I would like to sketch some of the ways
in which three of the best American writers since World War II play
variations on the traditional themes. In considering those variations we
will have to notice some of the sharp divergences from Anglo-American
tradition, but the surprising, or at least the more important, phenomenon is the powerful reassertion of traditional comparisons and contrasts.

Consider, for example, Saul Bellow's story "Mosby's Memoirs"
(1968). Here the point of view is that of a brilliant reactionary writer
whose opinions do not necessarily represent those of Saul Bellow.
Mosby himself admits at least once that both he and "the French intellectuals" were "quite wrong" in their generalizations about French and
American national character.[21] The narration does not contradict or
undercut Mosby's satirical representation of French pretensions. Mosby
complains that "the French" failed to oppose the Nazis' deportation of
French Jews—an outrage that he says was opposed not only in Denmark but in benighted Bulgaria! Yet even in the dismal, poor Paris
after 1945, "the French were even then ferociously telling the whole
world" that they had "the savoir vivre, the gai-savoir. Especially Americans," Mosby says, "haunted by their Protestant Ethic, had to hear
this. My God—sit down, sip wine, taste cheese, break bread, hear

music, know love, stop running, and learn ancient life-wisdom from Europe" (167).

As Henry James said long before Mosby, "It is a complex fate being an American," and one of its risks, he said, is "a superstitious valuation of Europe."[22] Saul Bellow's foolish Lustgarten, the incompetent would-be tycoon and smuggler, is superstitiously following not European religion or monarchy or feudalism, but modern European dreams of revolution. He is an ex-Trotskyist trying to make his fortune on the European black market after World War II. Bellow, through Mosby, scorns Lustgarten's ludicrously misplaced, doctrinaire Leninism, as well as his belated opportunism. Mosby depicts the penniless Lustgarten, evicted from his apartment and living in the brand-new Cadillac that he has imported just too late to be able to sell it for a great profit: "sleeping, covered with two coats, on the majestic seat, like Jonah inside Leviathan." And Mosby perceives that "this shoe salesman, in America attached to foreign doctrines, who could not relinquish Europe in the New World, was now, in Paris, sleeping in the Cadillac, encased in this gorgeous Fisher body from Detroit. At home an exotic, in Europe a Yankee. His timing was off" (170).

In the same story another American, a poet named Ruskin, insists that "America had had no history, was not a historical society. His proof was from Hegel" (171). That is, his proof of a statement about American society was not actual evidence about that society, but was taken from Hegel, who knew virtually nothing about American history, and whom Ruskin is misrepresenting.

Now although Ruskin, the target of Bellow's wit here, echoes a lament of Henry James, Nathaniel Hawthorne, and others, that Americans have no past, in a more important way Bellow marches brilliantly, originally, right in the path of Mark Twain, Henry James, and a dozen others. Not only does the naïf fool's misapplication of European doctrine here resemble Huckleberry Finn's hilarious misinformation about Henry VIII and his Declaration of Independence, "with all them Saxon heptarchies."[23] An even more striking similarity is the provincial author's demonstration that he himself has acquired the taste and the learning of the European intellectual before satirizing both the doctrine, if it is fallacious, and the ignorant character's comical misapplication of the doctrine. "Absurdly," Mosby says, "the college-bred dunces of America had longed for a true Left-Wing movement on the European model. They still dreamed of it. No less absurd were the Right-Wing idiots" (175–76). Bellow and his Moses Herzog are just as far above the college-bred dunces as the Philistine Mark Twain is above the hypocritical American pilgrims in *The Innocents Abroad.*

In Henry James's European novels, of course, the author displays his mastery not of European philosophical and political ideas, but of European manners and aesthetic techniques such as impressionism. In some ways Henry Adams might make a better parallel for Bellow— the Adams of *The Education of Henry Adams* rather than the two novels. But Bellow's concentration on the ideas is a modern way of making a point similar to James's. James's flawed heroes, Newman and Strether, triumph by demonstrating that they can behave in a Parisian drawing room, both by perceiving nuances and by behaving generously and gracefully. Similarly Moses Herzog, the title character of my favorite Bellow novel,[24] is often mad and desperate, but his crazy letters to the living and the dead reveal both broad learning and acute critical understanding. Herzog may be as comical in thinking for himself about modern philosophers as Mark Twain and Christopher Newman are in seeing for themselves the masterpieces of European painting. But Herzog and Bellow have read carefully, and at least some of their questions, like some of Mark Twain's, are perceptive. Herzog rebukes Nietzsche for celebrating "the power of the Dionysian spirit to endure the sight of the Terrible . . . , to learn from deep pain." When he asks Herr Nietzsche "a question from the floor," Herzog's simple human point is devastating: "For this higher education, survival is necessary." Herzog's criticism here resembles Herman Melville's remark that Goethe's command to live in the All would have no value for a man suffering a raging toothache.[25] In this mad but acute letter to the dead philosopher, Herzog tells Nietzsche that "humankind lives mainly upon perverted ideas" and that Nietzsche's own ideas, when perverted, "are no better than the Christianity you condemn" (388–89). And Herzog has similar rebukes for Spengler and Heidegger. Herzog lives in a realm that few American literary characters have ever inhabited, the republic of European thought that is represented by Montaigne, Marx, Comte, Tolstoy, Pascal, Proudhon, Rousseau, Spinoza, Kierkegaard, Hegel, and Whitehead. He even quotes Pascal, Tolstoy, and Hegel in a letter that would have baffled its addressee, Dwight D. Eisenhower (200).

Another way in which Bellow, despite all his learning, resembles the autodidact Mark Twain is in the combination of daring criticism with startling, blunt language. In this quality both Bellow and Malamud use their Jewish characters to confront the pretentious authority of high culture with the common perception and diction of a Jewish American, mixing blunt diction with elevated terminology. Listen first to the Connecticut Yankee Henry Morgan's critique of the repetitive narratives of medieval romance, told to him by the loquacious lady he has rescued:

> If she had had a cork she would have been a comfort. But you can't cork that kind; they would die. Her clack was going all day, and you would think something would surely happen to her works by and by; but no, they never got out of order; and she never had to slack up for words. She could grind, and pump, and churn, and buzz by the week, and never stop to oil up or blow out. . . . She never had any ideas, any more than a fog has. She was a perfect blatherskite; I mean for jaw, jaw, jaw, talk, talk, talk, jabber, jabber, jabber. [79–80]

Now consider Bellow's Herzog in only two of many examples. Here he attacks the modish pessimism of his boyhood friend Shapiro. Herzog begins with a memory of their enrollment in a seminar on Proudhon. Of Shapiro's affected diction he says:

> For a Russian Jew from Chicago's West Side that [exclamation] "How delightful!" was inappropriate. A German Jew from Kenwood might have gotten away with it—old money, in the dry-goods business since 1880. But Shapiro's father had had no money, and peddled rotten apples from South Water Street in a wagon. There was more of the truth of life in those spotted, spoiled apples, and in old Shapiro, who smelled of the horse and of produce, than in all these learned references. [91].

Soon Herzog takes on "Old Proudhon" and the seminar, and once again "old Shapiro" comes out superior. Here we recall that "kraut" in Anglo-American slang is a coarse epithet for German, the equivalent of "frog" for Frenchman:

Old Proudhon's visions of darkness and evil can't be passed over. But we mustn't forget how quickly the visions of genius become the canned goods of the intellectuals. The canned sauerkraut of Spengler's "Prussian Socialism," the commonplaces of the Wasteland outlook, the cheap mental stimulants of Alienation, the cant and rant of pipsqueaks about Inauthenticity and Forlornness. . . . We are talking about the whole life of mankind. . . . A merely aesthetic critique of history! After the wars and mass killings! You are too intelligent for this [Shapiro]. You inherited rich blood. Your father peddled apples. [96]

Herzog himself is not exempt from this kind of criticism. From a more formidable antagonist, who claims that "we're all whores in this world," he receives this crude rebuke:

"I know damn well *I'm* a whore. And you're an outstanding shnook, I realize. At least the eggheads tell me so. But I bet you a suit of clothes you're a whore too. . . . Who told you you were such a prince? Your mother did her own wash; you took boarders; your old man was a two-bit moonshiner. I know you Herzog and your *Yiches*. Don't give me that hoitytoity. I'm a Kike myself and got my diploma in a stinking night school. Okay? Now let's both knock off this crap, dreamy boy." [109]

The heart of the European theme in Herzog is in Moses Herzog's memory of the Jewish immigrant's experience in Montreal in the 1920s. This section begins with Herzog's memory of a ridiculously pathetic young Jewish couple who had eloped from Montreal to Paris, slept in ditches, read Van Gogh's letters aloud to each other. And when Herzog and the husband had visited the poor wife a few years later in a hospital for the insane, she had insisted on discussing nothing but "the shape of Valéry's images" (165). Against such mad preferences Herzog sets the traditions of the Jewish people.

Herzog's memory itself is the chief instrument that links him to a Jewish past, both in his family and in the distance. He remembers, for example, the prayers said at dawn in Montreal, in the home of his father, the incompetent bootlegger:

"*Ma Tovu ohaleha Yaakov . . .* "
"How goodly are thy tents, O Israel."
Napoleon Street, rotten, toylike, crazy and filthy, riddled, flogged

with harsh weather—the bootlegger's boys reciting ancient prayers. To this Moses' heart was attached with great power. Here was a wider range of human feelings than he had ever again been able to find. The children of the race, by a never-failing miracle, opened their eyes on one strange world after another, age after age, and uttered the same prayer in each, eagerly loving what they found. [174]

These memories tie his family to the Jewish European experience of suffering and hope. And his version of that experience, with the unique details of the household of his childhood, becomes a metaphor for "the human life" that he insists he owes to the powers that created him (270). He repeatedly refuses to wallow in what he calls "the mire of post-Renaissance, post-humanistic, post-Cartesian dissolution, next door to the Void." Everybody is in "that act," he says; even people "who had never even read a book of metaphysics were touting the Void as if it were so much salable real estate" (118). But his family's experience did occur, and his sympathetic memory of it is a central fact of his own current existence.

Bellow remarks in a recent interview that the Paris he lived in after the war was not the elegant old Paris of Henry James's heroine Madame de Vionnet.[26] Similarly the Europe in Herzog is not James's Paris; it is the Russia of Herzog's father. Jonah Herzog was no bogus dauphin or duke, as in Mark Twain's *Adventures of Huckleberry Finn*. No, Jonah was a bogus gentleman in Russia, with forged papers that allowed him to live among the gentiles and to squander great sums before his identity was discovered and he was jailed. His miserable failures in Montreal show that for him America is no refuge. Even when he hears of new horrors in the Europe from which he has escaped, he speaks of it as home: yet *in der Heim* things were even worse than in Montreal (178). Of the Russian Orthodox books with which Moses Herzog's wife has walled herself off from him in the marriage bed, Moses exclaims: "It's not enough they persecuted my ancestors!" (77).

Herzog's double consciousness, and the criticism that more mean-spirited characters throw at him, remind us of the dangers of mere sentiment, mere "potato-love," even in these touching, recurrent memories. But the memory itself, and the capacity to give individual suffering its dignity—these are humane qualities that distinguish Moses Herzog from the dehumanizing spirit of both the intellectual tradition and commercial American life. He resists the temptation to commit the easy sin of the modern intellectual: he refuses to hate the civilization that makes his life possible (370). But when he weeps at his father's funeral, his successful brother orders him not to "carry on like a goddamn immigrant!" (342). Feeling, then, is associated with that European memory. Again, Moses's philosophical sophistication teaches him, when he remembers his father's suffering, that in the context of the Holocaust "Father Herzog's claim to exceptional suffering" must be "abolished." "We are on a more brutal standard now, a new terminal standard, indifferent to persons" (184). But he does remember these insignificant personal histories. He must remember them. Unique though the Holocaust is, it brings Herzog into the confrontation that Herman Melville had presented in *Redburn,* by depicting a woman and her tiny children dying of starvation on a side street in Liverpool;[27] a confrontation that Mark Twain had presented in *The Innocents Abroad* and *A Connecticut Yankee,* and Hawthorne in contemplating the centuries of slaughter in Rome.[28] In this confrontation the American observer desperately seeks to maintain his belief in individual claims on human sympathy, against an almost timeless perspective that is forced on him by his view of the Pyramids or European history.

Moses Herzog is correct, then, when he remembers having believed that "his American credentials were in good order." As the class orator when he graduated from McKinley High School in Chicago, Herzog had quoted Ralph Waldo Emerson "to Italian mechanics, Bohemian barrel-makers, and Jewish tailors," the immigrant parents of Herzog's classmates.[29] He read them Emerson's declaration that "the main enterprise of the world, for splendor, . . . is the upbuilding of a man" and that "every man should be open to ecstasy or a divine illumination" (198–99). Even as a more sophisticated adult Herzog has deplored in Emersonian terms the petty, materialistic aims that President Eisenhower's Commission on National Purpose had recommended in the 1950s: "Eisenhower's report on National Aims, if I had had anything to do with it," Herzog says, "would have pondered the private and inward existence of Americans first of all" (205). Here he echoes Emerson's mid-nineteenth-century criticism of New England reformers: "No man can renovate society until he is himself renovated." Herzog's honest, complex memory is what redeems him—his sympathetic memory and his capacity to perceive human kindness even in his worst enemy, when that enemy treats a child kindly.

Being versus doing, then, is the subject to which we inevitably return, and once again we find that being is associated with the European experience—here the experience of the immigrant, the minority in America. In several of the best works by Bernard Malamud and James Baldwin, the discovery of being becomes a question of personal, national, and ethnic identity, but this question, with new twists here and there, reasserts central themes of the Anglo-American tradition with which we began.

Two superb stories in Bernard Malamud's *The Magic Barrel* (1958),[30] bring to Italy Jewish Americans who reenact the pilgrimage of James's and Mark Twain's innocents. In Malamud's characters, however, innocence is defined by a much larger ingredient of naïveté or moral unawareness than of relative purity. In "The Lady of the Lake" Henry Levin, a floorwalker at Macy's department store, assumes the name of Freeman when he comes to Italy in search of romance. The title itself echoes medieval romance and Sir Walter Scott's poem of 1810; and Freeman, like Mark Twain and James's Christopher Newman, has the sharp uninstructed eye that sees some things truly for itself but cannot distinguish original paintings from copies. Freeman dismisses with two little words the place where Napoleon is said to have slept—"a bed"—but even when the copies of paintings are excellent, he is disheartened by his inability to "tell the fake from the real" (123).

Like a number of American predecessors, Freeman sees the essence of European culture embodied in a beautiful woman, a Jewish caretaker whom he mistakes for an Italian aristocrat. William H. Prescott's Queen Isabella of Spain, Hawthorne's Beatrice Rappaccini, James's Claire de Cintré and Marie de Vionnet, Henry Adams' Virgin, and several of Hemingway's heroines—all give ironic depth to the description of Freeman's Isabella:

> She had, of course, the advantage of position—which included receiving, so to speak, the guest-intruder. and she had grace to lean on, herself also favored physically—mama, what a queenly, high-assed form—itself the cause of grace. Her dark, sharp Italian face had that quality of beauty which holds the mark of history, the beauty of a

people and civilization. The large brown eyes, under straight slender brows, were filled with sweet light; her lips were purely cut as if from red flowers; her nose was perhaps the one touch of imperfection that perfected the rest—a trifle long and thin. . . . Her past he could see boiling in her all the way back to the knights of old, and then some; his own history was something else again, but men were malleable, and he wasn't afraid of attempting to create certain daring combinations: Isabella and Henry Freeman. [113, 115]

Why, Freeman wonders, has she promptly asked whether he is Jewish. Having promptly denied being a Jew, he even manages to think of Jews in the third person: "Maybe she had once had some sort of unhappy experience with a Jew? Unlikely, but possible, they were now every-where." He waves away such speculations with a trite rhetorical ques-tion that has a special resonance here—because the phrase "ancient history" has a double meaning but also because the inverted question must surely be spoken in the tone of Jewish-American dialect, bor-rowed from Yiddish: "With ancient history," he says, "why bother?" (115).

Even after Isabella has shown him a tapestry depicting a leper in Dante's *Inferno* who had been damned because he "falsely said he could fly," Freeman asks a similarly revealing question—"For that you go to hell?" (123)—and he thinks of letting her "find out after she will have lived" as his wife "a while in the States" that being Jewish there is no crime; that in the U.S.A. "a man's past was, it could safely be said, expendable." Even after she has given as her reason for rejecting him her fidelity to her past, "the bluish line of distorted numbers" from Buchenwald on "the soft and tender flesh" of her exposed breast, he cannot quite utter the essential word: "'Isabella—' he cried brokenly. 'Listen, I—I am—.'" She has "stepped among the statues," and "in the veiled mist that had risen from the lake, . . . Freeman embraced only moonlit stone" (133).

Similar issues and a splendid comical version of some of the same techniques help to make Malamud's "The Last Mohican" one of my favorite short stories. Here Fidelman (a name which can be read as "faithful man") comes to Italy to write a critical study of Giotto. Wear-ing a tweed suit that is too warm for the September day, he comforts himself with the thought of the lighter suit in his suitcase as he takes his first look at a Roman piazza and mutters, "Imagine all that history" (155–56). With considerable self-approval, then, he imagines how he must look to any observer, but his exaltation fades as he perceives why he has thought of his appearance: a stranger is watching him. This is plainly his double—"give a skeleton a couple of pounds"—who has been "loitering" near the statue of Romulus, Remus, and the wolf. "Shalom," says Susskind the double, and Fidelman hesitantly replies, "'Shalom,' . . . uttering the word—so far as he recalled—for the first time in his life. . . . 'My first hello in Rome,'" he thinks, "'and it has to be a schnorrer'" (157).

Susskind is a kind of Jewish version of Herman Melville's Bartleby,[31] so thoroughly unwanted that even Israel will not let him stay there. Several of his most important exchanges with Fidelman consist of questions, with Susskind driving home the thematic point with a negative question that serves as a declaration. After Fidelman has good-humoredly declared Susskind "a Jewish refugee from Israel, no less," he adds, "Where else from, if I may ask?" Susskind replies, "Where else but Germany, Hungary, Poland? Where not?" And again when Susskind asks, "You wish a guide in Rome?" Fidelman replies with a question of his own—"Are you a guide?"—only to receive the unanswerable rejoinder, "Why not?" At last the interrogation turns to the subject of Giotto, and again Susskind has the last question, the most telling one so far. "You've studied his work?" Fidelman asks in some surprise, and Susskind answers, "Who doesn't know Giotto?" Fidelman is "secretly irritated," but he asks, "How do you happen to know him?" and the interrogative retort is even more succinct: "How do you?" (158–59).

Of course, it develops that the person who doesn't really know Giotto is Fidelman. The unlovable but inescapable Susskind, who not only has no spare suit but owns no suit at all, keeps asking Fidelman to give him his extra suit, then steals Fidelman's briefcase, including the first chapter of the book on Giotto. As Fidelman tries to escape both his tormentor and his guilty conscience by giving Susskind small, supposedly final gifts, he learns more and more about Susskind's miserable plight, and Susskind's rhetorical questions (as well as a few declarations) continue to instruct him about the presumption and shallowness of his own spiritual identity. Fidelman dreams of pursuing

Susskind in the Jewish catacombs, lighting the way with a menorah (which he thinks of only as "a sevenflamed candelabrum"); but the candles are blown out, leaving Fidelman "sightless and alone in the cemeterial dark" (170). His writing too, is blocked by the loss of his first chapter, "because he was lost without a beginning" (172). He does not come to "know Giotto" until his quest for the thief has led him in November through the old ghetto, an old synagogue, the Jewish section of the Cimetero Verano (including "an empty place" marked in memory of a man murdered at Auschwitz), and at last to the unheated hole in which Susskind lives. This "place," he thinks, is "probably no more than an ice-box someone had lent the refugee to come in out of the rain" (180).

Only after this experience, from which we are told that "he never fully recovered," does his unconscious mind bring together his Jewish heritage and the culture of classical and Christian art. He dreams of "Virgilio Susskind," who rises from an empty grave, asks him first whether he had read Tolstoy, then "Why is art?" and at last shows him the answer by leading him to a marble synagogue which contains a fresco by Giotto: St. Francis giving his gold cloak to an old knight in a thin red robe. From this dream that shows a modern American the essence behind the form, Fidelman awakes running, hurrying to bring both his literal and his spiritual suit to the poor refugee. He finds Susskind in the act of lighting a stub of candle with the last page of the missing chapter. This image may be intended as an ironic echo of Christopher Newman's magnanimous decision to throw an incriminating letter into the fire, and the moral point for Fidelman is the same as in Newman's "instinctive" turning, upon discovering that he has probably been outwitted, to see whether the letter has been completely destroyed.[32] Fidelman "savagely" opens the "pigskin briefcase" to look for his chapter, and then he chases Susskind through the ghetto, threatening to cut his throat. But the chutzpah that has characterized Susskind throughout the story persists even in full flight. This irritating survivor of European anti-Semitism has a familiar lesson for his American innocent: "I did you a favor," he insists. "The words were there but the spirit was missing." As "the ghetto Jews, framed in amazement in their medieval windows," stare "at the wild pursuit," Fidelman has "a triumphant insight" that moves beyond his unconscious dream and his deliberate gift. "Susskind, come back," he shouts, "The suit is yours. All is forgiven." But the refugee runs on, and the last line tells us that "when last seen he was still running" (182).

James Baldwin's attitude toward our subject has changed more than once in the decades since he published his autobiographical essays, *Notes of a Native Son, Nobody Knows My Name,* and *The Fire Next Time,* but I am especially interested here in the powerful reinforcement that his variations give to the traditional theme. He argues that the American Negro (the term accepted in polite usage thirty years ago) must be perceived as the representative American, because of the Negro's peculiar historical experience. The expatriate Baldwin who makes this discovery as a young character in several of the autobiographical essays, goes to Paris at least partly with the hope of liberating himself from the dreadful consequences of American racism. He shows us in the title essay in *Notes of a Native Son* that for him the worst of those consequences was a rage that brought him nearly to the point of murder when a waitress in a New Jersey restaurant told him, "We don't serve Negroes here."[33] Although he has already learned at his father's funeral in New York that he cannot be free of his Afro-American past, it is only in France that he learns he is also a plain American who has believed as innocently as James's Isabel Archer or Malamud's Henry Levin (alias Freeman) in the freedom of his essential self from historical complexity. At first, when he compares his experience with that of black Africans whom he meets in Paris, he finds that he cannot simply identify with the Africans. "He finds himself" caught up, he says, "in the same old battle: the battle for his own identity. To accept the reality of his being an American becomes a matter involving his integrity and his greatest hopes, for only by accepting this reality can he hope to make articulate to himself or to others the uniqueness of his experience, and to set free the spirit so long anonymous and caged" (121). And he soon comes to see that "in this need to establish himself in relation to his past he is most American, that this depthless alienation from oneself and one's people is, in sum, the American experience" (123). He even perceives that the history of this alienation may account for a "nearly unconscious assumption" which he considers typically American: the assumption "that it is possible to consider the person apart from all the forces that produced him" (136).

Yet he does not know or express the full significance of these discoveries until he has been imprisoned and charged with receiving stolen goods, a bed sheet which a fellow American has stolen from a Parisian hotel. As the days pass without any indication that the injustice will be corrected, Baldwin learns in the cold French prison that his assumptions differ astonishingly from those of his black fellow prisoners, all of whom are from Africa or Europe. He, it seems, has come to Europe with some of the assumptions of James's Lambert Strether. "The very word 'institutions,'" because American society "suffered so cruelly from the lack of them, had a pleasant ring," he says, "as of safety and order and common sense; one had to come into contact with these institutions in order to understand that they were also outmoded, exasperating, completely impersonal, and very often cruel" (140). The European and African prisoners, then, are not surprised by the cruelties, evasions, terrors, and delays of the French prison system. "None of them poured as much emotional effort into the fact of their arrest as I did: they took it, as I would have liked to take it, as simply another unlucky happening in a very dirty world" (151).

The last image of the narrative depicts Baldwin in a variation on an old American theme. Just as James's Christopher Newman listened to the chant of the Carmelite nuns in the rue d'Enfer and thought of the inhuman sequestration of his lovely Claire, so James Baldwin, having elected to go to Mass in the French prison on Christmas Day, finds himself locked in a frigid cubicle, "peering through a slot placed at the level of the eye at an old Frenchman"; this priest wears a hat, an overcoat, a muffler, and gloves, and he preaches to the freezing prisoners "the story of Jesus Christ's love for men" (158).

The complexity of innocence and of Baldwin's American identity becomes even more intricate in the last of my examples. The essay called "Stranger in the Village" narrates Baldwin's experience as the first black man whom the inhabitants of a Swiss village have ever seen. He describes his mixed feelings as his black presence in the snowy white square moves the delighted Swiss to touch his curly hair, and as innocent children call out *"Neger!"* when they see him. Like many nineteenth-century American characters, Baldwin associates European experience with the festival and the church. In the village's celebration of carnival, however, our black observer sees two blue-eyed Swiss children made up in blackface. He sees Swiss Christians drop coins into a box that is "decorated with a black figurine," and he learns that contributions to this box are said to "buy" the souls of African natives for Christianity. Last year, a Swiss woman tells him proudly, six African souls were "bought" with money from this village (163). Thus our naïf American learns that for Europeans the black man has always been an abstraction, whereas "in America, even as a slave, he was an inescapable part of the general social fabric" (170).

Baldwin's description of his mixed feelings gives his restatement of our theme a new intensity. But the most powerful statement of those feelings leads him into some logical difficulty. He declares that "from the point of view of power" these Swiss people

> cannot be . . . strangers anywhere in the world; they have made the modern world, in effect, even if they do not know it. The most illiterate among them is related, in a way that I am not, to Dante, Shakespeare, Michelangelo, Aeschylus, Da Vinci, Rembrandt, and Racine; the Cathedral at Chartres says something to them which it cannot say to me, as indeed would New York's Empire State Building, should anyone here ever see it. Out of their hymns and dances come Beethoven and Bach. Go back a few centuries and they are in their full glory—but I am in Africa, watching the conquerors arrive." [165]

Here is a new version of the old theme, the American lamenting his lack of a past. I have argued elsewhere that the way the illiterate Swiss are related to Dante, Shakespeare, and Michelangelo is much less significant than the way that Baldwin the literary artist is related to them, because the personal pronoun "I" that stands for Baldwin's identity must include the language and the traditional literary skills that he has mastered. The trope that places him in Africa five hundred years ago, waiting for the conquerors to arrive, expresses his feelings forcibly, but it contradicts his acute perception that Americans who refuse to "accept the black man as one of themselves" deny "his human weight and complexity." The trope also contradicts Baldwin's declaration that the battle for the Afro-American's identity "has long ago been won. The Afro-American is not a visitor to the west," Baldwin says, "but a citizen there, an American; as American as the Americans who despise him, the Americans who fear him, the Americans who love him" (173).

When Baldwin turns, then, to explain what the cathedral at Chartres says to him that it cannot say to the Swiss villagers, he appeals to the same kind of historical experience that we have seen in the fiction of Bellow and Malamud. The Swiss, he says, "have known God . . . longer than I have known him, and in a different way, and I am terrified by the slippery bottomless well to be found in the crypt, down which heretics were hurled to their death, and by the obscene gargoyles jutting out of the stone and seeming to say that God and the devil can never be divorced. I doubt the villagers think of the devil when they face a cathedral because they have never been identified with the devil" (174). When he warns that "the world is white no longer, and it will never be white again," he anticipates the conclusion to Malamud's novel *The Assistant* (1956): "All men are Jews." Here the so-called ethnic American writer echoes Thomas Paine, Herman Melville, and Walt Whitman in drawing a line through uniqueness to universality.

In their concentration on a so-called ethnic American's anxious relationship to the genealogical side of his cultural past and to the Western civilization they are addressing, Bellow, Malamud, and Baldwin are only three of the best contemporary American writers who play elegant, moving variations on an old American theme. In their work "innocence" often means not simple purity but naïveté, a naïveté verging on blindness and vulnerable to being corrupted by the provincial's desire to be accepted by the dominant culture. Their WASP predecessors in nineteenth-century American literature provided them with strong models for both the unconventional perception of the acute, limited outsider and the representative American Everyman whose essential being is enhanced by his confrontation of European history and European forms.

Notes

1. See, for example, Cushing Strout, *The American Image of the Old World* (New York: Harper and Row, 1963).

2. William Bradford, *Of Plymouth Plantation,* ed. Samuel Eliot Morison (New York: Alfred A. Knopf, 1952), pp. 3–4.

3. Thomas Hooker, *A Survey of the Summe of Church-Discipline* (London, 1658), p. [xvi].

4. Joel Barlow, "The Hasty Pudding," in *The Works of Joel Barlow*, ed. William K. Bottorff and Arthur L. Ford, 2 vols. (Gainesville: Univ. of Florida Press, 1970), 2:91.

5. See, for example, "Advice to Authors," in *The Miscellaneous Works of Philip Freneau*, ed. Lewis Leary (Delmar, N.Y.: Scholars' Facsimiles and Reprints, 1975), pp. [44–45].

6. Mark Twain, *The Innocents Abroad; or, The New Pilgrim's Progress* (New York: Signet Classics, 1966), pp. 207–8.

7. Nathaniel Hawthorne, *Our Old Home: A Series of English Sketches* (Boston, 1863).

8. David Levin, *History as Romantic Art: Bancroft, Prescott, Motley, and Parkman* (Stanford, Calif.: Stanford Univ. Press, 1959), chap. 2.

9. Ibid., p. 46.

10. Edwin Arlington Robinson, *Collected Poems* (New York: Macmillan, 1944), p. 348.

11. Mark Twain, *A Connecticut Yankee in King Arthur's Court* (New York: New American Library, n.d.), p. 83.

12. Mark Twain, *Adventures of Huckleberry Finn*, in *The Art of Huckleberry Finn: Texts, Sources, Criticism*, ed. Walter Blair and Victor Fischer (Berkeley and Los Angeles: Univ. of California Press, 1985), p. 137.

13. Mark Twain, *Innocents Abroad*, pp. 136–38.

14. Henry James, *The American* (New York: Viking Penguin, 1981), p. 67.

15. Yvor Winters, *In Defense of Reason* (London: Routledge and Kegan Paul, 1960), pp. 308–11.

16. Henry James, *The Portrait of a Lady* (London: Penguin, 1966), p. 201.

17. Ibid., p. 577.

18. Henry James, *The Ambassadors* (New York: Rinehart, 1960), pp. 1–2, 348–49.

19. See Abraham Cahan, *The Rise of David Levinsky* (rept. New York: Harper and Row, 1945), and Anzia Yezierska, *Hungry Hearts* (Boston and New York: Houghton Mifflin, 1920) and *Bread Givers* (Garden City, N.Y.: Doubleday, Page & Co., 1925).

20. Herman Melville, *Typee: A Peep at Polynesian Life*, ed. Harrison Hayford et al. (Evanston and Chicago: Northwestern Univ. Press, 1968), p. 125.

21. Saul Bellow, *Mosby's Memoirs and Other Stories* (New York: Viking, 1968), p. 159.

22. Henry James to Charles Eliot Norton, Feb. 4, 1872, in *Henry James Letters*, ed. Leon Edel, 4 vols. (Cambridge: Harvard Univ. Press, 1974),

1:274. James Baldwin quotes this famous line in the opening sentence of "The Discovery of What it Means to Be an American," in *Nobody Knows My Name* (New York: Dell Books, 1961).

23. Mark Twain, *Huckleberry Finn*, p. 199.

24. Saul Bellow, *Herzog* (New York: Fawcett, 1965).

25. Herman Melville to Nathaniel Hawthorne, June 1, 1851, in *The Letters of Herman Melville,* ed. Merrell R. Davis and William H. Gilman (New Haven: Yale Univ. Press, 1960), pp. 130–31.

26. Martin Amis, interview with Saul Bellow, *London Observer,* Dec. 11, 1983, p. 25.

27. Herman Melville, *Redburn, His First Voyage,* ed. Harrison Hayford et al. (Evanston and Chicago: Northwestern Univ. Press, 1969), pp. 180–84.

28. Nathaniel Hawthorne, *The Marble Faun; or, The Romance of Monte Beni* (New York: Dell Books, 1960), p. 28. Cf. pp. 296–97.

29. For illuminating comparisons of Bellow and Emerson, see Daniel B. Shea, "Emerson and the American Metamorphosis," in *Emerson: Prophecy, Metamorphosis, and Influence,* ed. David Levin (New York and London: Columbia Univ. Press, 1975), pp. 54–56, and M. Gilbert Porter, "Hitch Your Agony to a Star: Bellow's Transcendental Vision," in *Saul Bellow and His Work,* ed. Edmond Schraepen (Brussels, 1978), pp. 73–88.

30. Bernard Malamud, *The Magic Barrel* (New York: Vintage Books, n.d.).

31. Herman Melville, "Bartleby, the Scrivener," in *Piazza Tales* (New York, 1855).

32. James, *The American,* p. 449.

33. James Baldwin, *Notes of a Native Son* (Boston: Beacon Press, 1955), p. 96.

Index